Operating Signals, Points and Level Crossings

A MECHANICAL, ELECTRICAL AND ELECTRONIC GUIDE FOR RAILWAY MODELLERS

D1225374

Operating Signals, Points and Level Crossings

A MECHANICAL, ELECTRICAL AND ELECTRONIC GUIDE FOR RAILWAY MODELLERS

Clive Heathcote and A. Anderson

THE CROWOOD PRESS

First published in 2014 by
The Crowood Press Ltd
Ramsbury, Marlborough
Wiltshire SN8 2HR

www.crowood.com

British Library Cataloguing-in-Publication Data
A catalogue record for this book is available from the British Library.

ISBN 978 1 84797 863 9

Disclaimer
The author and the publisher do not accept any responsibility in any
manner whatsoever for any error or omission, or any loss, damage,
injury, adverse outcome, or liability of any kind incurred as a result of
the use of any of the information contained in this book, or reliance
upon it. If in doubt about any aspect of railway modelling, including
electrics and electronics, readers are advised to seek professional
advice.

Designed and typeset by Guy Croton Publishing Services,
Tonbridge, Kent

Printed and bound in Malaysia by Times Offset (M) Sdn Bhd

CONTENTS

INTRODUCTION AND ACKNOWLEDGEMENTS

Points signals and level crossings are generally all under the control of a signalman. Things changed so little on the railways that a signalman from the 1870s could have stepped into a 1950s signal box and operated it. Since then railways have undergone rapid modernization and things have changed extensively.

This book tries to explain how to model the operation of a real railway as it seems much more satisfying to understand why things are how they are. We have tried to include a lot of practical information about how to control signals points and level crossings, from the simplest methods to the more complex.

We hope the reader will be able to extend the ideas within this book to suit the circumstances of his model railway. For this reason we have tried to put in detailed explanations of how everything works. We would like to thank Neil Wint for his help with DCC control. Also thank you to Peco for supplying us with photographs of their products. Finally, thank you to the Churnet Valley Railway for kindly guiding us around their signal box and for filling the Churnet Valley with steam trains.

CHAPTER ONE

POINTS

After constructing the baseboard, planning and laying down the track is an important stage in building a model railway. To enable your rolling stock to run on a variety of routes, putting in points is essential.

A point is defined as 'a section of track used to direct a train onto two or more alternative routes'. It is sometimes, particularly in America, known as a switch or a turnout. Designing your model train layout is much easier than on the real railways. In the past the track plan had to be approved by a railway inspector, who in the early days was usually an army man from the Royal Engineers. Safety was important and standards were very stringent when passengers were involved. This affected how the railways laid out their track and signalling. Often with model railways the limited space available is the main concern, but if you bear these points in mind the model railway will look more realistic.

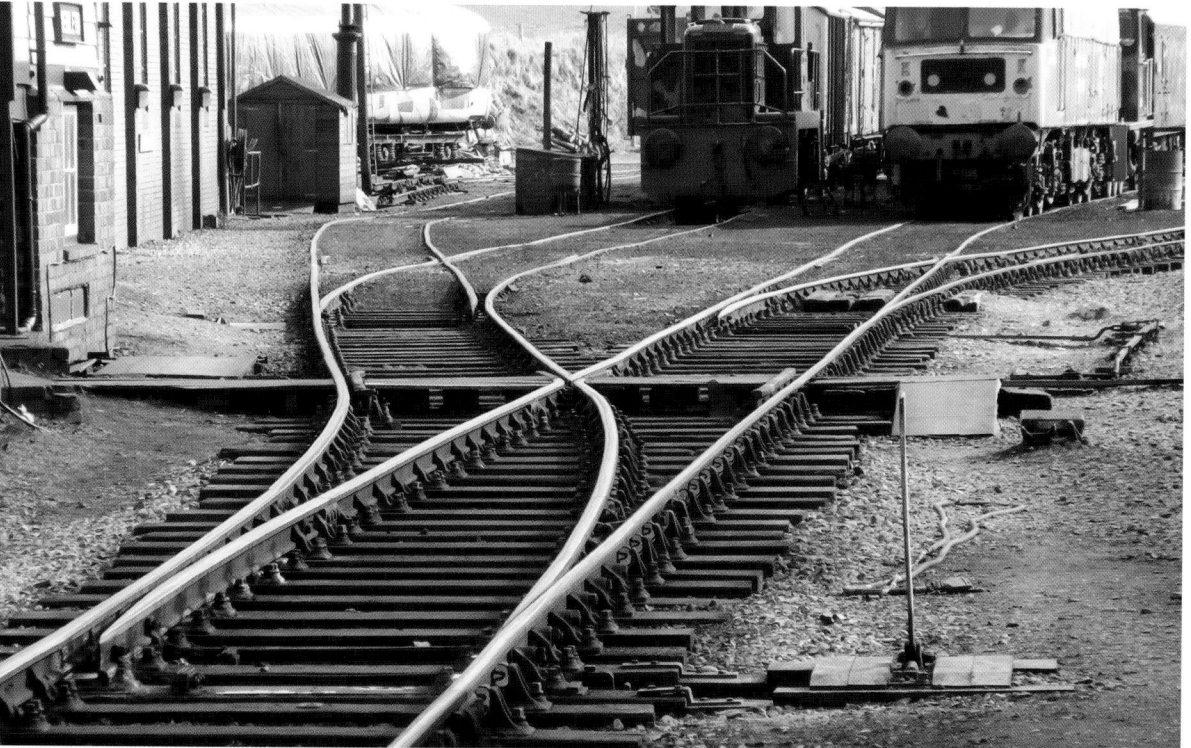

Full-sized railway points at Cheddleton Station on the Churnet Valley Railway in North Staffordshire. The points allow four sidings to lead into one line. The point at the front of the picture is operated by the white hand lever on its right. The second nearest point is operated from the signal box, which can be seen on the left of the picture. The point rodding from the signal box passes under the line and is protected by a wooden cover. It then goes alongside the track and joins to the point tie bar by an angle crank.

TYPES OF POINTS

RIGHT HAND AND LEFT HAND POINTS

Several types of points are in use on the railways. Simple standard right hand and left hand points are more common because they are more economical to make and maintain. With a right or left hand point, one track is straight and the other is curved. The radius of the curve on the tracks can vary. The bigger the radius of the curve, the faster the train can run over the points. Model railway track is often available with a choice of radius: large radius looks more realistic and gives better running but the points are substantially longer.

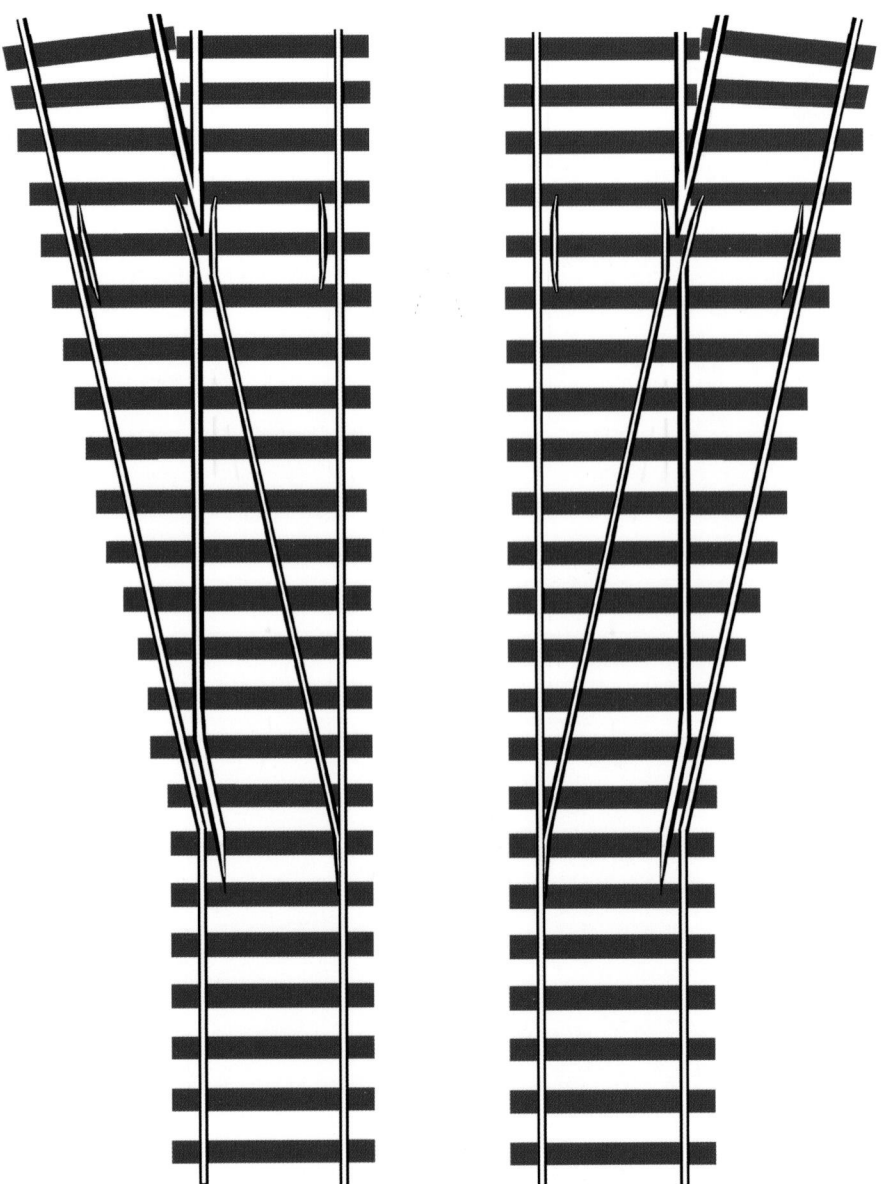

Left hand point refers to the side of the point the track diverges at, shown here on the left of the diagram. Generally the straight portion of the point will be on the main line to allow for a faster route. Sometimes the main line is on a gradual curve and the diverging route will then be at a sharper radius.

Y POINTS

Y points are very similar to left and right hand points. The difference is that both diverging tracks curve away in opposite directions. An advantage to this is that the tracks diverge in a shorter distance. Since the point takes up a shorter length of space, this is a big advantage on smaller model railways.

POINT ON A CURVE

Where the main line is on a gentle curve, then this type of point is required. These points can be very useful for saving space on model railways as they allow the line to split into two before a straight piece of track is reached.

Y point. Since both tracks curve away from each other they separate more rapidly than a left or right hand point. This makes a worthwhile ploy when saving space.

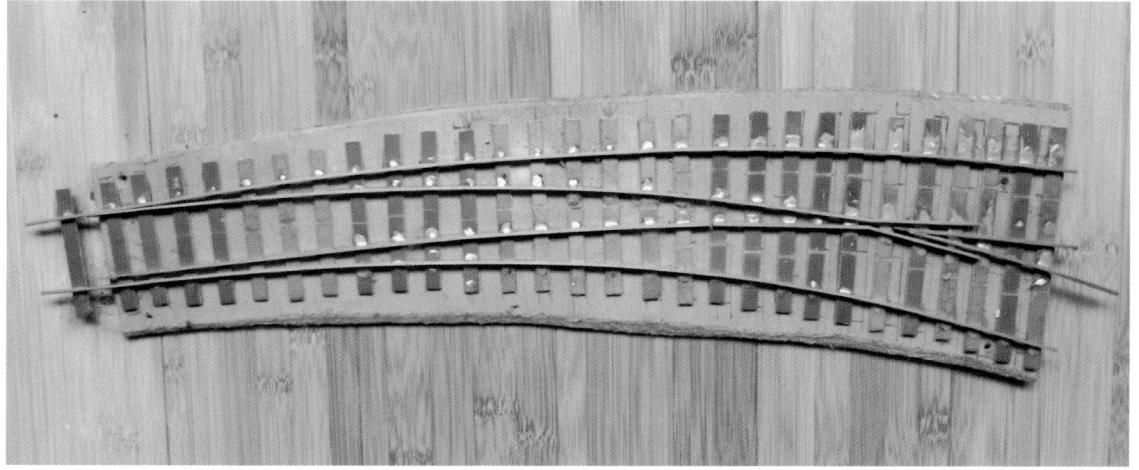

An O gauge home-constructed model of a right hand curved point built by one of the authors. Both tracks curve to the right. Strips of copper clad fibreglass are used for the sleepers. This is the material used to make circuit boards and is readily available. It allows the rail to be soldered to the sleepers. An advantage to building your own track is that it can be made to any radius to allow flowing curves of track.

DIAMOND CROSSINGS

Diamond crossings are also used particularly at junctions, but these offer no challenge to the modeller as they contain no moving parts.

The accompanying diagram shows a double junction, where two double-track lines meet. It consists of two left hand points and a diamond crossing. This is a very common track arrangement on full-size railways. Until recent times safety regulations required a single-track branch line to diverge from a double-track line using a double junction rather than a crossover and point.

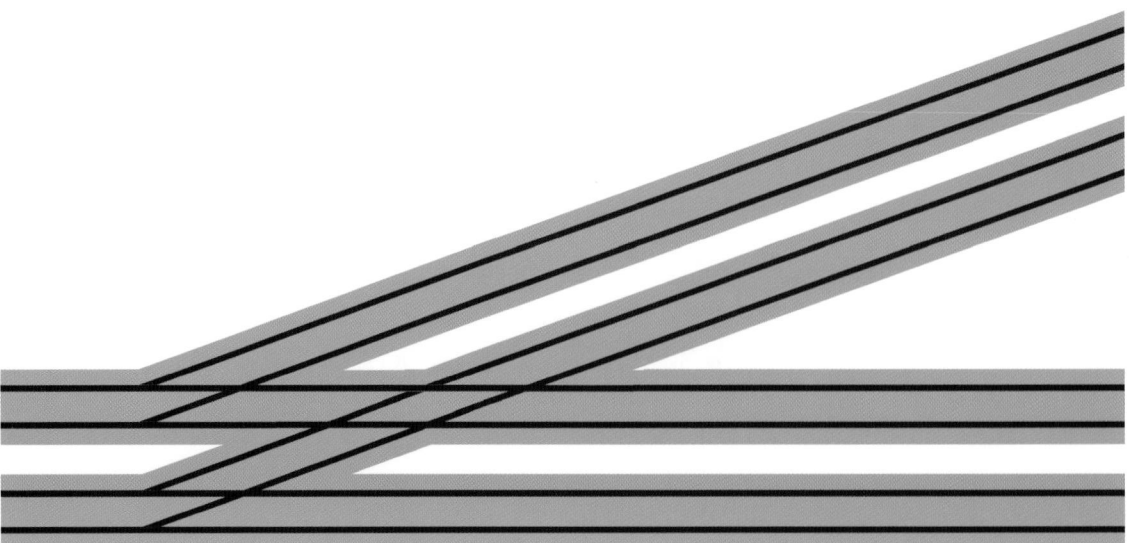

A double junction with two left hand points. The junction could equally have two right hand points. Manufacturers arrange the sizes and angles of their track so that formations such as these are easily assembled and the distance between the tracks are consistent to allow room for the model trains to pass.

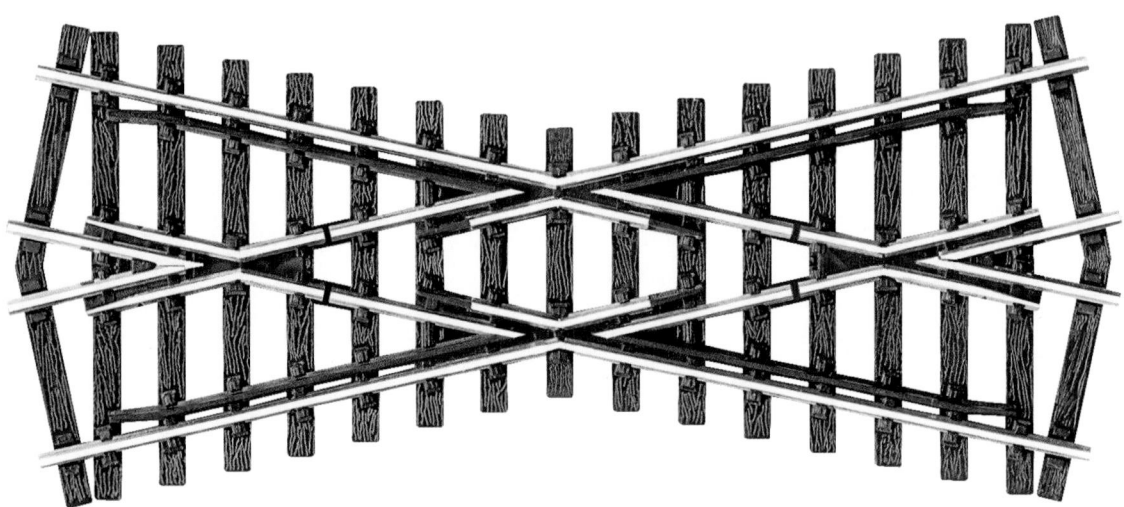

A 00 gauge model diamond crossing manufactured by Peco. You can see that is has two electro frogs as the nickel silver rails meet to form a V-shape rather than ending in a plastic moulded V-shape frog.

SINGLE AND DOUBLE SLIPS

Where space is restricted, for example at stations, single and double slips are used to save space. Single and double slips are actually diamond crossings with moving parts. With a diamond crossing a train approaching from A can only travel to D, whereas with a single slip a train approaching from A can travel to C or D, depending on how the point blades are set. Note there are two sets of point blades and two point motors are required. However with a single slip a train approaching from B can only travel to C.

Double slips have extra point blades to allow trains to travel from B to C or D, as well as A to C or D. Again two point motors are used to operate a double slip. The same track routing could be obtained by using two simple left or right hand points end to end. Although this would be simpler, it would take an extra length of track to achieve, hence the space-saving advantage of double slips.

B 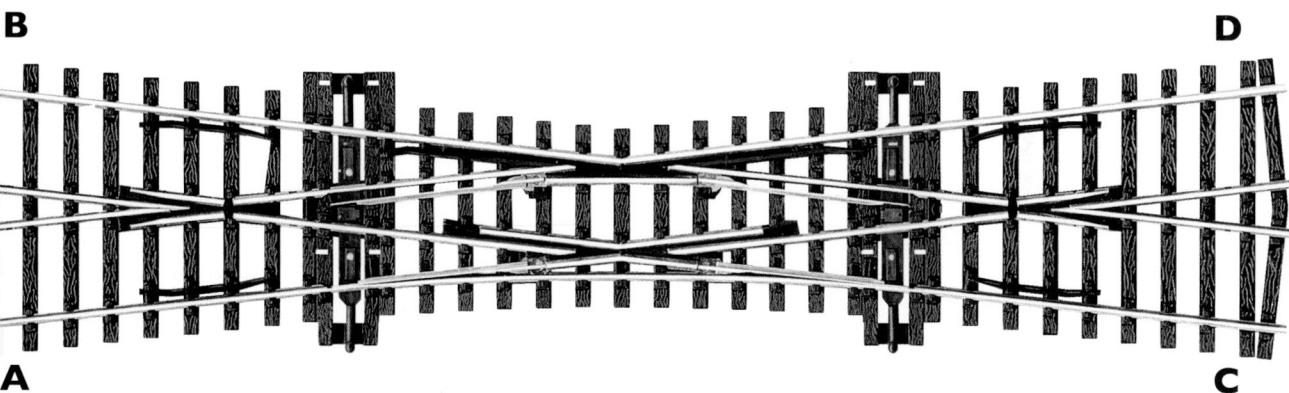 D

A C

Single and double slips are a lot more complicated than ordinary points. This is why they are only used when there is insufficient space to use a simpler arrangement with left and right hand points. At the approaches to busy stations, however, a lot of lines need access to a number of platforms, so this might be the only way to arrange the lines in the limited space available. PECO PUBLICATIONS

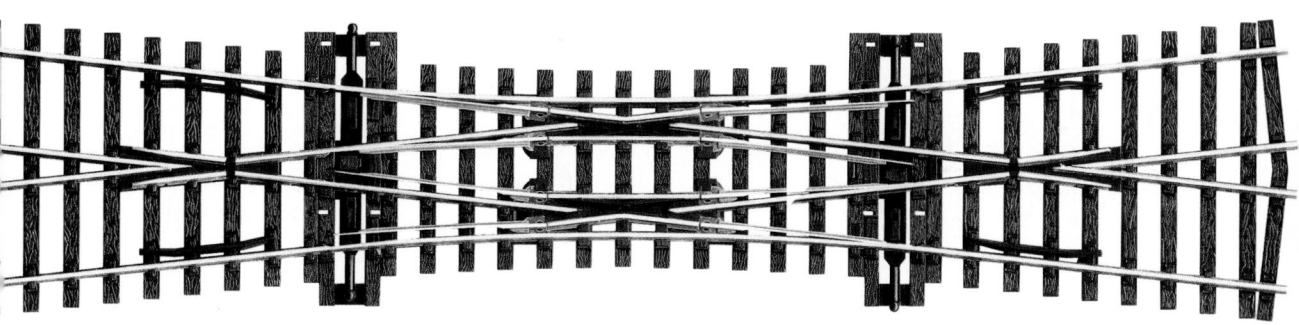

A model double slip point manufactured by Peco. There are two tie bars each moving four point blades. Two separate point motors, one for each tie bar, are required to work the double slip.
PECO PUBLICATIONS

THREE-WAY POINTS

In goods yards and marshalling yards three-way points are sometimes used to save space. They are seldom used on main lines for safety reasons because they are more complicated than standard left and right hand points and so not suited to a train crossing at high speed. Three-way points also have two sets of point blades and require two point motors.

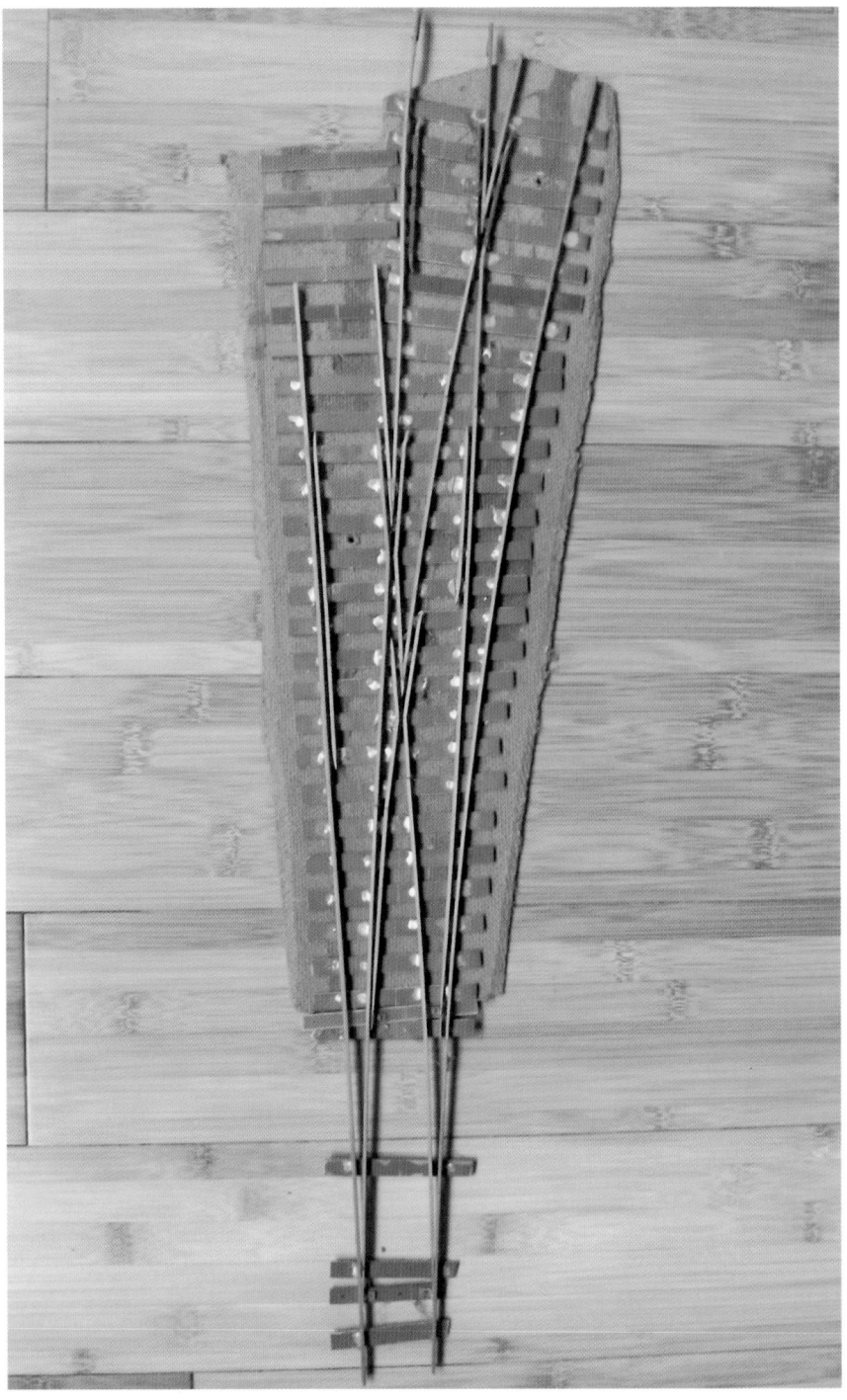

A three-way point allows the track to split into three in a shorter length than with two standard points. Two point motors are required for the three-way point. It has been constructed in the same way as a curved point.

CATCH POINTS AND TRAP POINTS

Catch points and trap points look the same but serve different purposes. Catch points are used on steep gradients in case a train splits in half and the rear portion rolls backwards down the hill. Their job is to derail the runaway. It is better to derail the train before it reaches tremendous speeds at the bottom of the hill. Trap points are used where a siding joins a main line. Their purpose is to prevent a collision with a train or wagons encroaching on the main line. When the point is set to the main line, the trap point is then set to derail the train. It is not so essential that such safety features are present on a model railway but the model looks more realistic if they are. It is rare that modellers go to the trouble of making these work.

A catch point at Cheddleton Station on the Churnet Valley Railway. If there were a runaway train or wagon on the left hand track, the catch point would derail the train before it could reach the right hand main track, so preventing obstructions on the main line. Interlocking in the signal box makes it impossible to set the main line point unless the catch point is set to derail in this way. When the main line point is set to the left hand track, the catch point can then be changed to allow trains to pass across it. Sometimes instead of using a catch point a normal point is used, followed by a short section of track, a sand drag to slow the train and a buffer stop.

OPERATING POINTS

LEVERS IN A SIGNAL BOX

Traditional railway lines were operated by lots of signal boxes instead of a centralized power box; points were operated by a signalman pulling a lever in a signal box. There are only a very few lines that retain this type of operation. Levers for points and signals are distinguished by colour but otherwise look the same. The levers are coloured black for points and blue for facing point locks. Home signal levers are coloured red and the levers for distant signals are yellow in colour. Spare or disused levers are painted white. Levers for operating gate stop locks for level crossings are brown in colour. There are even black and white chevrons on the levers that operate mechanisms to place detonators on the track in case of fog. When the train wheels hit the detonators, the explosion alerted the driver to come to a stop. It would be an appropriate touch to colour the switches on your model railway control panel using the same scheme. You can obtain coloured rubber covers for toggle switches.

Inside a small signal box at Consall Forge Station. Several different coloured levers can be seen. On each lever is a brass plaque with a number that corresponds to the signal or point on the diagram above the instrument shelf. The function of the lever is also identified by its colour. The cloth hanging on the lever, which is pulled forward, is used by the signalman to stop sweat corroding the metal lever. Signalmen were usually allocated a particular signal box to work in and they treated this as a home from home, keeping it immaculate. One of the authors visited a signal box during British Rail days and discovered the signalman had installed a sofa and cooker. The telephone that communicates with other signal boxes along the line can also be seen, as well as the block instruments used to pass control of the train between signal boxes.

Points in sidings were often controlled by the shunter or guard using a lever alongside the point, as here at Cheddleton Railway Station. The point blades and the tie bar that connects them together can just be seen. This arrangement is safe enough for slow-moving goods trains shunting in sidings but it would never be allowed on passenger-carrying main lines where the point must be interlocked to the signals and under the control of a signalman. Models of these levers can be obtained.

POINT RODDING

Signal box levers are connected to the point by steel bars. This is known as point rodding and can be seen running alongside railway lines.

Cosmetic plastic injection point rodding parts are available in 4mm scale from Wills. Etched brass components are also available for making point rodding. In larger scales it may be possible to make working point rodding from fine brass bar.

INTERLOCKING FRAME

On the ground floor of a traditional signal box is an interlocking frame. This is a mechanical device that prevents points being moved until the appropriate signals have been put to danger. There is a limit to how far away the point could be from the signal box due to the friction of the steel bars over the supports. For this reason some stations have signal boxes at each end of the station.

GROUND FRAME

Sidings some distance from the station have their own signal box. If the sidings are seldom used there will be a ground frame instead. A ground frame is a bank of levers that is only unlocked when a railway guard or shunter is required to carry out shunting manoeuvres. This should be operated by the guard travelling on the train. Off the main line points on sidings might be operated by levers alongside the point.

Mechanical signal boxes had their levers connected to the points by the square section rodding shown here. Semicircular cranks were used to change the movement through ninety degrees to connect with the point tie bars.

A ground frame with three levers for operating three points. The numbers in front are not part of the ground frame but are a speed limit for the engine driver.

ELECTRIC POINT MOTORS

In more recent times electric point motors have been used, allowing points to be operated over great distances from a single signal box known as a power box. A signal box of this type can control many miles of railway route.

DOUBLE TRACKS

The majority of railways in Britain are double-track lines; trains travel on the left as on the roads. The line going towards the major city is always known as the up line and the other track is called the down line. In the USA, in contrast, the tracks are called Eastbound and Westbound, as most routes are transcontinental.

FACING AND TRAILING POINTS

While trains on British double-track main lines travel on the left track, in many other countries trains travel on the right. In the Channel tunnel one track passes beneath the other so that the trains resurface on the correct side for the country they arrive in. As trains always travel in the same direction along a track, a point will always be arranged either to split the line or cause two lines to converge. Facing points are where the lines split and trailing points are where the lines converge.

Facing points enable the train to travel either route and so if the signalman makes a mistake he could send the London express into the back of a siding full of wagons. When a trailing point is used if a mistake is made or a fault occurs with luck the train carries on, without luck it only derails. Mechanical problems with a facing point may cause the point blade to move slightly and it is more likely to derail the train than if this happened with a trailing point. On a trailing point most likely the wheels would push the point blade back into place. In the interests of safety trailing points were always preferred to facing points.

INTERLOCKING

On passenger lines, as well as having a lever to move the facing point, the signalman has a second lever to apply a lock to the point blades. This is called a

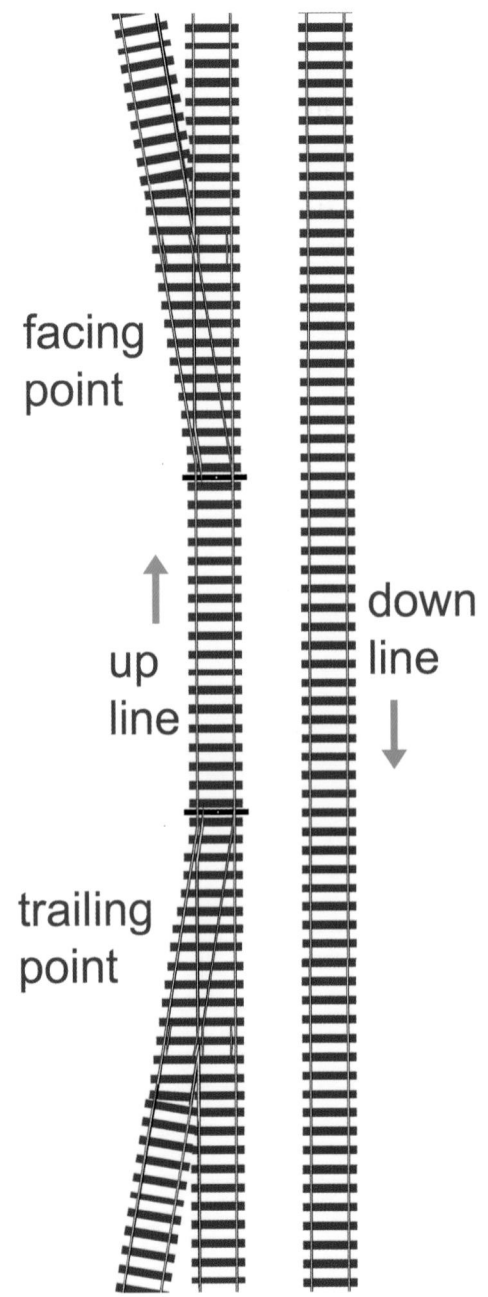

A trailing and a facing point on the left hand track of a double line.

facing point lock. Until both are in the correct position, the lever to move the signal to clear will not operate. This is an example of interlocking. If you look at old station plans you will find that nearly all the points are trailing points. However, on modern railways facing points are used more extensively to simplify operation.

CROSSOVERS

Crossovers are often present on double-track lines. One reason for this is that when engineering work is carried out on one of the lines, trains will need to be able to cross to the other line. Because of the dislike of facing points, crossovers are nearly always made of trailing points. The train has to reverse over the crossover to reach the other line.

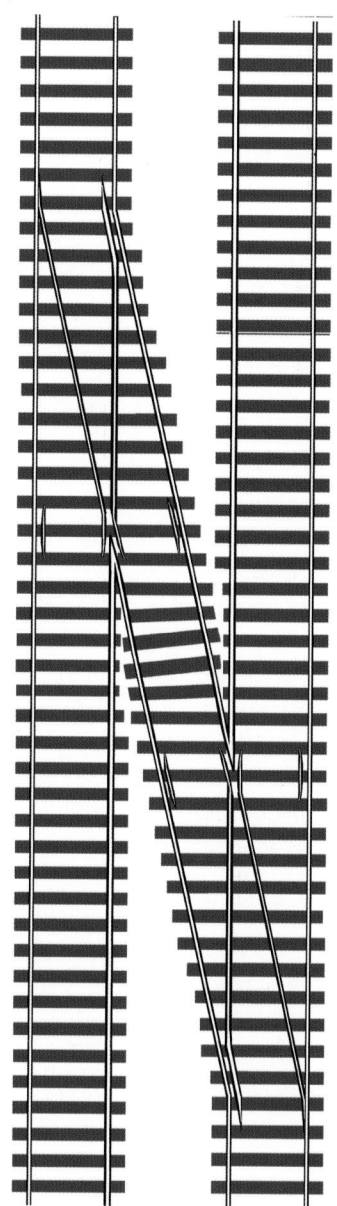

A trailing crossover for trains running on the left. This is by far the preferred option rather than having facing points.

CHAPTER TWO

HOW TO GET YOUR POINTS MOVING

Manufacturers of points produce them ready assembled or in kits. Some modellers build their own points. Some manufacturers, such as Kato, produce track with the motor built into the point, while others build point motors specifically to fit their own points. To some extent the type of point determines the best way of activating it.

The moving parts of the point are called the point blades. There is one for each rail and these are linked together by the point tie bar. Generally the activating mechanism is linked into the tie bar.

MOVED BY HAND

An advantage of hand-operated points is that they are cheap and simple, but they have the disadvantage that you might accidentally knock rolling stock on the adjacent track. Large model railways will provide excessive exercise as you run to change the points at the end of the room. On small layouts some modellers arrange pieces of stiff wire, such as bicycle spokes, protruding out from the edge of the baseboard. These have a mechanical linkage to the tie bar and the point can be changed by sliding them a few millimetres in and out.

MOVED MECHANICALLY WITH A LEVER

Manufacturers such as Gem and MSE produce working model lever frames based on the lever frames in real signal boxes. The lever is connected to the point tie bar by piano wire (fine steel wire), which is available from model shops specializing in radio-controlled aeroplanes. To overcome problems with the wire bending when it is pushing, the wire can run inside a plastic or brass tube in a similar way to the brake cable of a bicycle. This method of operation is satisfying because it is close to how the real points of a full-size railway operate. The length of the wire needs to be exact. For portable layouts it is difficult to cross baseboard joints because the wire needs to be disconnected when the baseboard is taken apart.

MEMORY WIRE

If you want to build your own point motor, memory wire is worth investigating. Memory wire, also known as muscle wire, is an alloy that shrinks about 5 per cent, whatever its diameter, when heated by an electrical current. As it cools it returns to its original length, provided there is a spring to tension it. It will do this around a million times. It is available in diameters ranging from 5 to 50 microns. As a micron is one thousandth of a millimetre, memory wire is finer than a single human hair. One type of memory wire is Nitinol, an alloy of titanium and nickel, and it is reasonably easy to obtain.

The speed at which the point blades move over depends on how quickly the memory wire heats up and cools down. To make it cool more slowly, a plastic tube can be threaded over the wire to provide some heat insulation. Although good results can be obtained there are some snags. You cannot solder the memory wire because its properties are destroyed if it gets too hot; crimping is the best alternative as it needs to be connected to an electrical supply. The other difficulty is that it is quite fiddly to work with something so fine. You need to control the current through the wire so that it doesn't get too hot. This is usually done by using a regulated power supply and a resistor. The resistor's value will depend on the voltage of the power supply and the diameter and length of the memory wire. Most kits supply tables to

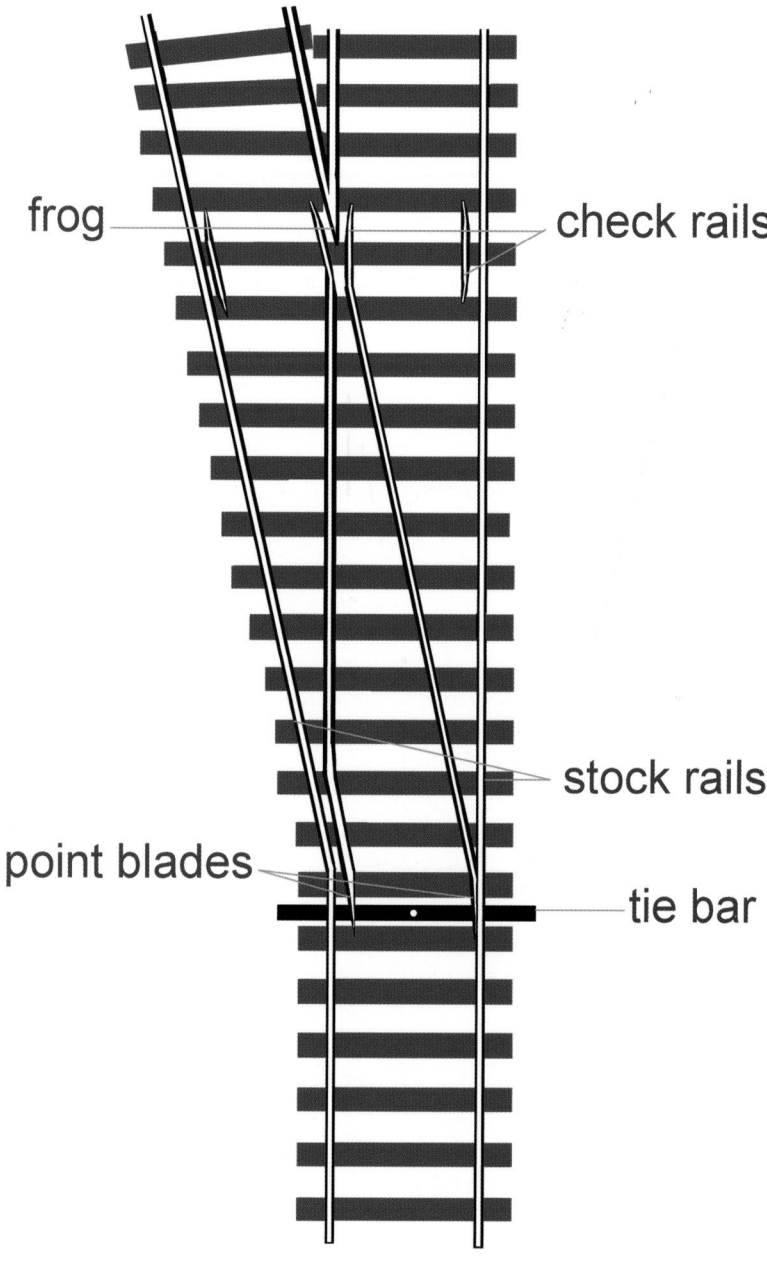

frog

check rails

stock rails

point blades

tie bar

The parts of a point. The check rails are intended to guide the wheel flanges through the gap in the track at the point's frog.

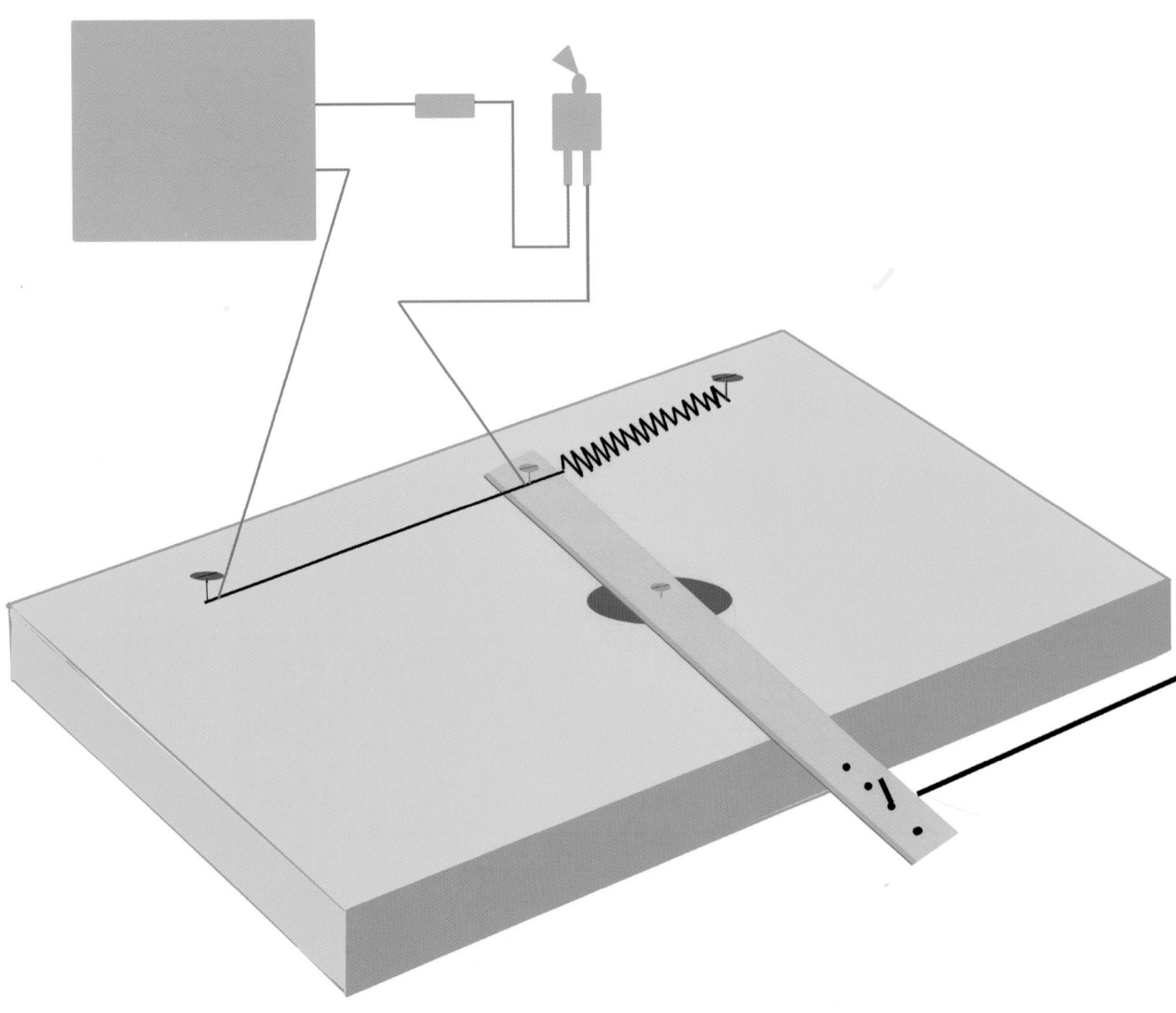

This diagram shows a power supply supplying current to the memory wire, using a switch to connect and disconnect this current. The resistor shown is necessary to limit how much current flows. As the memory wire heats up it will shorten and so pull the blue lever towards it. At the other end of the lever is a mechanical connection to the point's tie bar. When the current is turned off by the switch the memory wire will cool; as it expands, the spring will pull the lever back to its original position.

enable you to work this out. C+L Finescale supplies a kit containing memory wire and all the necessary accessories, including springs and cranks.

SOLENOID POINT MOTORS

These provide a very popular way of operating points, probably because they are readily available, simple to set up and modestly priced. If you use connectors on the wires to the point motors, the baseboard can easily be taken apart. The disadvantage is that the solenoids move the point blades over too quickly, creating an unrealistic effect. The point motor usually consists of two solenoids (electro-magnets) side by side with a ferrous metal rod in the centre, all built into one unit. As the solenoid point motor is not continuously powered it is most suited to points with a locking mechanism, such as a spring, to hold the point blades in place. To move the solenoid requires a large

current. If the solenoid were continuously powered it would get very hot and might burn out. To prevent this, the electricity must be applied in a short burst of typically half a second. When the current is switched through one of the solenoids, the rod is attracted and pulled sideways towards it. In other words, activating one solenoid moves the rod to the left and activating the other solenoid moves the rod to the right. Fixed in the rod is a metal pin that fits in the tie bar and moves the point blades, thereby altering the setting of the point. When the pulse ceases, the point is held in place by a tiny spring built into the point.

Popular manufacturers of double solenoid point motors are Peco, Seep and Hornby. Peco point motors are designed to clip underneath the point. This type of fitting solves any problems with alignment, but it does require you to make a hole in the baseboard that will need disguising, possibly using a thin strip of card.

The Peco solenoid point motor clips to the underside of the point and so requires a hole in the baseboard to fit the point motor into. Connections can be made to the brass connector on the side of the point motor either by soldering or using wires fitted with spade connectors. PECO PUBLICATIONS

A surface-mounted point motor clipped to a 00 gauge point: both are manufactured by Peco.
PECO PUBLICATIONS

Peco recently started manufacturing a surface mounting point motor that clips onto the side of the point. This is easier to use but makes your model railway look less realistic, unless disguised.

Seep point motors do not require a hole in the baseboard, just a slot under the tie bar. It is more difficult to align the point motor as you are working under the baseboard, but a jig can be purchased or made to help you align it. The Seep motor is held under the baseboard by two screws. It seems to work better if there is a little slack in the screws as it binds if they are too tight. Peco and Hornby both also make side-fitting solenoid point motors, but these are located on top of the baseboard alongside the point. They are easier to fit but present the problem

of how to disguise them. The common solution is to place a hut over the top and if you have a lot of points you may end up with a shanty town.

SWITCHING SOLENOID POINT MOTORS

Standard switches are not suitable for switching point motors as they would cause the current to flow continuously. There are five common ways in which a short burst of current can be achieved.

Momentary Switches

These are toggle switches that have internal springs to return the switch's lever to the central position immediately after release. In the central position the

Tracks stretching into the distance and signals showing both red and green on this sizeable and extensive model railway.

Four toggle switches. The levers are all in the upright position, where no connections are made. Gentle finger pressure pushing them to either side will make a connection.

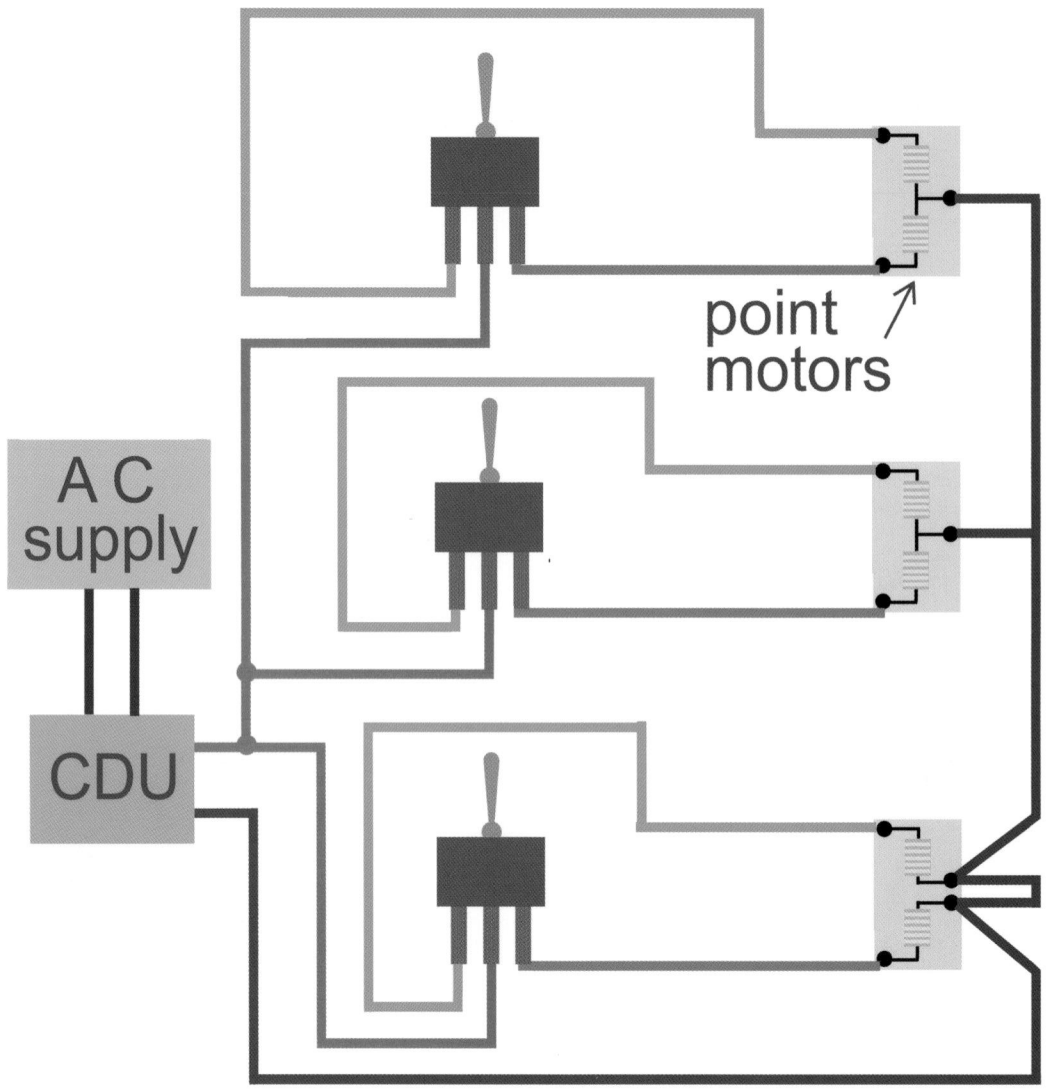

Three point motors wired to a CDU by toggle switches. The blue connection from the CDU goes directly to one end of each coil on the point motors. The manufacturer has internally linked the ends of the two coils on the upper two point motors, but on the lower point motor this has not been done so the modeller needs to make the extra connection, as shown in the diagram. Seep point motors have the internal connections, while Peco's do not. When the switch is moved to the left the green wire is energized, activating the lower coil. When it is moved to the right the turquoise wire is energized, activating the upper coil. The direction the solenoid point motor moves in depends upon which coil is energized.

switch makes no contact and electricity will not flow. The switch lever can be temporarily held in the left or right position. The switch can be wired so that it corresponds to the movement of the point.

Stud and Probe

A method of switching points called stud and probe can be used. The point motor is wired to metal studs located on the control panel. The point motor's

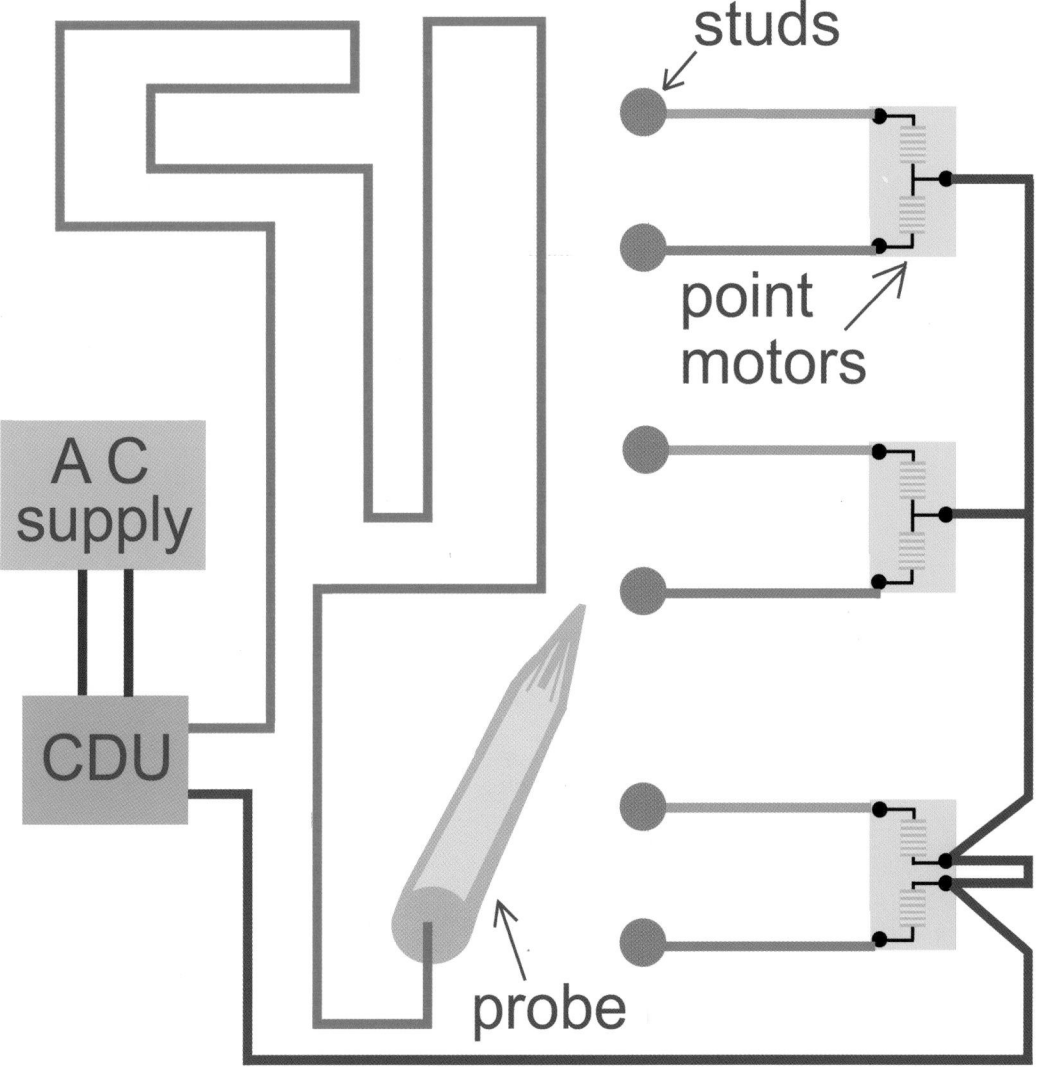

Diagram showing how the studs are wired to three point motors. When the probe is touched onto one of these studs, electricity will flow through the coil of the point motor, so moving the point. The diagram shows a CDU, but this may not be necessary if you are switching only one point at a time and the points can be switched directly with the 16V AC supply. Stud and probe is a good method for switching three-way points as you can have a separate stud for each of the point's three positions. It is also a very economical method of switching points. Although the method of operation is different, the wiring for stud and probe follows exactly the same pattern as wiring momentary switches. The difference is that, instead of the red wire going to every common of each switch, as shown in the previous diagram, it simply goes to the single probe.

power source is connected to a probe via a length of flexible wire. The point is moved in the direction you wish by touching the probe onto the relevant stud.

Peco supplies the parts to build a stud and probe system. The studs are part number PL18, to which the wires to the point motors are crimped. The firm also supplies a probe (part number PL17). It is fairly easy, however, to use nuts, bolts and washers for the studs. The wire can be trapped by washers between two nuts on the rear side of the control panel. Probes

can be constructed by fitting a piece of metal, such as brass, inside the casing of a ballpoint pen.

Push-button Switches

Two push-to-make push-button switches are required for each standard point. Push-to-make switches have two contacts that are electrically disconnected until they are pushed, when the two contacts become electrically connected. An advantage of push-button switches is that three-way points can have one push-

The six push-button switches shown here are available with different coloured buttons. There are two solder connections on the bottom of each switch. These solder connections become electrically connected when you push the button.

button for each direction. Connections are usually made to these by soldering.

Passing Contact Switches

These are roughly based on the shape of the lever inside a signal box and similarly the lever has just two positions. As the lever is pushed from one position to the other, contacts are made inside the switch and then broken. This supplies the necessary short burst of power to the point motor. They are easily made up into a bank of switches replicating the levers inside a signal box. Passing contact switches have the advantage of indicating the positions the points move to. They would be out of place on a diagrammatic control panel because of their inappropriate size and shape, but you could cut away the back of a model signal box and place the levers inside it.

Both Hornby (code RO44) and Peco (code PL26B) produce passing contact switches. The Peco switch utilizes spade terminals so that the wiring can be done by crimping the connectors onto the end of the wires, which may help those who are not confi-

The resemblance of Peco passing contact switches to signal box levers is particularly apparent when a number are put side by side. Even though the lever is not in the central position, the switch has been designed so that no connection is being made. The connection is only made while the lever is being moved from one end to the other. PECO PUBLICATIONS

dent with soldering. Hornby switches have the wire already attached.

DCC Accessory Decoders

As well as controlling the speed and direction of the trains, the DCC controller can operate point motors. Digital command control (DCC) is a system

A ZTC DCC controller. As well as controlling the engines it can also be used to control the points. It sends digital signals along the rails to the accessory decoder, which in turn produces the electrical output to the point motor. To the right is a subsidiary hand-held controller for a second operator.

A Hornby DCC controller being used to change a point.

that sends digital information along with electrical power using the track's rails. Each engine can be controlled independently as it contains a chip with a unique address. In a similar way modellers with DCC model railways can use the DCC system to switch their points. To do this a DCC accessory decoder is used.

Two wires connect from the track to the accessory decoder, then the accessory decoder is wired to the point motors. The accessory decoder takes the information transmitted by the controller's DCC signal and produces the relevant bursts of current to the point motor.

Most accessory decoders operate four point motors, although Lenz has a version to operate six.

Some point motors also have a built-in accessory decoder. Another factor to look at is how the accessory decoders are programmed. Some accessory decoders, for example, require you to remove every engine from the track before the accessory decoder can be programmed with its address. The programming is necessary to give each point a unique number so that it can be operated independently. The more basic accessory decoders operate solenoid point motors, whereas more sophisticated decoders can also operate slow motion point motors. Although the point motors can be controlled directly from the DCC controller, this requires pressing at least three buttons, which seems laborious compared to just flicking a switch.

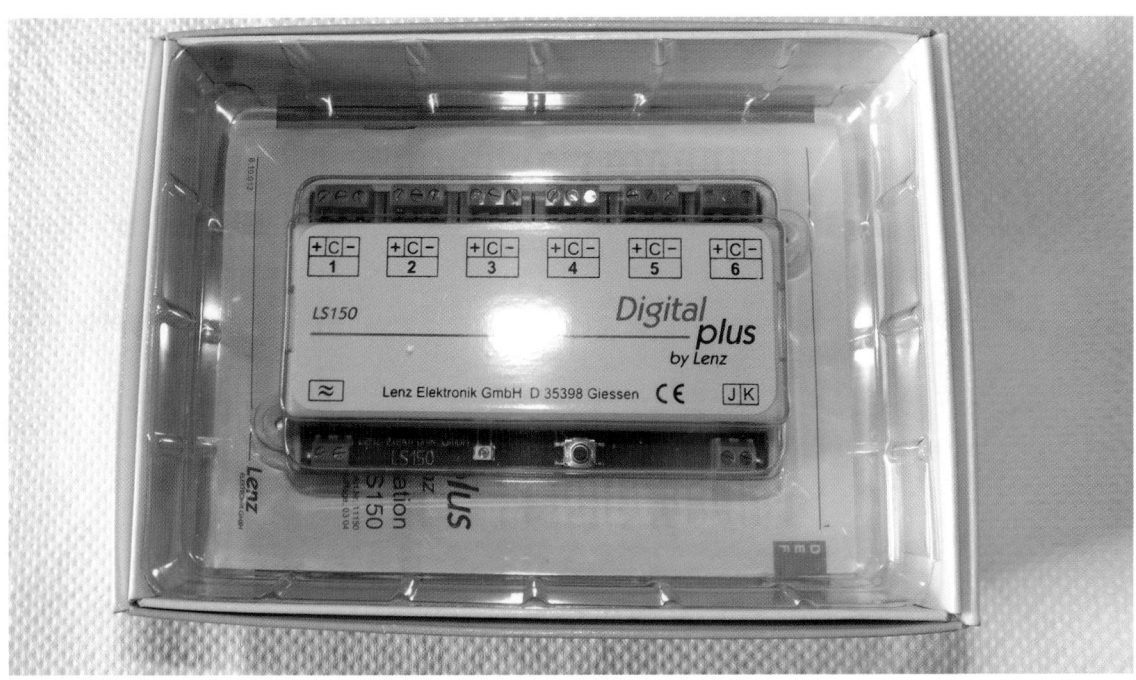

ABOVE: *The Lenz DCC accessory decoder can control six point motors, which are connected to the six three-way terminal blocks at the top of the unit.*

BELOW: *This Digitrax Accessory Decoder controls four point motors. All DCC components are made to conform to certain electronic specifications. This means that you can get the DCC controller from one manufacturer and it will work with any other manufacturer's DCC Accessory Decoder.*

Hornby Railmaster software enables a track plan of your layout to be drawn and displayed on a laptop's screen. Once this is done you can use a mouse to click on points and signals on the screen and the laptop will communicate this information to the DCC system, changing the points and signals on the model.

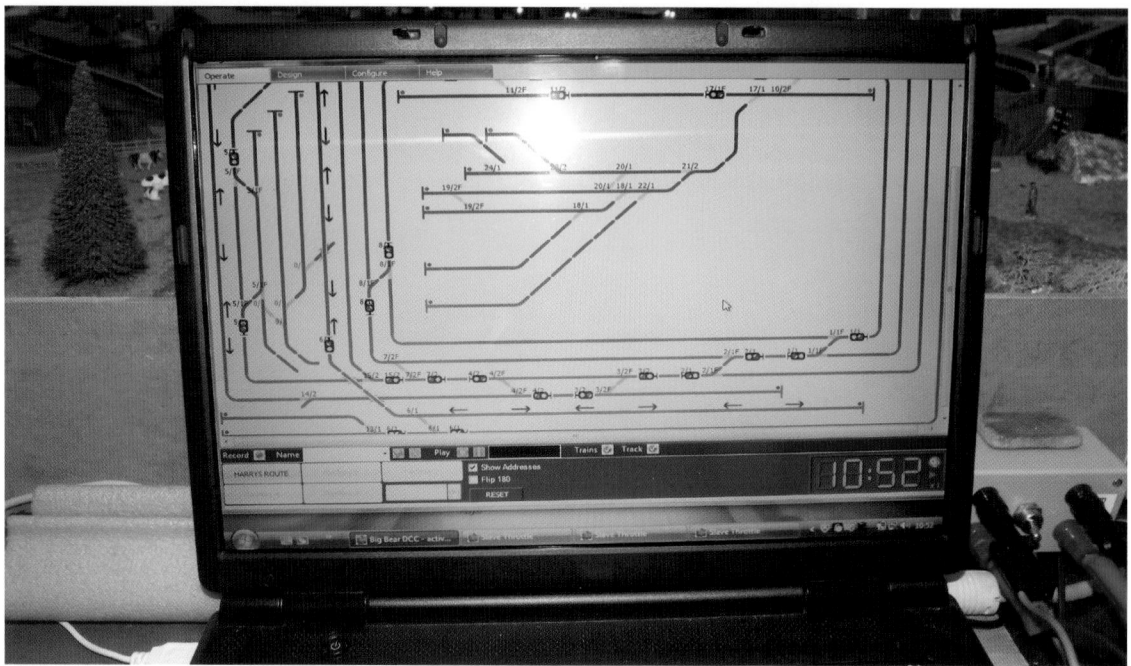

A larger view of the laptop screen clearly shows how all the points have a unique number. This is the address with which the accessory decoders have been programmed. This number can also be entered in the DCC controller via its keypad to change the points. In the bottom left-hand corner of the screen can be seen the words HARRY'S ROUTE. Clicking the mouse on this will cause the points to change to the route already programmed by Harry. When you select a route in this way the points change one by one to avoid the current surge that would occur if the points all changed at once.

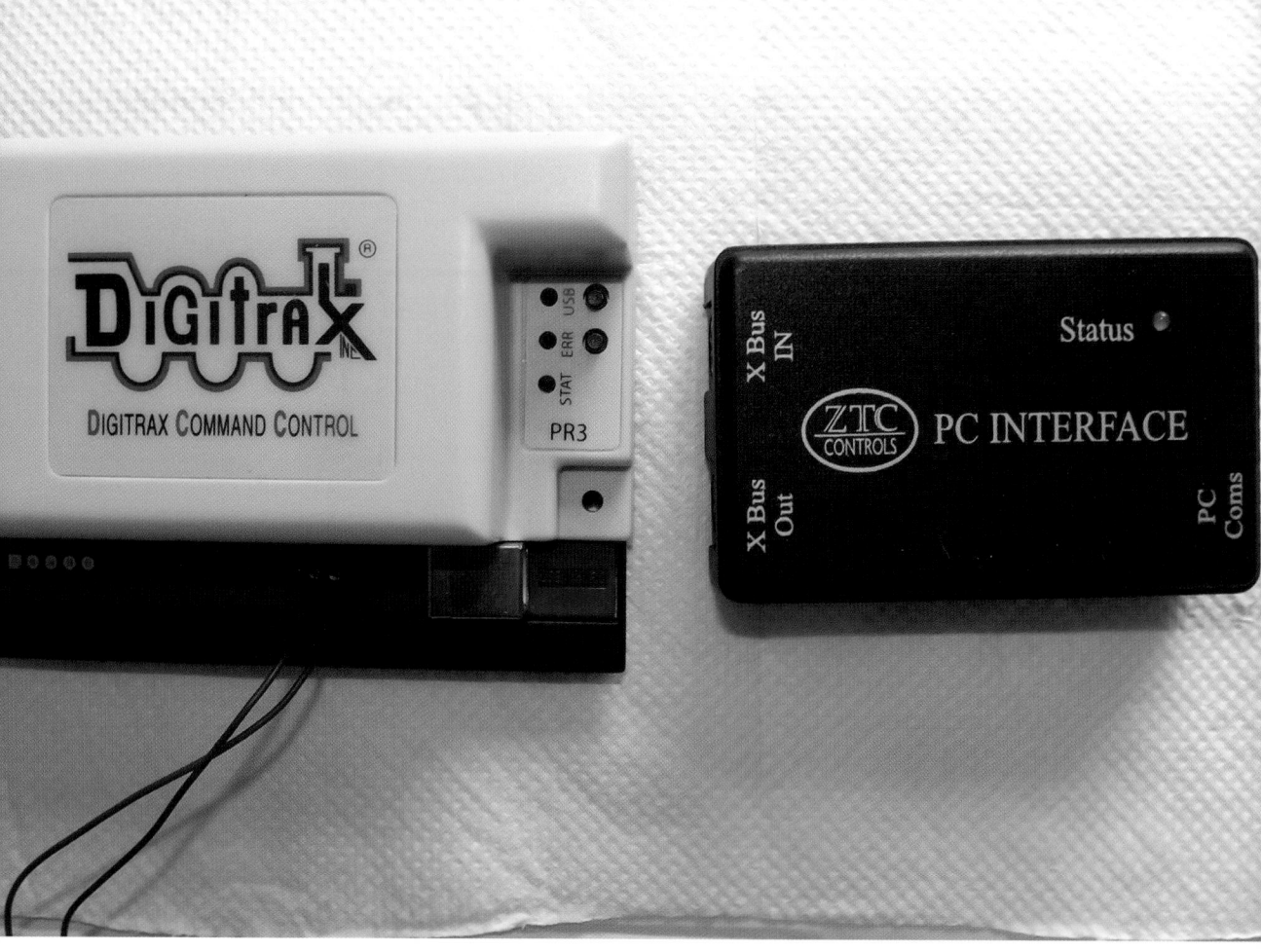

Two computer to DCC interfaces: (left) the American Digitrax; (right) the British ZTC. Unlike the accessory decoders, the interfaces must match the manufacturer's controller.

You can, however, connect a PC or laptop to the DCC system. This allows the layout plan to be displayed on the screen and the points to be changed with a mouse click. You can even set up the computer so that clicking on a button with the mouse sets any number of points to change to a preprogrammed route.

To connect the PC or laptop to the DCC controller you generally need an interface box. An exception to this is Hornby's Elite controller, which connects directly to the computer with a USB cable.

There is a choice of software to load onto a PC to allow you to draw a track plan of your layout and control the points. Some of this software, such as JMRI (Java Model Railroad Interface), is free and can be downloaded from the internet. Other software programs to look at include Big Bear, Railroad & Co. and Railmaster. The last of these is supplied by Hornby and there is the option of using smartphones as extra controllers.

Using a computer rather than banks of switches to control your model railway is rather like the difference between a signalling power box and a traditional signal box. In other words, it is the difference between pulling levers and clicking a mouse. It is a matter of preference as to which you find more satisfying.

The underside of the baseboard showing two Hornby DCC accessory decoders. As each accessory decoder controls four point motors there are quite a number of wires. Cable ties have been used to tidy them up.

CHOOSING BETWEEN THE METHODS OF SOLENOID POINT CONTROL

Control Panel

The type of control panel you plan to have is a factor in your choice of point motor switch. Diagrammatic control panels, also known as mimic control panels, have a track plan of the layout with the switches positioned on the image of the points they control. Momentary toggle switches, stud and probe or push-button switches are most suitable for these. Passing contact switches are better if you prefer to have the switches arranged in a bank rather like in a traditional signal box. A large number of passing contact switches, however, will make it difficult to remember which point motor each one operates. This could be overcome by numbering each one and having the points numbered on a diagram. This is the method used by full-size signal boxes. The levers in a signal box are painted different colours depending on what they operate. The levers also have a brass number on them corresponding to the number on the diagram above them.

Three-way Points

If you are using three-way points you may find stud and probe or push-button switches are more intuitive to use than toggle or passing contact switches as you only need to press one button or touch one stud to set the route. If you were to use toggle switches or passing contact switches you would need to operate two for some routes. The accompanying diagram shows the wiring for setting the route with single-switch operation.

Which Way the Points are Set

Passing contact switches have the advantage that the position of the lever shows the direction of the point. With other methods you cannot see which way the point is set unless it is close enough to view. A way to overcome this is to use a Point Indicator board. This is an electronic circuit board that senses the pulses to the point motors and uses this to light one of two LEDs, which show which way the point is set. These LEDs can be wired into the control panel. Point Indicator boards are available from All Components and Heathcote Electronics. Similarly,

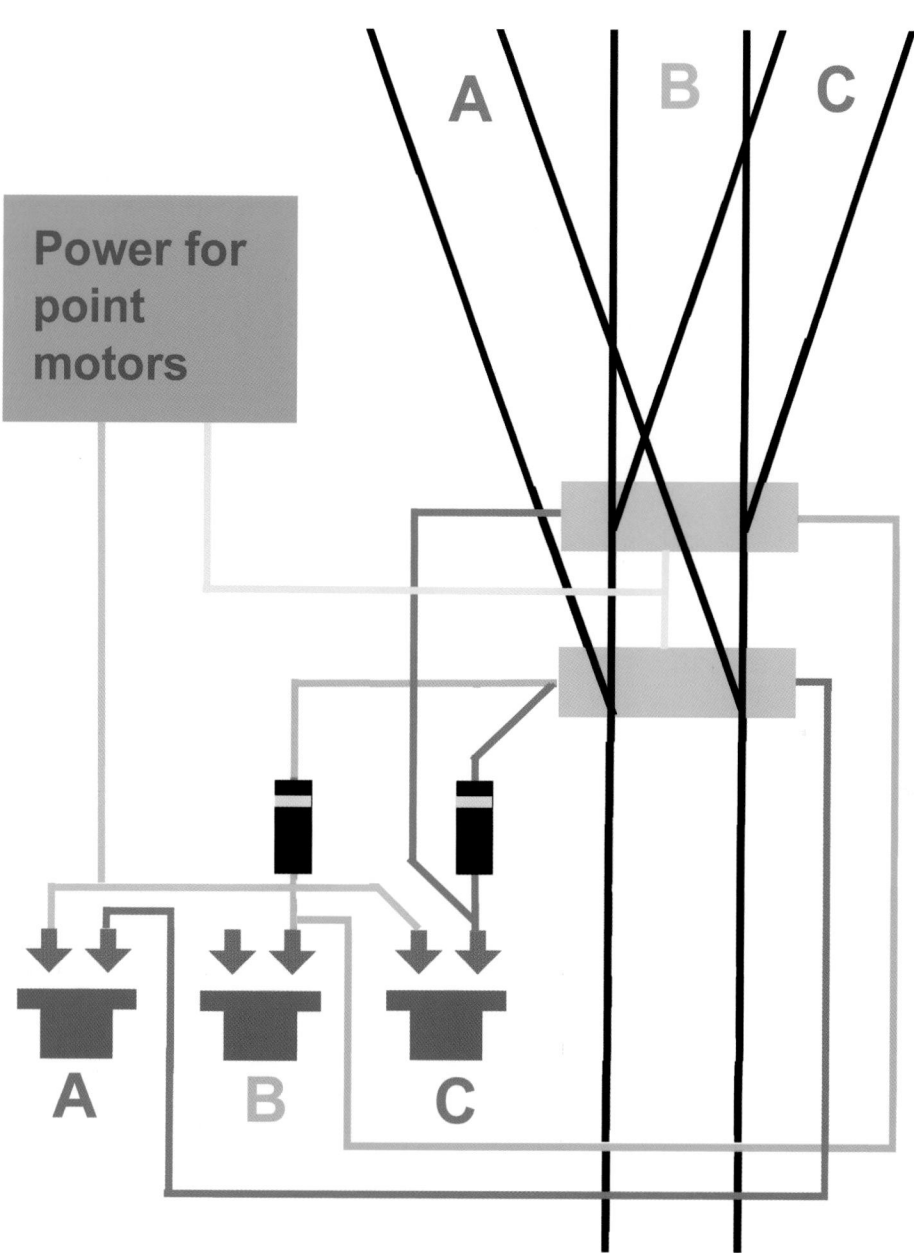

This diagram shows how to wire a three-way point to be operated by a single press of one of three push-buttons. Push-buttons B and C both operate two solenoid point motors. They share a connection. To prevent unwanted backfeeds, two diodes have been used.

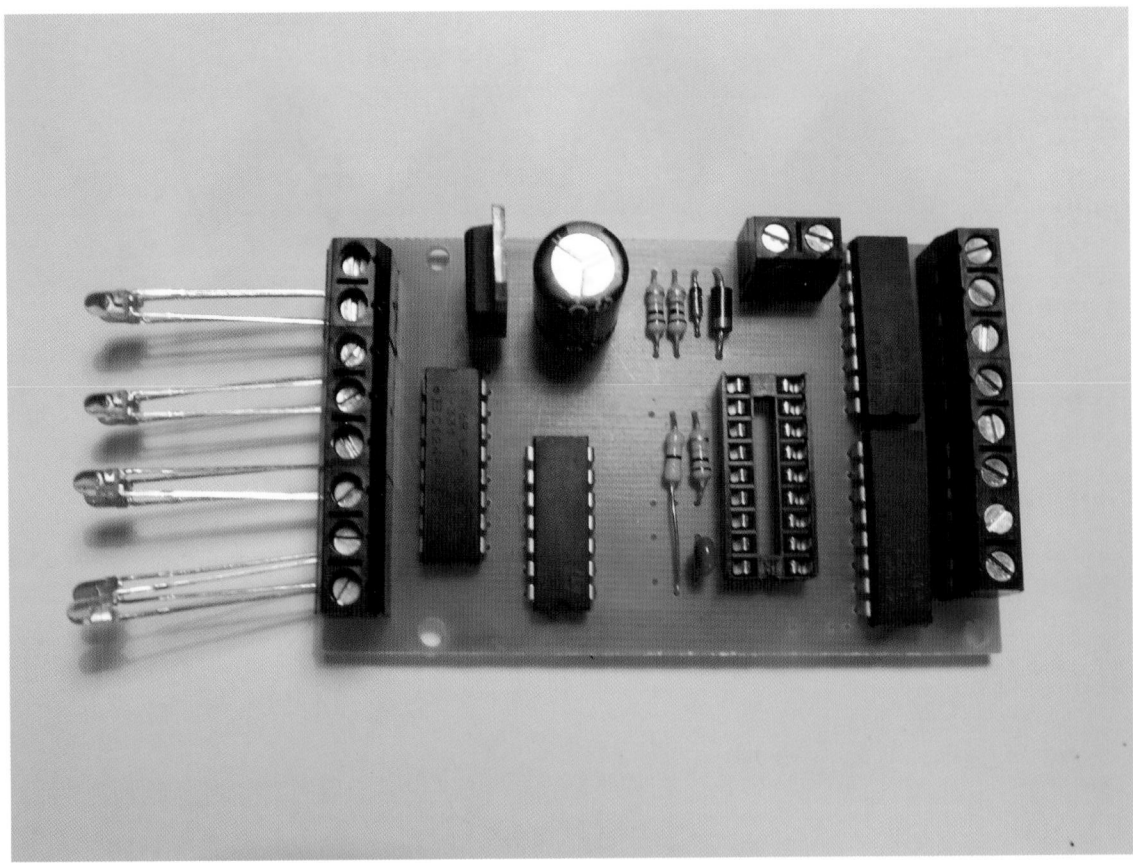

The Point Indicator here shows the setting of four solenoid point motor-operated points. There are a pair of LEDs in the terminal blocks for each point. These are unscrewed and wired to the control panel. The terminal blocks at the opposite side of the Point Indicator board are wired to the switches operating the points. The two-way terminal block is used to connect power to the Point Indicator board.

you can light pairs of LEDs to show the points setting by wiring the LEDs to a contact changed by the point's movement.

DCC Accessory Decoders

One advantage to DCC accessory decoders is that if you use controllers linked by radio or infrared you can switch the points from wherever you are standing in the railway room. DCC and passing contact switches are the two most expensive methods of controlling solenoid points. Using DCC decoders has the advantage that a control panel with switches is not required, which saves time on wiring. You may, however, find that not having a

control panel is a disadvantage because a series of apparently unrelated buttons have to be pressed on the DCC controller to change the point, whereas if the DCC system is linked to a computer the track plan can be displayed on the screen and the points can be operated via a mouse. A further possibility is that DCC controllers can be programmed so that pressing a series of buttons sets up a complete route for a train. Another factor to be considered is that on a large model railway a train can be followed by its operator with a handset that can also operate the points from anywhere in the room, whereas the presence of a control panel confines the operator to one place.

POWER FOR SOLENOID POINT MOTORS

Solenoid point motors can be powered by AC or DC electricity. Although you can buy an uncased transformer to step down the mains electricity to 16V AC, this is a dangerous option unless you are qualified to work with mains electricity. Live mains will be exposed and if you get the connections wrong, rather than decreasing the voltage, the transformer will increase it potentially up to 3,000V. Cased transformers supplied by companies such as Gauge Master take care of all of the safety concerns. A lot of model railway controllers have an accessory output built into them. This is often 16V AC and is intended for working solenoid point motors. Personal experience shows that 16V is a good choice as 12V struggles to move a solenoid point motor.

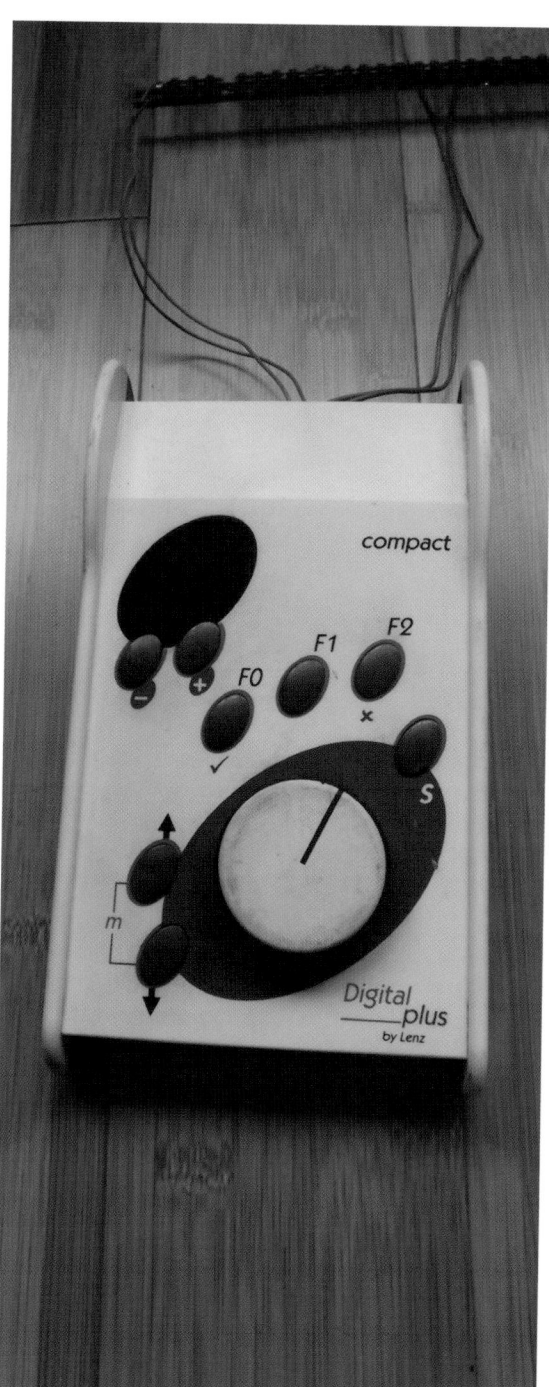

The written specification on this transformer indicates that it is a mains to 15V transformer. The two 120V windings would be connected together for the UK. Connecting the wires and securing everything in a safe box is a job for a qualified person because the mains connections are exposed.

This DCC controller can be used to change the points as well as controlling the direction and speed of the locomotives. It can also operate the signals and even sound effects on board the engines.

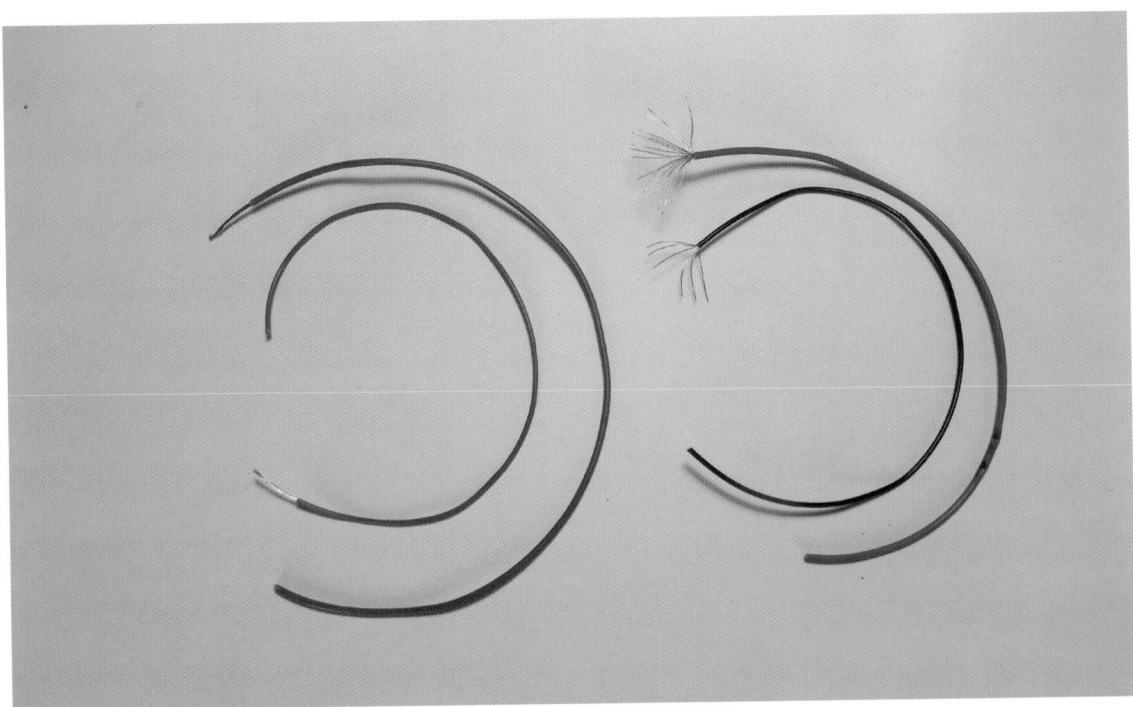

The ends of the black and red wires have been stripped of insulation and splayed out to show that the 3 amp rated red wire has thirteen strands of conductor and the 1.4 amp rated black wire has seven strands of conductor. Wire can also be obtained with a solid core. The disadvantage to this is that it is easily broken if bent a few times. This is particularly likely to happen where it has been stripped as it breaks along minute nicks left from the strippers if bent backwards and forwards.

As well as a suitable voltage, solenoid point motors require several amps of current. Thicker wire is needed to carry this large current. Generally wire consisting of a number of strands is more suitable for wiring model railways because it is flexible and less likely to snap off at the joints. The description 100m 7/0.2mm on a reel of wire or in a catalogue indicates a 100m length of wire consisting of seven strands of 0.2 mm diameter wire. This wire would carry 1.4A of current. Wire labelled with 16/0.2mm carries 3A of current. Most wire is made of copper as it is highly conductive and reasonably inert (meaning, for example, that it doesn't oxidize easily). Even though copper is very conductive it is not perfect and the longer the piece of wire the greater its resistance will be. For one point motor wired six feet away 1.4A wire is probably sufficient, but two point motors wired twenty feet away, working at the same time, will need 3A wire.

Because of the large currents, if you are switching several point motors at once you almost definitely will need a CDU.

Capacitor Discharge Unit (CDU)

Solenoid point motors consume power only when they are switched. It does not matter how many point motors you have, it matters how many you want to switch at the same time. To switch several points simultaneously requires a large current. Three point motors are going to require three times as much current as a single point motor. To supply this current would require a large and therefore heavy and expensive transformer. The large current, though, is required for only a short length of time, less than a second. You can use a CDU to produce a pulse of large current from a small transformer. The heart of a CDU is a capacitor, which stores electrical charge. A small transformer will charge up the capacitor over a number of

The large cylindrical electronic component seen here is the capacitor. This is the heart of the CDU, storing up the electrical charge ready to be released when the points are switched.

seconds, enabling a momentary large current to be discharged when you throw the switch to operate the points simultaneously. A toilet cistern is a good analogy. It takes a long time for the cistern to fill from the mains water supply but only a very short time to flush the bowl when the handle is pushed.

Another good reason for using a CDU is to protect the point motor coils from burning out. Once the CDU has discharged the large amount of current, it cuts off further current to the point motor until the switch is opened. If the current were to flow continuously, for example if the switch got stuck, the point motor coil could overheat and burn out.

There are numerous manufacturers of CDUs but the important factor is the size of the capacitor, measured in microfarads. A useful one to have would be rated at 4,700 microfarads or greater. A CDU with two 4,700 microfarad capacitors powered from 16V AC should switch at least six point motors simultaneously. To increase the number of point motors being switched the voltage that charges the

CDU could be increased to 24V. This should double the number of points you can switch, providing the wire can handle it.

As the point motors are only powered momentarily, you need no more power for a large number of points if they are switched individually.

DIODE MATRIX

So far we have explained how to wire a switch to a single point motor. It may be that you want to be able to press a single push-button switch to cause a number of points to change to a set route.

The diagram overleaf shows push-button switch A wired to set the route to track A, push-button switch B wired to set the route to track B, and push-button switch C wired to set the route to track C. All the connections to the two point motors are shown in the diagram. Look at the green coloured wire. The electricity can flow from switch B to switch C and so the right hand solenoid point motor will try to move in both directions at once.

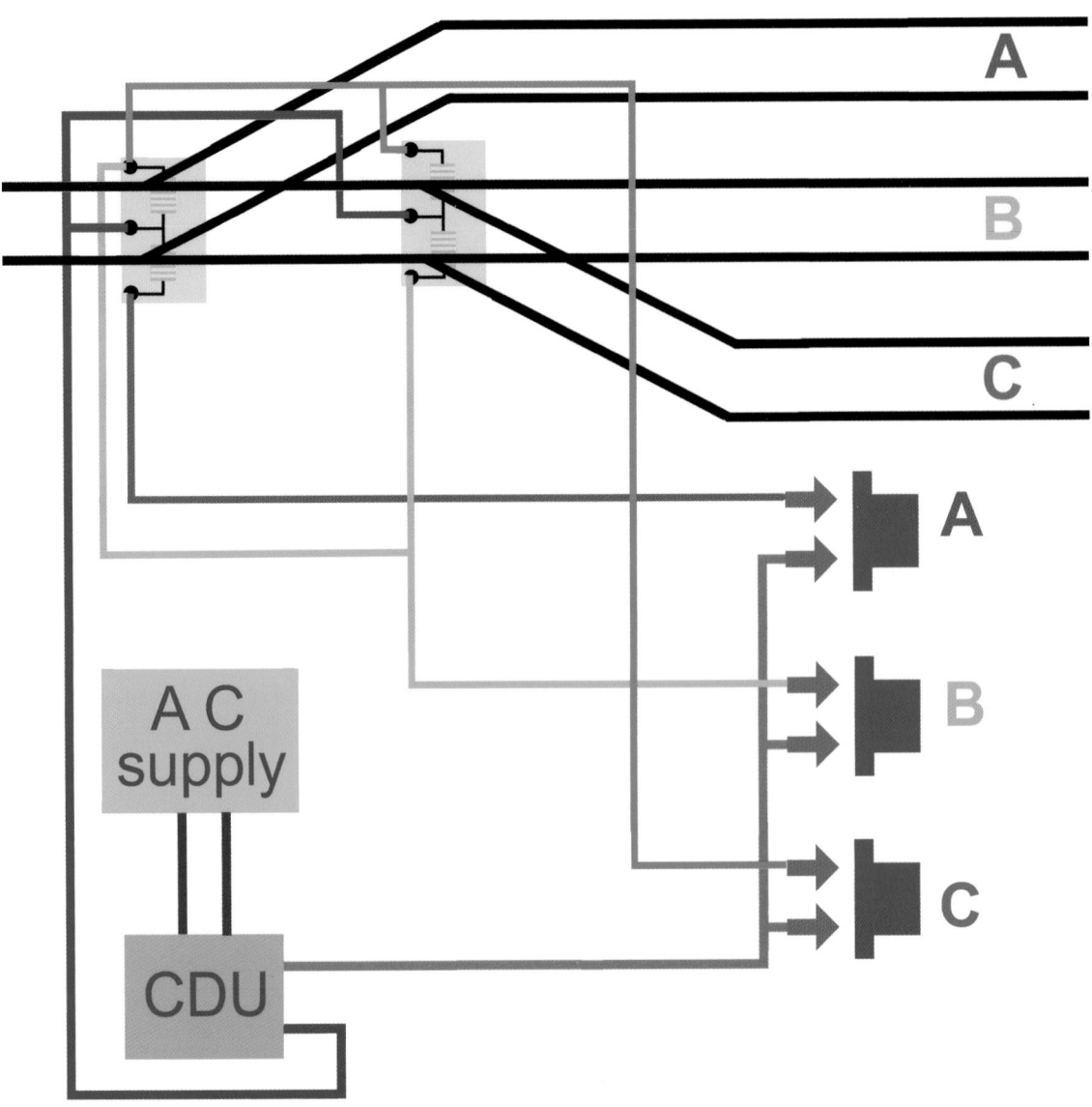

This diagram shows an attempt to wire three push button switches A,B and C to select the route to either siding A, B or C. For example, if you press push button C the upper solenoid of both point motors is energized and the points are pulled into place for the train to run into siding C. However, there is a snag.

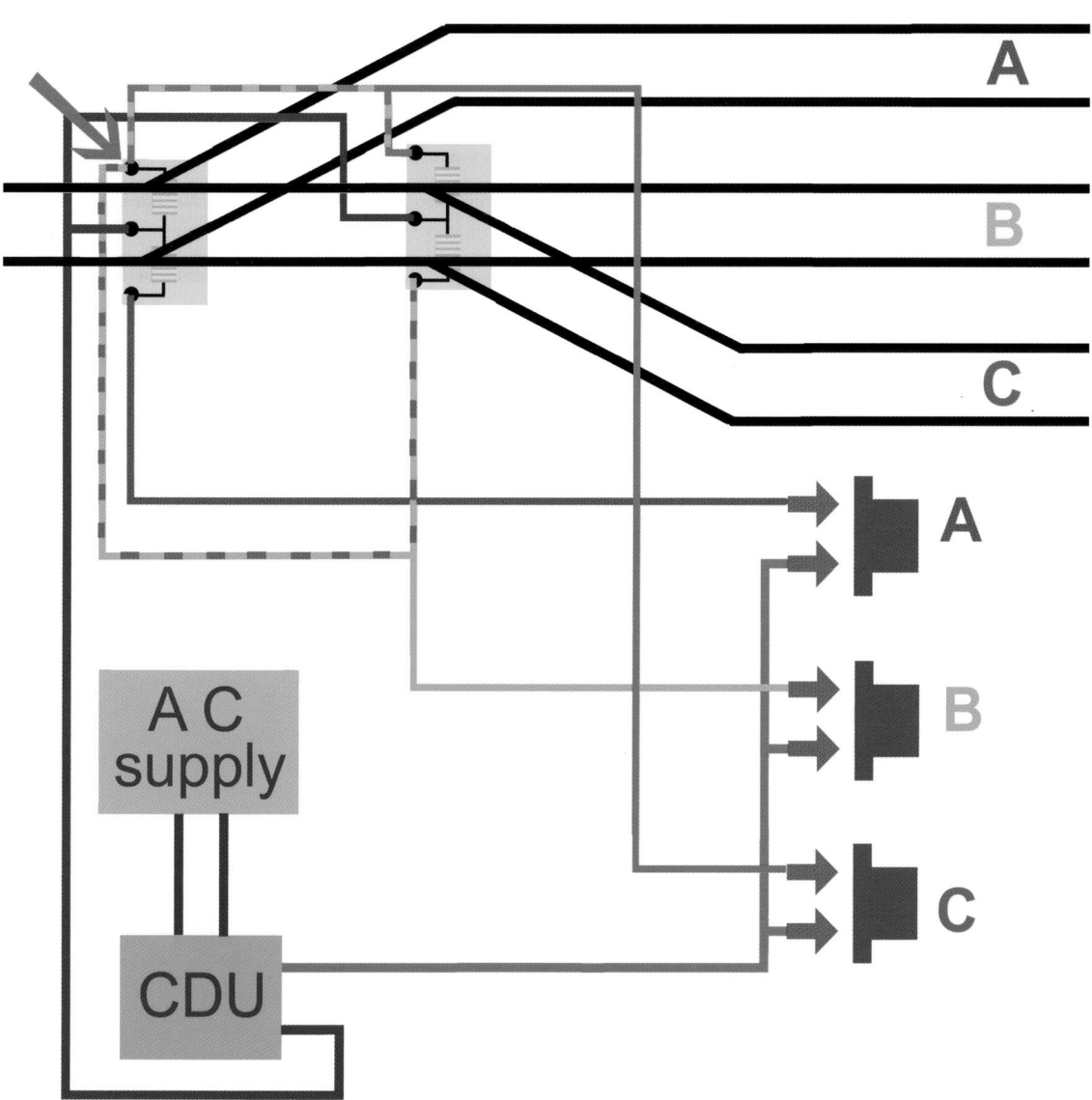

This diagram shows the problem. Both the green and orange wire connect to the same solenoid.
When you press either switch B or C both solenoids on the right hand point motor become energized.
This will prevent the point motor working.

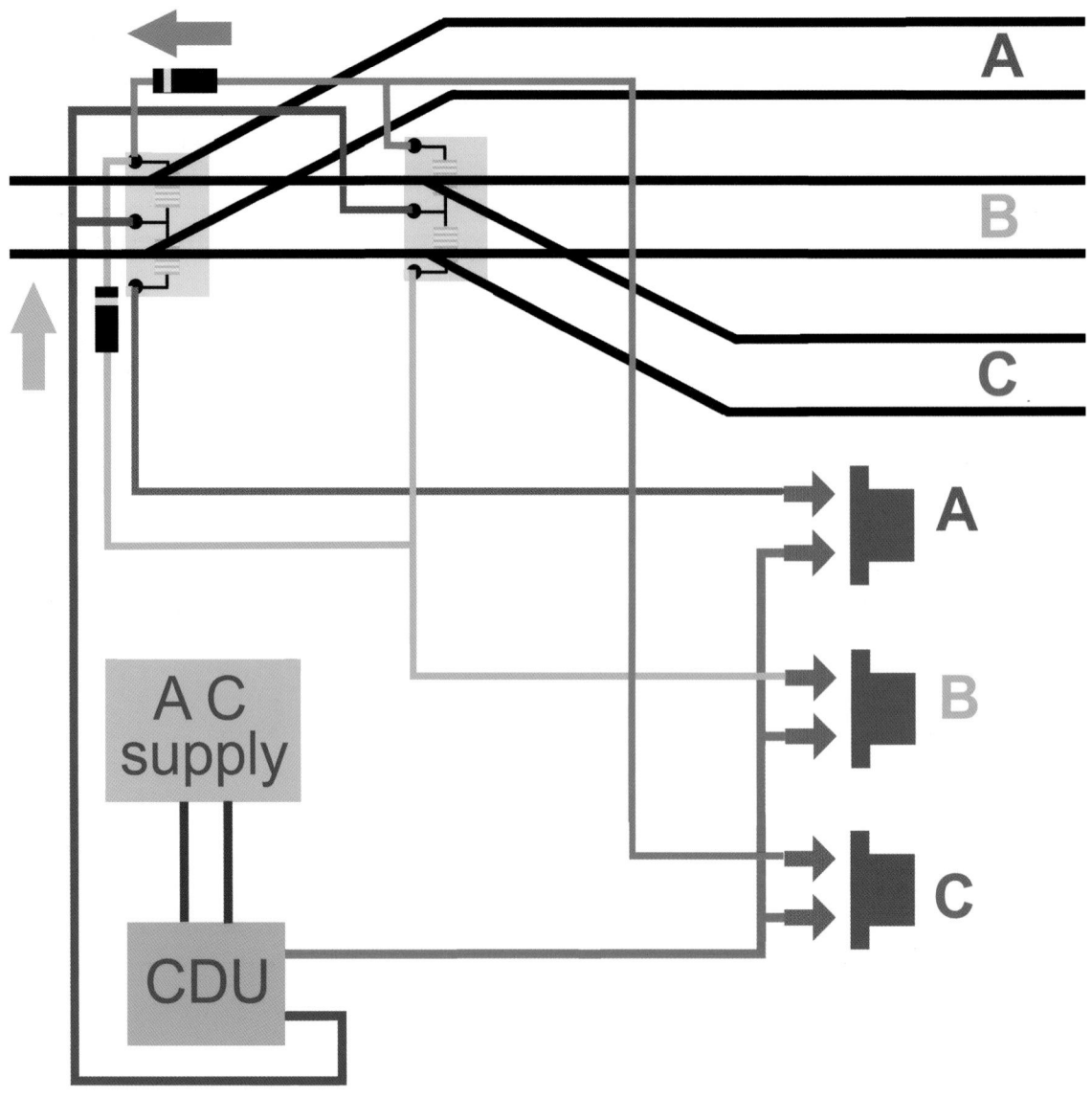

This final diagram shows how placing two diodes prevents the two solenoids of the point motor from being energized at the same time.

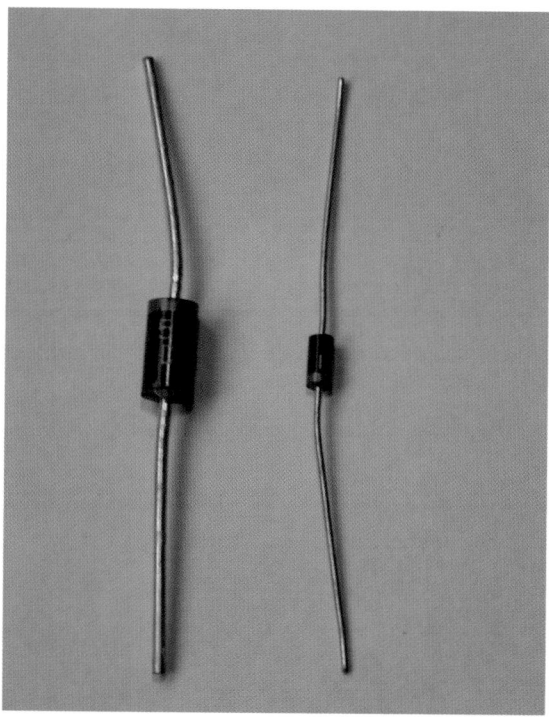

A 3 amp rated diode, such as the one shown here, is suitable for building diode matrixes. Its manufacturer's part number is 5N401 and it costs only pennies.

You can see that when push-button B is pressed, the electricity is flowing in the wrong direction down the green wire. The problem could be prevented if we had a one-way valve for electricity. A diode behaves as a one-way valve.

The typical diode seen here has a silver band, although other colours are sometimes used, to mark the cathode (negative) end. This silver band marks the direction in which the electricity is flowing.

The two legs of the diode are intended for soldering into a printed circuit board, although for model railway use there is no reason why you cannot solder a wire directly to the diode's legs. Alternatively, you could use a connector, such as a chocolate block, to make connections.

If you study the final diagram you will see that the problem has been solved and the electricity can now flow towards the solenoid point motor, but not away from it. This is a simple example of a diode matrix, but the idea can be used for more complicated situations.

SLOW MOTION POINT MOTORS

These are used by modellers who are not satisfied with point blades suddenly flicking across when operated with solenoids and who want to achieve a more realistic point movement. Slow motion point motors contain a DC electric motor driving either a series of gears or a threaded rod to convert many revolutions of the motor into a small movement for operating the point. To change the route of the point the polarity to the electric motor is reversed, causing the motor to turn in the opposite direction. The motor continues to turn until it has pushed the point blade against the stock rail. The motor stalls when it cannot turn any more. The motor is designed so that it is not damaged by a current flowing through it when it is not moving and also to have a low current when stalled. Keeping the motor powered ensures the point blade is firmly pressed against the stock rail, improving the electrical connection between the two and reducing the chance of derailments. Points with a built-in spring that does the job of pressing the point blades against the stop rails may operate more smoothly if the spring is removed. A 12V DC supply is normally used for slow motion point motors. The polarity is usually reversed by using a double pole, double throw switch.

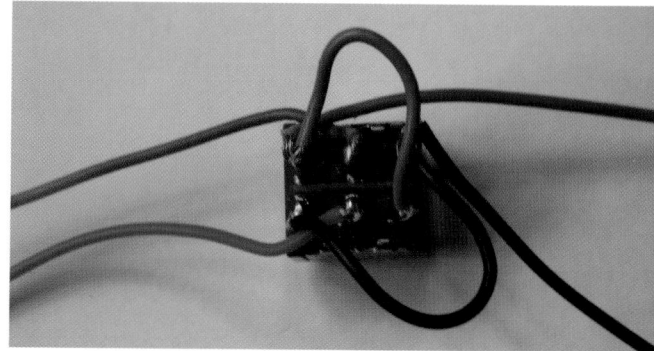

Wires can be soldered to the lugs on a double pole, double throw switch to make it reverse polarity and so reverse the direction of rotation of the DC electric motor inside the slow motion point motor. Power comes in along the black and green wires and travels to the point motor along the red and black wires.

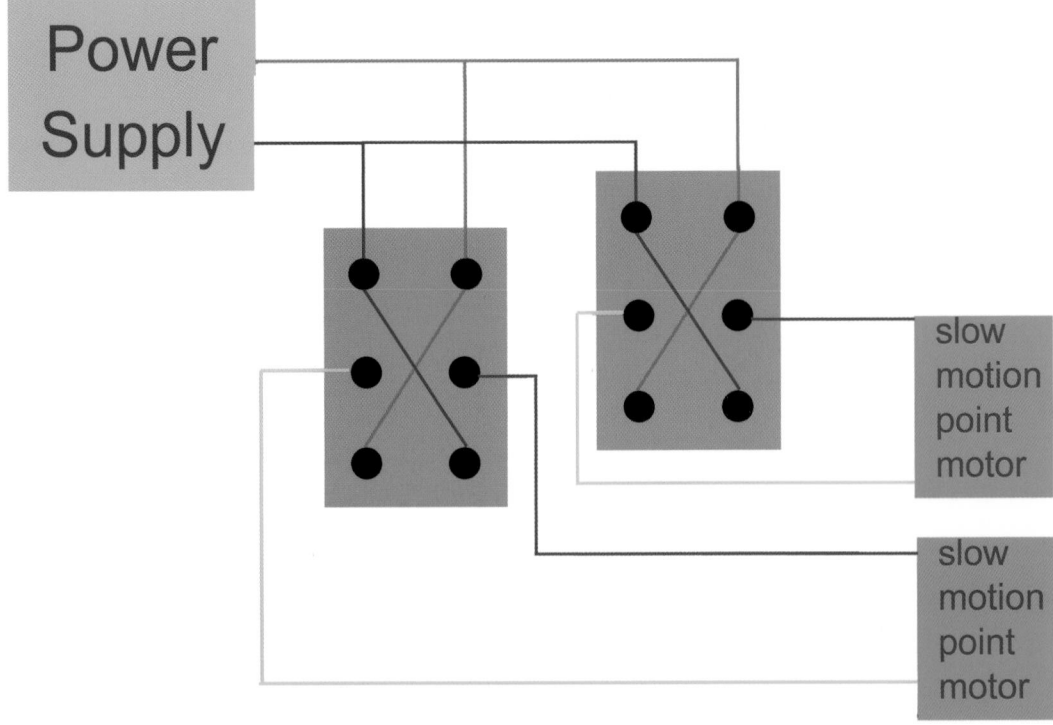

This diagram illustrates the same wiring as shown in the previous photograph, with two point motors operated by a single power supply. This can easily be extended to more point motors, although there will be an upper limit as each point motor is continually powered.

TYPES OF SLOW MOTION POINT MOTORS

Some factors to think about if you wish to use slow motion point motors are dimensions (particularly the depth below the baseboard), how quiet or noisy it is in operation, voltage and current consumption and how easily it can be used with DCC. Price and availability are also important as some types are manufactured overseas. The number of contacts built into the slow motion point motor may be important for those who want to incorporate features such as signal interlocking. Several types of slow motion point motors are available, including:

- **Traintronics CM-TT300**. This has a built-in DCC decoder, but it will also work with 12V DC.
- **Tortoise Slow Motion Point**. This point motor consists of a cube of plastic containing a DC electric motor geared down to produce a strong slow arm movement. This point motor has been popular for many years and requires an added decoder to operate with DCC.
- **Fulgurex**
- **Lemaco**
- **Cobalt**. This has a built-in DCC decoder but can also be operated manually with a switch.
- **Tillig**. Uses a threaded rod instead of gear wheels.
- **Little Jemmy**. This is available in kit form and uses an AC supply with momentary switches.

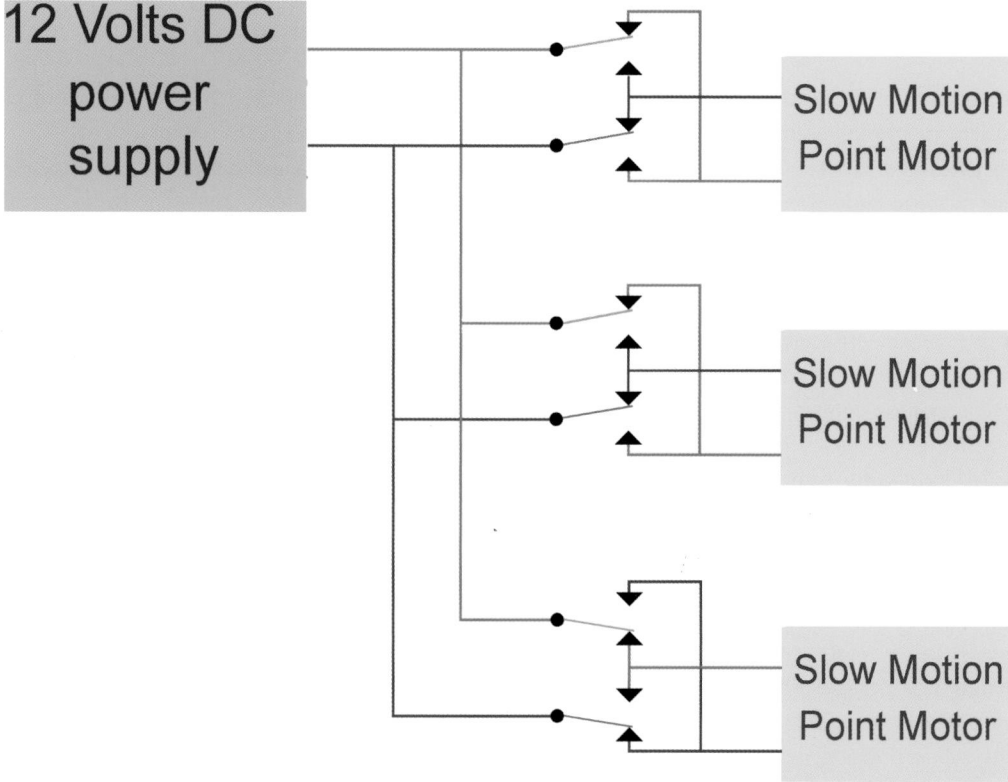

Three double pole, double throw switches wired to operate three slow motion point motors. It should be apparent that this idea can easily be extended for larger numbers of point motors. In this diagram the contacts inside the switches are shown. This makes it easier to see what happens when the switches are thrown.

POWER FOR SLOW MOTION POINT MOTORS

Slow motion point motors require a DC voltage of typically 12V. If you reduce this voltage slightly the points will move over more slowly. A simple and inexpensive way to reduce the voltage is to add diodes into the supply wire. The voltage will be reduced by 0.7V for each diode inserted. As all the slow motion point motors are continuously powered, the more point motors you have the greater the current the power supply will have to provide. The manufacturer should state the current consumption of the slow motion point motor. Multiply this by the number of point motors you use to check that your supply is adequate.

Switching the Polarity of a Slow Motion Points Motor

To move a point, the polarity to the slow motion point motor needs to be reversed. This is achieved by using a double pole, double throw switch.

A double pole, double throw switch is a switch made up of two sets of changeover contacts, both of which are mechanically moved by a single lever. These contacts are isolated from one another. The accompanying diagram shows a power supply connected via switches to three slow motion point motors. The switches have been switched to different positions. The diagram shows how the polarity of the slow motion point motor has been changed. On the reverse side of the double pole, double throw switch there are six studs intended for attaching wires by solder.

SERVO MOTORS

Servo motors have many applications for model railways, particularly for moving points, signals and both level crossing gates and barriers. One of the advantages of using a servo motor to control points is their small size. They can also make the points move at the slow speed of a real point in contrast to the less realistic rapid movement of the solenoid.

Whereas ordinary electric motors simply rotate while they are powered, servo motors have an arm that rotates to a position determined by an electrical signal. Inexpensive good quality ones are made for radio-controlled models, for example for moving the rudder of a radio-controlled boat.

Three wires connect to a servo motor: two are for power but the third sends the electrical signal to tell the servo motor which position to turn to. The servo motor can move its arm over a total angle of approximately 270 degrees. There are two main types of servo motor: the older design of analogue servo and the modern digital servo. Although there are advantages to the digital type, it is more expensive and the analogue type is perfectly acceptable for most model railway uses. Both types, however, use the same control signal so they are interchangeable. Servo

motors come in various sizes but the size described as miniature is very suitable for model railways.

You do, however, need an electronic control board to produce the electrical control signal. These are designed to give selectable speeds and choice of servo arm position. They only require an on/off switch to be connected to them. Servo motors are controlled by a pulse width modulated signal (PWM). This simply means that every twenty milliseconds a pulse of voltage is fed into the motor. The width of this pulse is proportional to the angle the servo motor turns to. Therefore a wider pulse equates to a greater clockwise position of the servo motor arm. While the pulse stays at the same width the arm will remain stationary. When the width of the pulse changes the servo motor arm moves rapidly to the new position determined by the new width of pulse. The other two wires carry 0V and 5V to power the servo motor.

Inside the servo motor there is a DC (direct current) electric motor and gear wheels connecting the motor to the servo motor arm. These gears are arranged so that it takes many rotations of the motor through a series of gears to produce a small movement of the servo motor arm. This gives fine control of the arm's movement and increases the servo arm

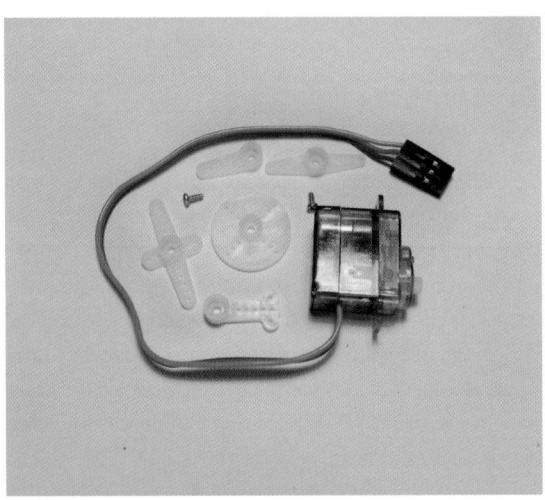

A servo motor with the assortment of arms supplied with it. The arms are called horns by radio control modellers. They clip onto the rotating part on the right of the servo motor and are secured by a small screw.

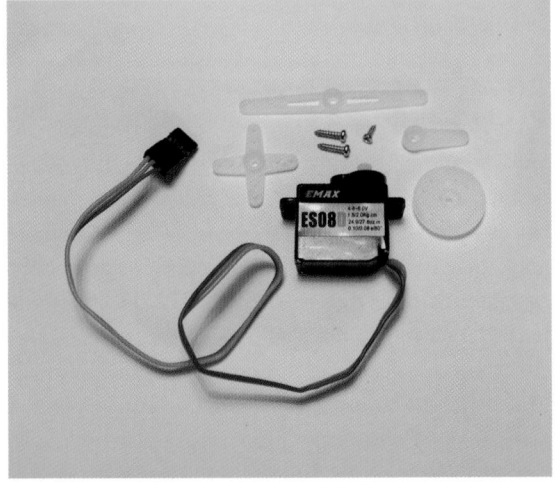

A servo motor made by a different manufacturer, showing the three wires going to the connector attached to the control board.

The underside of the baseboard. As the servo motor arm rotates, the fine steel wire will move from side to side. This will cause the fine wire to rotate in the hole in the baseboard. Another crank bent into the wire on the upper side of the baseboard moves the point's tie bar.

strength, known as torque. In other words, the arm of the servo exerts a lot more force than the motor on its own would exert

The servo motor arm is connected internally to a potentiometer, which is a resistor with a contact that slides along it. This contact is moved by the servo motor arm. One end of the resistor is connected to 5V and the other end is connected to 0V. As the contact is moved by the servo motor arm, the voltage on the contact is gradually changed from 5V to 0V. In the centre position the voltage will be 2.5V.

The potentiometer converts the mechanical movement of the servo motor arm into an electrical signal that is compared with the electrical control signal sent from the control board. When the two match, the arm has reached its required position.

LINKING SERVO MOTORS TO POINTS

The servo motor can be mounted above or below the baseboard. If you wish to mount a servo under the baseboard it will be linked to the point's tie bar by stiff wire. A hole is made in the baseboard for the wire to rotate in. The end of the wire is bent at right angles twice to make a Z shape, the end of which fits into a hole in the tie bar. You now have in effect a crank, a small rotation of which will give the necessary sideways movement to move the tie bar. Underneath the baseboard the wire is again bent at 90 degrees, leaving about 3cm at the end, which fits into a hole on the servo motor's arm. With this arrangement a large movement of the servo motor's arm converts to small movement at the tie bar and of the wire. Doing this makes the movements slower and less jerky.

SOURCES OF SERVO MOTOR CONTROL BOARDS

- **Heathcote-Electronics**. Single and dual servo motor controllers are available, together with servo motors and servo motor mounting brackets.
- **MERG (Model Electronic Railway Group)** produces a kit for its members.
- Some DCC point decoders, for example those made by **ESU** and **Team Digital**, have the option to operate servo motors.

CHAPTER THREE

LIVE FROGS, DEAD FROGS AND ELECTROFROGS

Some point motors have a number of electrical contacts that switch over with the point's movement. These can be used to operate signals, switch the point's frog polarity, to give an indication of the point's setting and for use in various interlocking schemes.

Some point motors already have these contacts built in, such as Seep solenoid point motors and many of the slow motion point motors. More information about how signals may be operated with the point motor's contacts may be found in Chapter 5. A

The contact worked by the point wired to switch 12V DC to the coil of the relay. When the relay coil is connected all the relay's contacts are switched over. If the relay does not have enough contacts, the point's contact can be wired to additional relay coils wired in parallel.

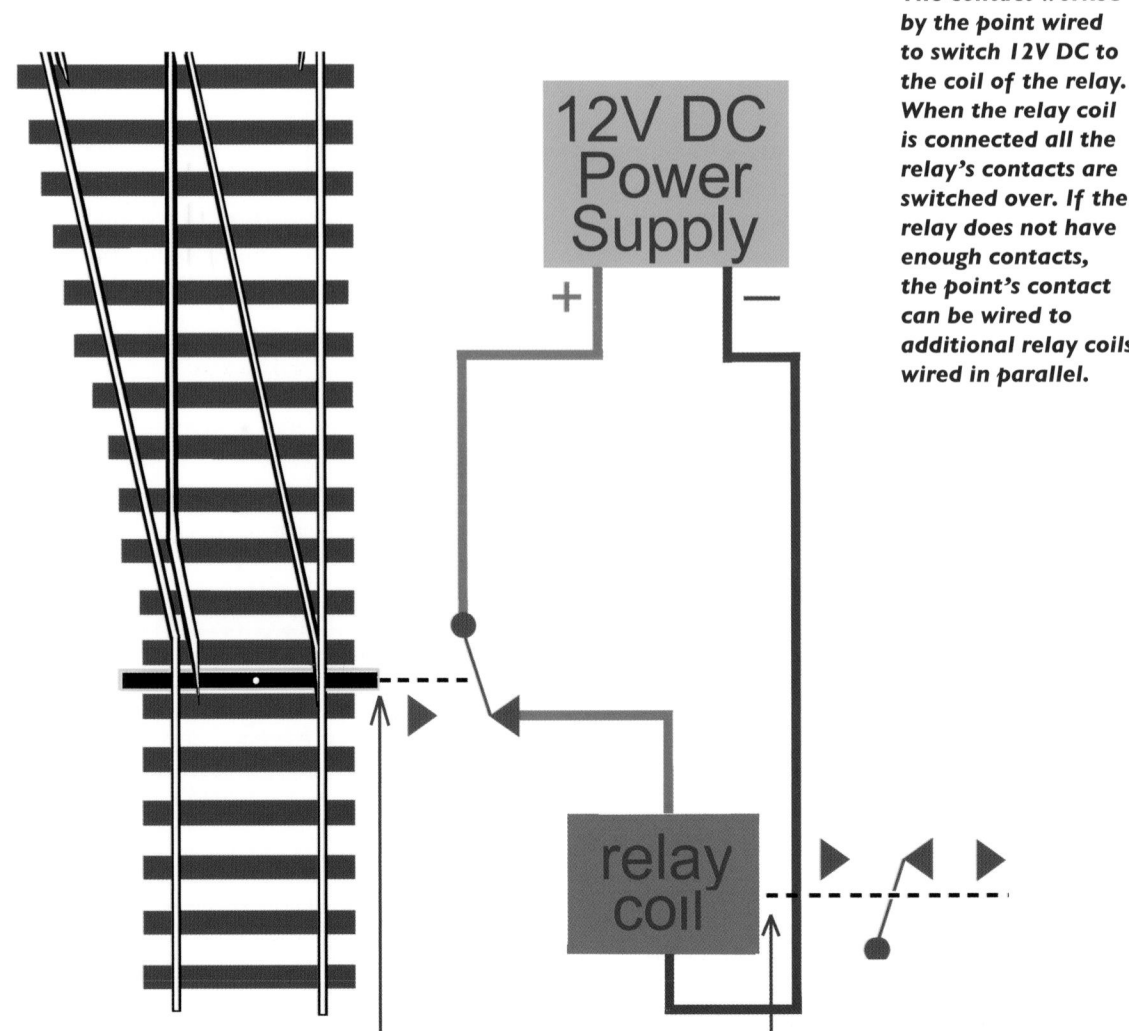

12V DC Power Supply

+   −

relay coil

Seep point motor, for example, has just a single pole, double throw (changeover) contact, but you may require more contacts than this. The conventional way to achieve this is to use the contact on the Seep motor to operate one or more relays. Relays can have a number of poles, so you can produce as many contacts as you wish. (For more information about relays, see Chapter 8.)

The reason for having many different poles is to keep electrical circuits separated from each other. If, for example, an LED signal circuit and a circuit for switching the frog were not separated in this way, the signal could be damaged by the high current to the frog.

MICROSWITCHES

If your point motor has no contacts these can be added by using microswitches. A microswitch is a switch operated mechanically by a lever. The lever is spring loaded. A typical example of the use of a microswitch is a fridge light. When the fridge door opens the spring-loaded arm of the microswitch is released and the contact is closed, thus lighting the light bulb.

I have used microswitches with Peco point motors by mounting them under the baseboard on a block of wood. The microswitch arm is easily adjusted to be pushed by the point motor pin, which fortuitously

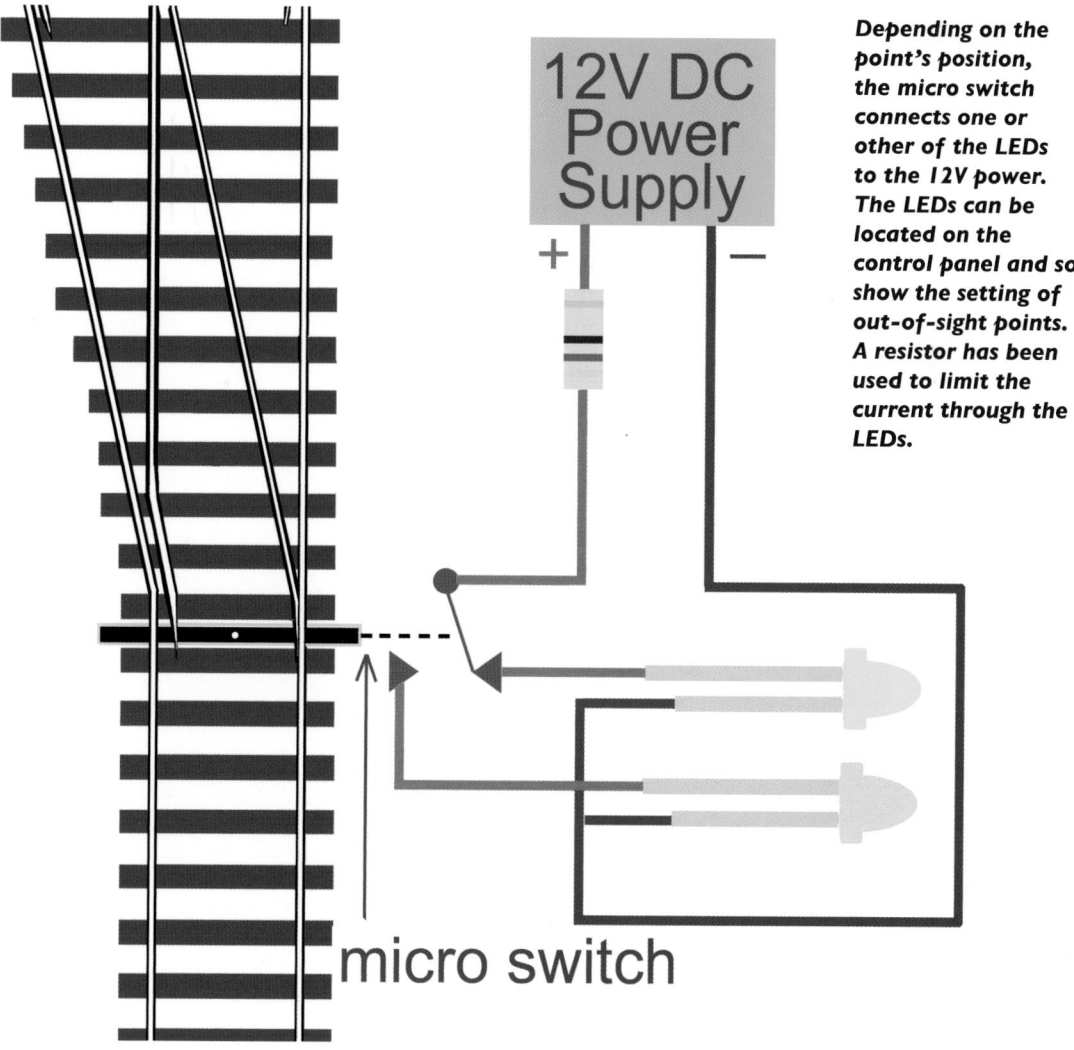

Depending on the point's position, the micro switch connects one or other of the LEDs to the 12V power. The LEDs can be located on the control panel and so show the setting of out-of-sight points. A resistor has been used to limit the current through the LEDs.

12V DC Power Supply

micro switch

The frog on a full-size point at the disused sand sidings near Froghall, Staffordshire, where sand was loaded for transport to the Pilkington glass factory. The point is made using bullhead rail. More modern track uses flat bottom rail, which does not require the chairs that can be seen attached to the sleepers.

extends below the point motor. Contacts worked by the points are useful for lighting a pair of LEDs on a control panel to show the position of a point.

LIVE FROGS AND DEAD FROGS

The two main ways in which points are wired are known as live frog and dead frog. Frog refers to the V-shape where the inner rails meet in a point.

In order for a train to move both rails must be at different polarities: a positive voltage and a negative voltage. To someone sitting on a model train facing in the direction in which the train is moving, the basic wiring convention is that the left-hand rail is always a negative voltage and the right-hand rail therefore is always positive voltage. Looking at the accompanying diagram, you will see that the frog needs to change voltage depending on the route taken.

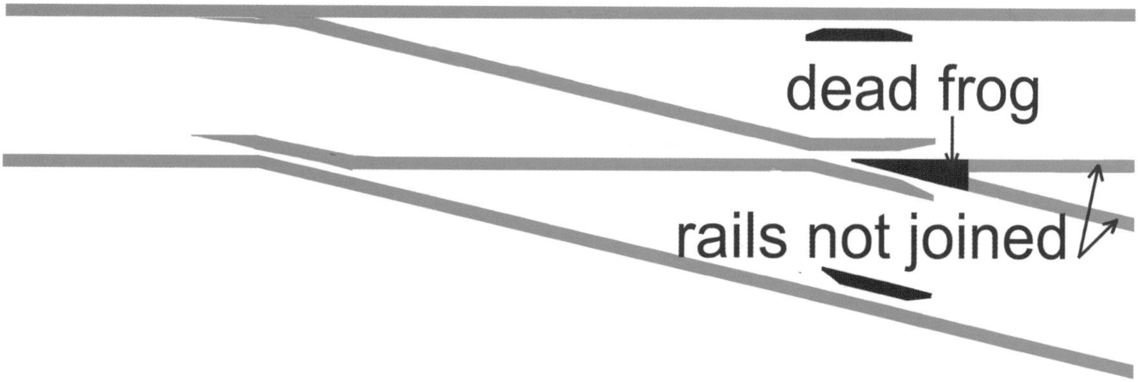

dead frog

rails not joined

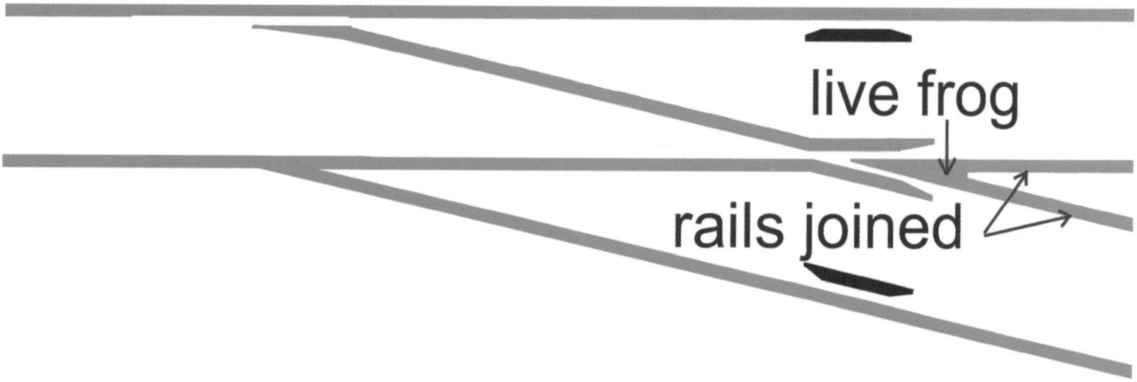

live frog

rails joined

The upper point has a dead frog marked in grey. Although this makes the wiring simpler, the disadvantage is that locomotive wheels crossing the frog cannot pick up electricity. This is more of a problem for four-wheeled engines as only one wheel is left to pick up on that side of the train, because two are on the opposite rail of the track and the third is on the frog. A spot of dirt on the track or slightly uneven track may deprive the locomotive of power.

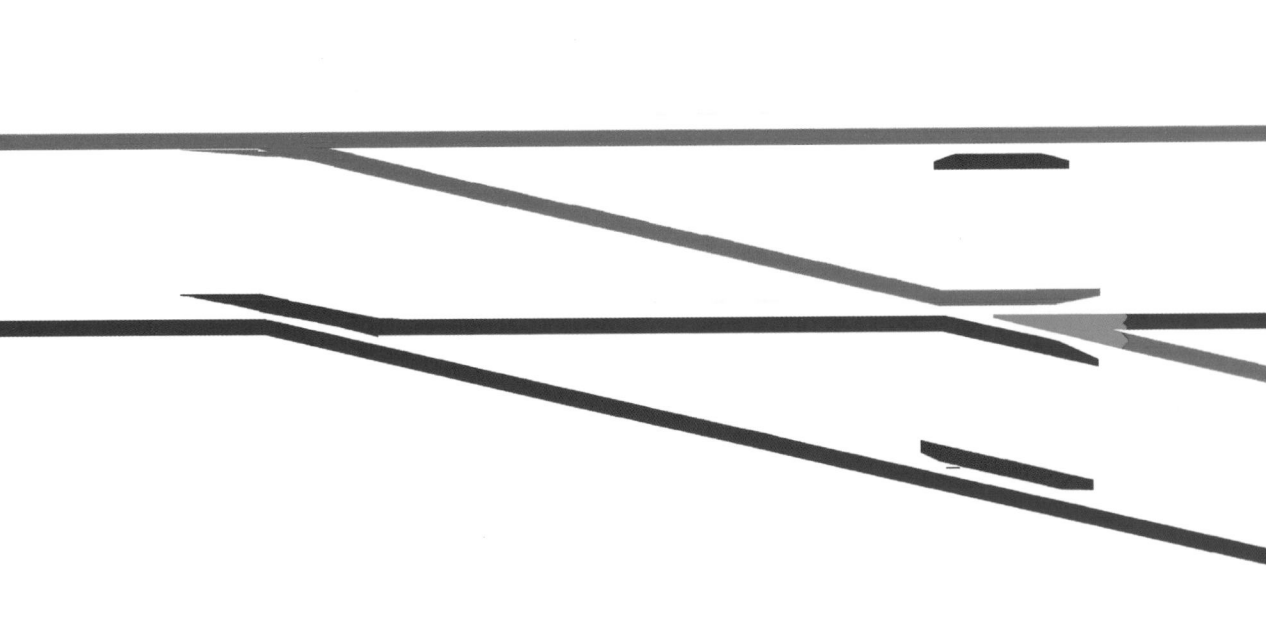

This diagram shows how the dead frog separates the polarity of the rails at the frog end. A live frog would have the rails joining the frog at the same polarity.

DEAD FROG POINTS

The simple way for model track manufacturers to evade this conundrum is to mould the frog in plastic insulation, entirely avoiding the problem of switching the frog's voltage. The manufacturer builds the points so that the rails connecting to the frog are electrically connected to the point blades. These are called dead frog points. Peco's trade name for this type of point is Insulfrog. Dead frog points are easier for the railway modeller to wire than live frog points.

Dead frog points can work in two ways. The first ensures that the route not selected is dead (not electrified) and the route selected is live (electrified). The second method ensures that both routes – the selected and the not selected – are always live (electrified). The reason you may want to make a line dead when it is not selected, for example, is if the point is leading to a siding. Using this type of point means that you can leave a train in the siding and it will not move until the point is set for it to leave. An alternative scenario is illustrated by the diagram of a terminus station, which can be full of trains that do not move until required. Some manufacturers, such as Kato, make points for which you can select which of the two types of operation you want.

If there were no disadvantages with dead frog points (Insulfrog), they would be used all the time and Peco would not have to make two types of points. The problem with dead frog points is that some engines, such as a small shunting engine with just four wheels, are going to have one wheel on the plastic frog as they move across the point. This wheel cannot pick up current. This leaves only one wheel on that side of the train to pick up electricity, which can result in erratic running.

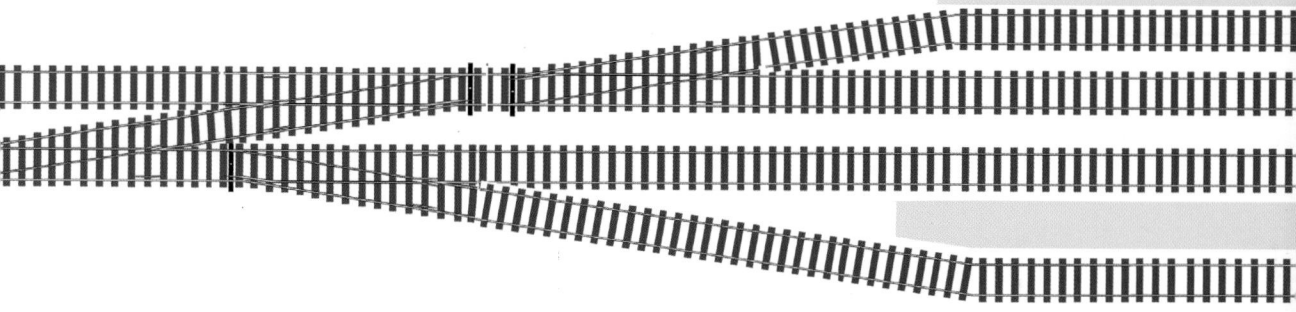

In a large terminus station there can be a number of trains waiting to depart and several trains that have just arrived. Using points to isolate the track makes it simple to replicate this. This is not a problem with DCC as trains can be stopped on live tracks. Indeed, DCC modellers prefer to have all the tracks live.

LIVE FROG POINTS

Live frog points, called Electrofrog by Peco, give superior smooth running across the points, but this is at the cost of some electrical complications. Both point blades and the frog are electrically connected together, but the stock rails only connect to the point blade that is touching them. With live frog points, when the point blades touch the stock rail the electricity to the frog will be at the correct polarity for the route the point is set to.

The problem, however, is that the route to which the point is not set will have both tracks at the same polarity. If there is an engine on this track it will not move, even though both rails may be at 12V. Each rail must be at a different voltage for electricity to flow from one rail to the other through the engine's elec-

tric motor. This can be a good outcome as it makes the route dead, but problems arise with some track plans such as passing loops. If the points are set for two opposing routes, one frog will be negative and the other frog will be positive, and the connecting rail joining these together will result in a short circuit. The controller will cut out and all the trains will come to a standstill.

The solution is to use insulation breaks on the two centre lines. These breaks can be made by using plastic rail joiners.

When using Electrofrog points make sure the power feeds to the track are always at the single-track ends of the points and use insulation breaks where points face each other. Drawing a diagram of the track should help you solve these electrical conflicts.

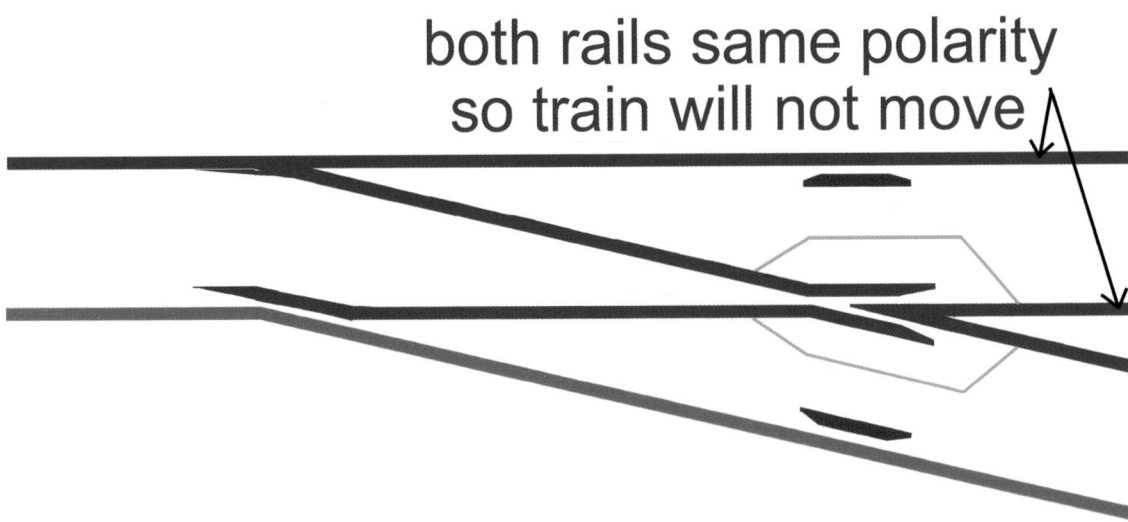

both rails same polarity so train will not move

The polarity of the frog depends upon which rail the point blades are touching. The result of this is that one track will have both rails at the same polarity and the train will not move. This may not be a problem for a siding, but it complicates track wiring when there are points facing both directions as the feed cannot come from the double-track end.

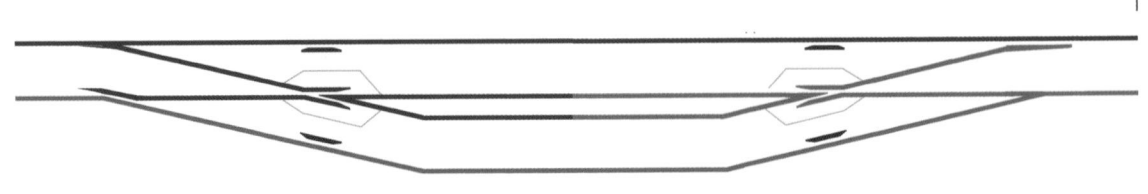

This diagram shows that the train will not run on either track because the point settings produce the same polarity on each rail.

POINT BLADE CONTACTS

The electrical switching to the frog relies on the point blade making a good contact with the stock rail. Factors such as dirt can make this contact unreliable. It seems to be a greater problem with N gauge than 00 gauge. A more reliable electrical feed to the frog can be obtained by using a contact worked by the points movement. In fact, as well as switching the frog some modellers modify their points by making isolation breaks in the point blades, so that the ends of the point blades can be electrically bonded to the adjacent stock rails. This overcomes another problem that, without this modification, both point blades are at the same polarity and this can cause short circuits if a metal wheel bridges the

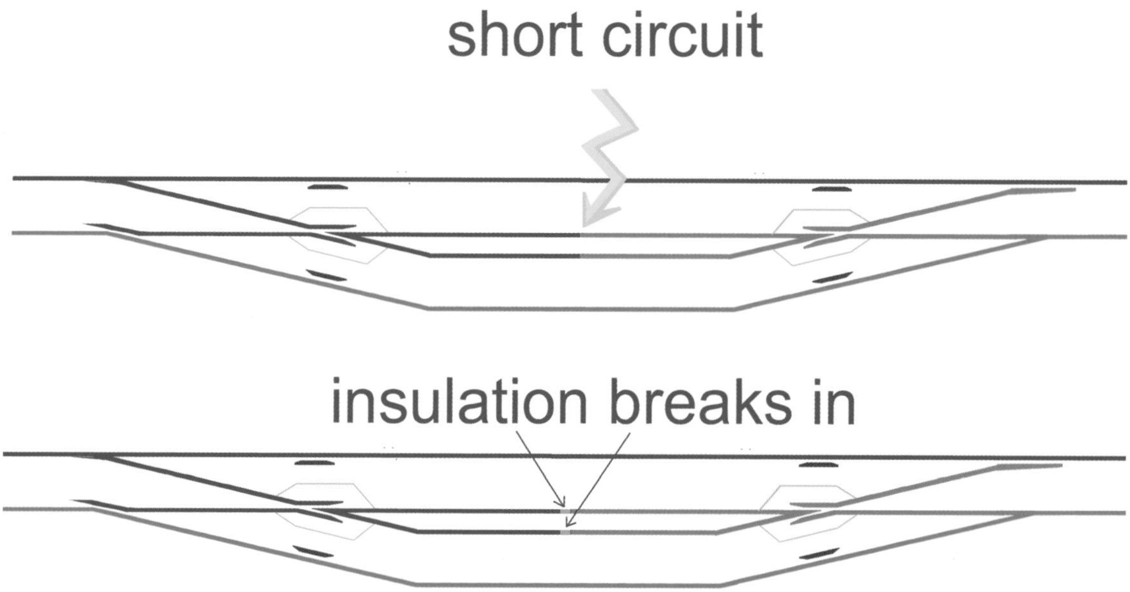

short circuit

insulation breaks in

Using live frog points can sometimes result in mysterious shorts. When both points are set to opposite lines the frogs are at different polarities and the centre tracks connecting them together give a short circuit. The lower diagram shows that the problem is solved by using insulation breaks. Insulating fish plates are made for these breaks, although the rails can simply be cut with a slitting saw in a mini-drill and the gap filled with insulating material such as epoxy glue. This may be simpler to achieve if the track is already laid.

gap between the stock rail and the open point blade. With DCC this short circuit cuts out the controller, so bringing all the trains to a stop. As a result many DCC modellers think this modification to the points is essential.

AUTOMATIC OPERATION OF POINTS

So far we have described how to operate the points via a human being, but it is possible to make the points work automatically with the movements of trains. An example where you might want to do this is where you have a train running automatically backwards and forwards. If you were to add a siding at one end, then by changing the points when the train arrives you could make the point change so that a second train departs. This allows two trains to travel alternately up and down the line under automatic control. The IRDOT-P unit made by Heathcote Electronics is suitable for this and will switch solenoid point motors.

There are other situations in which you may want the points to switch automatically. You can arrange automatic storage sidings so that when one train arrives another one leaves. Also with reverse loops it is very convenient to have the points change over automatically as the train runs round the loop. Passing loops can be arranged so that the points change automatically, either for both trains running in the same direction or both trains running in opposite directions. As well as controlling the points, electronic controls will automate the trains' movement and stopping time and control the signals.

A different approach to automating the points for users of DCC is to have all the points controlled by DCC decoders and to link up the DCC system to a personal computer. Various makes of software are available to enable you to run your railway automatically, including the points. A popular software package is Railroad & Co. by Freiwald Software. Hornby has recently released its own software and includes a USB connection on its DCC controller.

CHAPTER FOUR

A BRIEF HISTORY OF SIGNALLING

Signals that change realistically on a model railway as the train goes by look very effective. Railway signalling is the result of years of effort to make the railways safe while allowing an increasingly fast and more frequent train service to run. The very early railways used diverse methods of signalling. Men with flags, baskets full of hot coals that were hoisted in the air and rotating balls on posts are just some of the methods used. Trains were dispatched at intervals at least five minutes apart on the assumption that they would not catch each other up, but considering the unreliability of early engines this was quite a dangerous idea.

The situation became more standardized by the 1870s as the use of lower quadrant signals and the splitting up of the line into sections for safety became widespread. The main line was split into sections, each under the control of a signal box. Only one train at a time was allowed to be in a section. The signalman did not release a train into the next section until its signalman sent a message to say it was empty. These sections were called block sections and made the railways much safer. The many railway companies of that time tended to have their own design of signals, signal boxes and other infra-structure, which was manufactured in their own workshops where they made virtually everything else they needed.

The railways became run down during the First World War as the railways' resources were diverted into the war effort. To regenerate the railways,

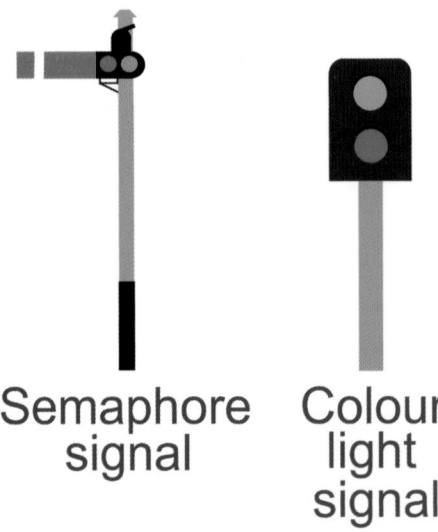

Semaphore
signal

Colour
light
signal

The types of signals you choose to use on your model railway set the region and time period, adding a lot of atmosphere. Although a few semaphore signals are still used, colour light signals generally make your model railway appear more modern.

nationalization was considered and rejected and it was decided to merge the 120 separate railway companies into just four: the LMS (London Midland and Scottish), LNER (London and North Eastern), SR (Southern Railway) and GWR (Great Western Railway), although the last of these had existed as a company since 1833 and simply absorbed companies within its territory. Each company produced a distinctive new design of signal to be used throughout its own network. With the exception of the GWR the change was made from lower to upper quadrant semaphore signals at this time. The legacy of this history is that, since signals last a long time, some examples of the older signals remained in use into the days of British Rail. The railways again became run down during the Second World War but this time they were nationalized after the war on 1 January 1947. The British Railways semaphore signal was almost a copy of the one already in use with the LMS.

Colour light signals came into use in the 1920s. The first four-aspect colour light signals were installed in 1926 on the Southern Railway in conjunction with the electrification of lines. The London and North Eastern Railway installed four-aspect signals in 1935 to overcome problems with the braking distance when running the Silver Jubilee at fast speeds between King's Cross and Newcastle. Most new signalling installations now use colour light signals but there are exceptions: in Scotland a radio system has replaced conventional signals on some single track lines.

SEMAPHORE SIGNALS

Semaphore signals consist of a moving arm generally activated mechanically by a linkage from a nearby signal box. For conditions of poor visibility a lamp is lit and can be seen through filters that move with

A small signal box positioned at the end of a station platform. On the upper floor, where the signal levers are, many windows were provided to give the signalmen a good view of what was going on. The interlocking equipment is located on the lower floor of the signal box.

The type of semaphore signal first designed by the LMS Railway and continued in manufacture by British Rail. This type of signal is upper quadrant with a tubular steel post. Every week the signalman would climb the ladder on the signal to refill the paraffin lamp behind the signal arm. The photograph also shows how semaphore signals can vary a great deal in height. Tall semaphore signals are intended to make the signal arm visible to the driver from a distance.

the signal arm. This allows a red or green light to show for home signals and a yellow or green light to show for distant signals. Because oil lamps have a very yellow coloured light, a blue filter is used to produce a green light. The part of the signal containing the filters is called the spectacle plate.

HOME SIGNALS

Both upper and lower quadrant home signals show danger, telling the driver to stop, when they are in the horizontal position but display clear differently, as shown in the accompanying diagram.

Stop signals have red arms with a white band when viewed from the front, and white arms with a black band when viewed from the back. Semaphore signals needed to be seen at night and in poor visibility, so an oil lamp is fixed to the signal post. Attached to the signal arm is a pair of filters arranged so that from the front a red light is seen when the signal is at danger and a green light when the signal is at clear.

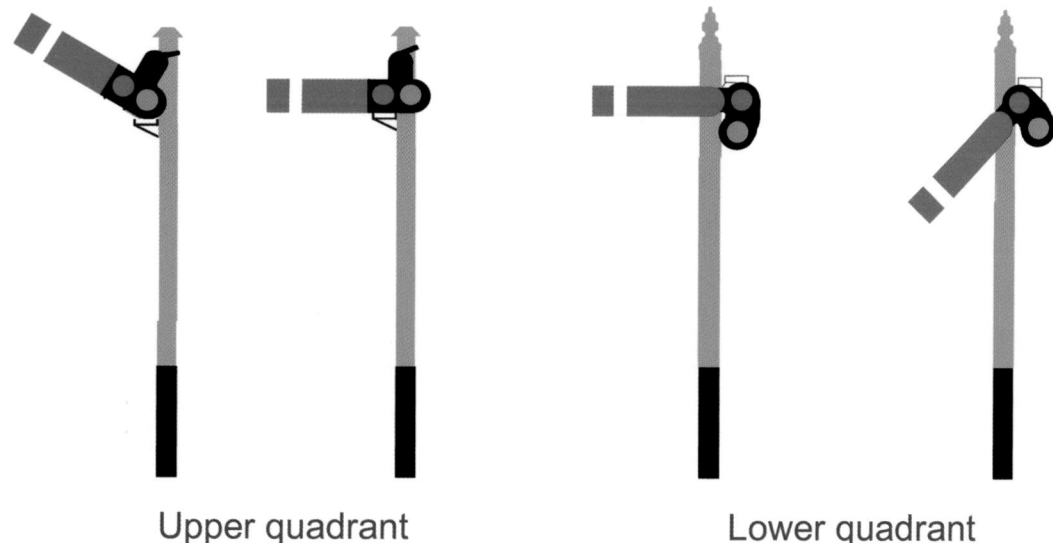

Upper quadrant   Lower quadrant

Home signals can be recognized by the red colour of their arm. Both the upper and lower quadrant semaphore signals have the same indication for danger (stop). In the past railway companies experimented with three-position semaphore signals, but they did not continue with them. One reason may be because the mechanical nature of the signal arm's linkage tended to expand in hot weather, leading to ambiguous signals.

DISTANT SIGNALS

Trains take a long distance to stop. By the time the driver of a fast train sees a signal it is usually too late to stop without passing the signal and so possibly crashing into any train in the next block. To give the driver warning of the position of the signal ahead, distant signals are located around a quarter of a mile before the stopping signal. When distant signals are in the horizontal position this does not mean the train is to stop, but it serves as a warning for the driver to start braking since the next home signal may be at stop. In some circumstances where the train is always going to have to travel slowly, fixed distant signals are used. These have an arm that is permanently fixed in the horizontal position. Distant signals are distinguished from home (stop) signals by colour (yellow with a black chevron on the front and white with a black chevron on the back) and by the notch cut in the end of their arm. Signals viewed from the back are ignored by the train driver. Distant signals show green or yellow lights through the filters on their spectacle plate.

The reverse side of a distant semaphore signal. Note the notch cut out of the arm to identify it as such.

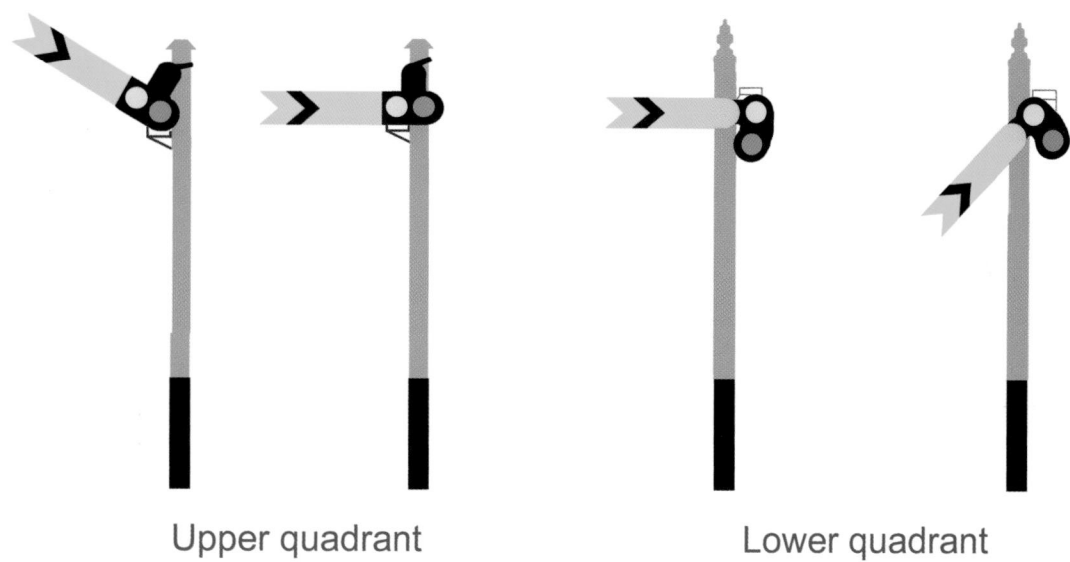

Upper quadrant   Lower quadrant

Distant semaphore signals are recognized by their yellow arms. When the arm is horizontal it indicates that the driver will find that the next home signal is set at danger, so the train will pass distance signals with horizontal arms but probably start slowing. Another difference between home and distant signals is the colour seen through the spectacle plate: home signals show red and green and distant signals show yellow and green.

INTERLOCKING

For safety there is a mechanism to prevent signals being set to clear when points along the train's route are set to derail the train or the next section is occupied. This is known as interlocking. In a mechanical signal box points were usually moved mechanically by a rod running from the lever in the signal box. On main lines the points would be interlocked to the signals. This was a mechanical arrangement of tappets and rods on the lower floor of the signal box arranged so that the signal could only be moved to clear when the points were correctly set to its route. Modern signal boxes use relays or even computer software to provide the interlocking.

HOW THE SIGNALS WERE OPERATED

Semaphore signals were usually placed on the left-hand side of the track. Originally signals were left at the clear position, but accidents resulted when the signal arms iced up in this position, preventing the signalman from moving the signals to danger to stop the train. It was realized that it was much safer to leave all signals at danger until a train was approaching. The signal would then be set to clear, provided the route ahead was correctly set and clear of obstructions. Immediately the train passed the signal the signalman returned the signals to danger.

JUNCTIONS AND DIVERGING LINES

At a junction two or more signal arms are used to show the driver which route is set. Usually the less important route (branch line) has a signal arm at a lower height than the more important route (main line). This tells the engine driver which way he is being sent as there may be a sharper curve on one route at the junction compared to another and so he may need to be alerted to the need to slow down. As well as home signals, two distant arms may be used on the distant signal ahead of these home signals. This gives the driver advanced warning of his route. This latter type of signal is known as a splitting distant.

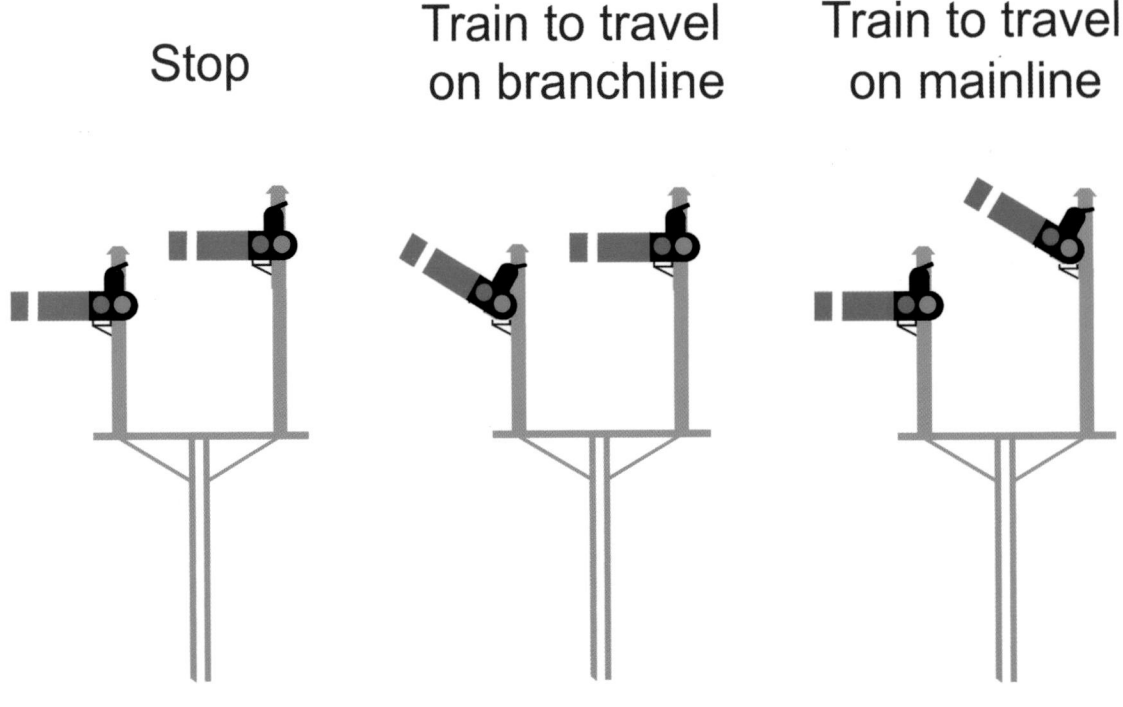

You can never have both the signal arms at clear as the signal interlocking will prevent this. The signal needs to indicate which route is to be taken.

SIGNAL BOUNCE

Semaphore signals are controlled by a wire running from the signal box to the signal. In the signal box the wire is connected to a long lever. Typically the signalman would pull the lever in two pulls, resulting in a pause midway as the signal arm was raised to clear. When he was pulling the signal to clear he would have to pull against all the counter-weights, but much less effort was needed when returning the signal to danger and the signal arm would tend to fall more quickly and bounce. The further away the signal was from the signal box the more the tendency there was to bounce, due to slack in the connecting wire.

There is a limit to how long the wire between signals could be because of the friction over the connecting rollers. This meant there had to be plenty of signal boxes and they all had to communicate with each other. This was done by telegraph, hence the reason for telegraph poles alongside railway tracks.

A busy railway track will have several short block sections one after the other. To make the signals fit the space available, the distant signal for a later block section often shares the same post as the home signal for the current block section. The home signal arm is always placed above the distant signal arm.

The railway had their own telegraph and later telephone system between signal boxes. Wires were also required for the block instruments to be interconnected between signal boxes.

COLOUR LIGHT SIGNALS

Some early signals had a single bulb with a filter that moved mechanically to change the colour. These were called searchlight signals. Later signals had a separate bulb for each colour and no moving parts.

Colour light signals consist of two, three or four lights on a post and are usually controlled by a single signal box controlling a large area of lines. These signal boxes are called power boxes.

Colour light signals have advantages over semaphore signals. Their lights are more powerful, particularly as they are focused into a narrow beam and can penetrate fog much better than an oil lamp. They are also more easily seen against obstructed backgrounds. There are no mechanical parts in modern colour light signals so they are more reliable and unlike semaphore signals, with the friction of mechanical wires running over pulleys, there is no limit on the distance they may be from the signal box.

The number of aspects refers to the number of colour lights on the signal: a three-aspect signal, for example, would have red, yellow and green lights. Apart from being called green, yellow (instead of amber) and red, the lights are arranged in a different way to road traffic lights. The red light is at the bottom so that it is at the train driver's eye level.

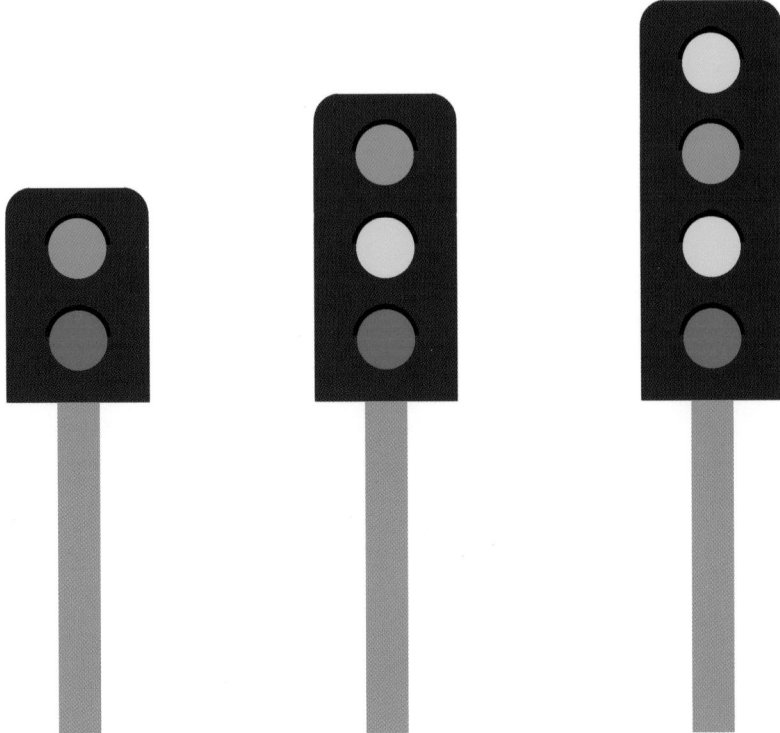

Two-, three- and four-aspect colour light signals. Notice that the red light is always at the bottom at the driver's eye level. The posts, unlike semaphore signals, are generally all the same height for this reason.

A modern four-aspect signal located on the platform at Blythe Bridge Station, Staffordshire.

TWO-ASPECT COLOUR LIGHT SIGNALS

Sometimes colour light signals were a direct replacement for semaphore signals that had reached the end of their life, for example if the post had rotted. A two-aspect red and green colour light signal would replace a home semaphore signal and a green and yellow colour light signal would replace a distant semaphore signal. Sometimes the distant signals were colour lights and the stop signals semaphore, the reason being that the distant signal may be 1,000 yards from the signal box and it was a great effort to pull the signal on and off due to the friction of all the cables.

THREE- AND FOUR-ASPECT COLOUR LIGHT SIGNALS

The accompanying diagram shows how four-aspect signals change as a train travels along a line. Initially the signals are all at green. When the train passes the first signal it changes to red. As the train travels along it always leaves a red signal behind it. Following trains are warned of this by a yellow and then a double yellow before the red signal. It takes a long distance for trains to stop. The signal displays yellow to warn the driver that the next signal is at red. For very fast lines it is necessary to warn the driver that the next signal is at yellow by displaying a double yellow. Signals with the double

The sequence of colour changes in the signals as Stephenson's Rocket travels down the West Coast line.

yellow are called four-aspect. Red, yellow and green signals are called three-aspect. Because there is no advance warning of a signal being at yellow with three-aspect signals, a longer braking distance is needed. The signals need to be further apart than with four-aspect signals or the trains need to travel at lower speeds, meaning that fewer trains can occupy the line. Therefore four-aspect signalling is necessary on busy lines.

JUNCTION ROUTE INDICATORS/ FEATHERS AND THEATRE INDICATORS

In the early days of colour light signals, junctions were signalled with two signal heads on the post, copying the method used at junctions by semaphore signals.

More recently, however, a different method was adopted for colour light signals to show the route at junctions. This uses route indicators, also known as feathers because of their appearance. Feathers consist of a row of five white lights, which are illuminated when the point is set to the diverging route and the line ahead is clear. If the diverging route is blocked (signal at red) then the feather is not lit. If there is more than one diverging route, then extra feathers are added to the signal. The angle of the feather gives an indication of the direction the diverging route leaves at.

On the approach to a large station there may be many routes the train can take. In these situations a theatre indicator might be used to show the train's route. A matrix of lights illuminates to show a number or letter corresponding to the platform number or route the train is to enter.

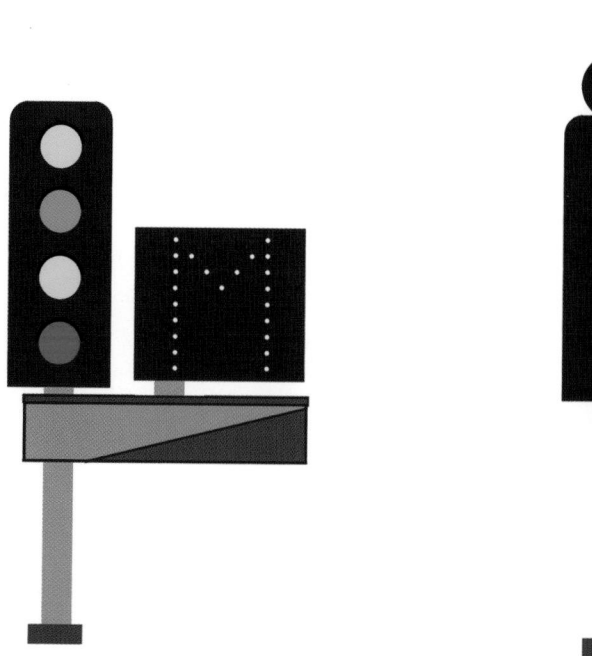

On the left of the diagram is a colour light signal with a theatre indicator. A matrix of lights can display letters or numbers to tell the driver which track he is being routed to. They are commonly used at large stations where they will tell the driver which platform number he is arriving at. A feather is shown on the right. This is positioned at an angle to correspond with the actual tracks. If there is more than one route, extra feathers are fitted to the signal.

GROUND SIGNALS

Also known as shunt signals, these are used for shunting and low speed manoeuvres such as controlling an engine running around its train or trains backing across crossovers or into sidings. Early ground signals had small versions of the semaphore arms used on stop signals. As well as being on posts near ground level, they are sometimes fixed low down on the post of a normal signal. Shunt signals display red for stop and white for clear. The modern light version has two whites for clear and a white and red for stop. The other type of signal shown with a yellow bar or light is often used where a point leads either to the main line or a headshunt. It may be passed when the yellow line is horizontal or the yellow light is lit, provided the points are set to the headshunt, but may not be passed if the points are set to the running (main) line. A headshunt is a siding provided for shunting the trains backwards and forwards without having to use the main line.

SINGLE-TRACK LINES

These still require signals at the terminus station and at passing loops. Extra safety measures were necessary on single track lines, however, where there was the possibility of a head-on collision. One method was to use a token for each section of line between passing loops. A train had to be in possession of this token before being allowed on the token's section of line. Where trains passed the drivers would exchange tokens.

SIGNAL GANTRIES

At busy railway locations it can be impracticable to find enough space for the large number of signals that may be required. To overcome these problems, signals are fitted to a gantry crossing above the track. A gantry is in effect a small bridge with signals on short posts fixed to it. The signals may be either sem-

shunting disc

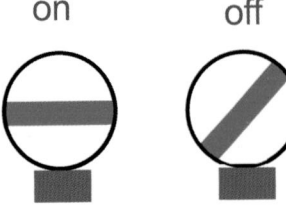

position light shunt signal

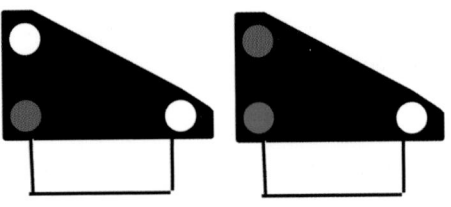

yellow shunting disc

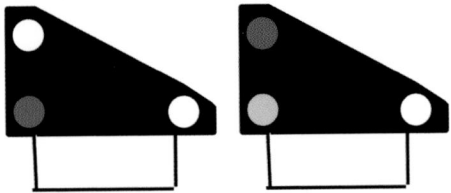

Mechanical and colour light ground signals.

aphore or colour light and have exactly the same purpose as signals on posts. Dapol makes a plastic kit and various model signal manufacturers supply the signal heads so that they can be fitted to model gantries.

CONCLUSIONS FOR MODELLERS

Adding signals to your layout will enhance the effect you can create. The ability to model signals realistically requires a basic understanding of how they operate, as well as an understanding of how to wire them. There are two main types of signal, home and distant, and these may be either semaphore or two-aspect colour light. Trains stop at home signals when they show danger, but the purpose of distant signals is to give the train driver warning about the aspect of the next signal so that he has enough stopping distance. Semaphore signals show only two aspects – danger or clear – but colour light signals may show two, three or four aspects. Signals remain at red or danger unless the line ahead is clear, when they change to green or clear. Signals showing yellow indicate caution as the next signal may be red; a double yellow signal indicates that the sections of the line further ahead may not be clear and gives a faster train time to slow down. The date of your layout will be a factor influencing your decision to use colour light or semaphore signals.

Semaphore signals are at danger unless they need to be at clear. Colour light signals are at clear unless a train has recently passed by.

Factors to consider when installing realistic signalling on your model railway include:

- **The date in which the model is set.** Up-to-date models can use the colour light signals with safety cages. Older models would use safety ring colour light signals. Minor secondary lines, however, may still be using semaphore signals up to the present day.

- **Location.** Before the First World War the majority of signals were lower quadrant and some of these signals were still in use in the 1960s. From then until the creation of British Railways, the regional railway companies had different designs of signal: the GWR used lower quadrant signals, while the other three companies used upper quadrant. Wooden signal posts can be recognized by their square cross-section and gentle taper. Apart from wood which was the most common signal post material before the First World War, railway companies used different materials resulting in the different appearances of the signals. Typically, the Southern Railway had concrete posts or posts built out of old rail, the LNER had steel lattice work , the LMS tubular steel posts and the GWR changed over to tubular steel posts.

- **How busy the line is and how fast the trains run.** A busy mainline will have four-aspect colour light signals. A more subtle difference would be that a busy line with semaphore signals would have the signals closer together. A stop signal would then share its post with the distant signal for the next stop signal along the line. A less busy line would have the signals spaced further apart, so the distant signals would stand on their own.

CHAPTER FIVE

OPERATING SEMAPHORE AND COLOUR LIGHT SIGNALS

HOW TO GET YOUR SEMAPHORE SIGNALS MOVING

Many of the methods used for moving points are also useful for moving semaphore signals.

USING WIRE IN TUBE

A model mechanical lever based on a full-sized lever in a signal box is used to move the signal by a linkage of fine steel wire. To enable a push as well as a pull movement, the wire may have to be inside a brass or plastic tube.

An alternative to wire in a tube is a similar method using cotton and elastic bands, which overcomes the push problem. The components for this method are supplied in some of the Ratio semaphore signal kits, which also include plastic mouldings to make up a working lever modelled on the levers inside signal boxes. Another variation uses fine steel wire to pull the signal arm and a coil spring close to the signal to pull the signal arm in the opposite direction. On full-size signals, instead of a spring, a counter-weight pivoted on the lower part of the signal post is used.

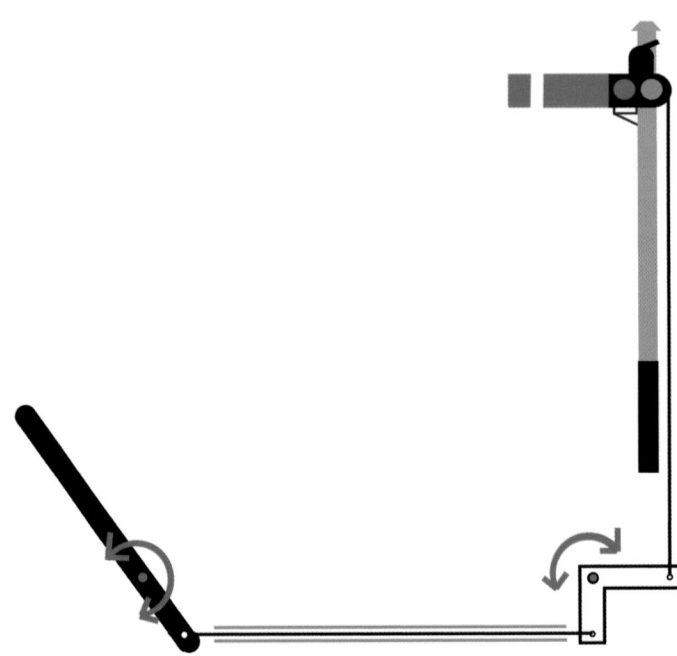

How to change a signal mechanically using a wire in a tube. The angle crank changes the direction of the movement. Using the tube allows the wire to travel around gentle curves between the lever and the signal.

These methods of operating signals have the disadvantage that the mechanical method of interlocking is very intricate to build and inflexible to change. It is very much easier to use electrical controls for interlocking. It is difficult to automate signals if they are operated mechanically. Electrical controls are also much more suitable for automating the signals.

SOLENOIDS

Solenoids, which are electromagnets that move when electrically powered, can be used for operating signals. These might be solenoid point motors or home-made solenoids. The disadvantage of using solenoids to operate signals is that the sudden movement they produce is very unrealistic for signals. Years ago Hornby OO motorized their signals in this way and you can still probably buy them second-hand.

SLOW MOTION POINT MOTORS

Slow motion point motors move slowly and so give a more realistic movement to the signal's arm. It is necessary to incorporate mechanical stops so that the arm cannot move past its danger and clear positions. It is more complicated to use slow motion point motors for interlocking because they require double pole contacts to control their movement, since the electrical supply needs to be reversed to move them in the opposite direction.

SERVO MOTORS

This is a popular method for working semaphore signals. Servo motors are fairly small and so are easily fitted. The size is particularly important if the signal has more than one arm. Both the limits of the movement and the speed are easily adjusted. Sophisticated

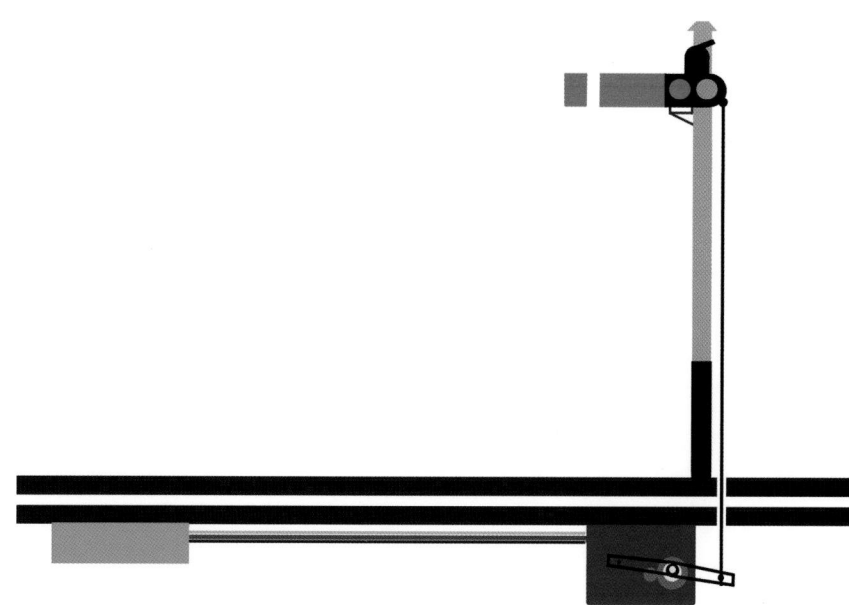

Servos are well suited to controlling semaphore signals. They are fairly small so can be easily fitted under the baseboard and it is simple to connect their lever to the signal arm with some stiff wire. There is actually a balance weight at the bottom of the signal's post and it would be quite feasible to make this move as well. In the diagram the servo is shown plugged into a servo control board.

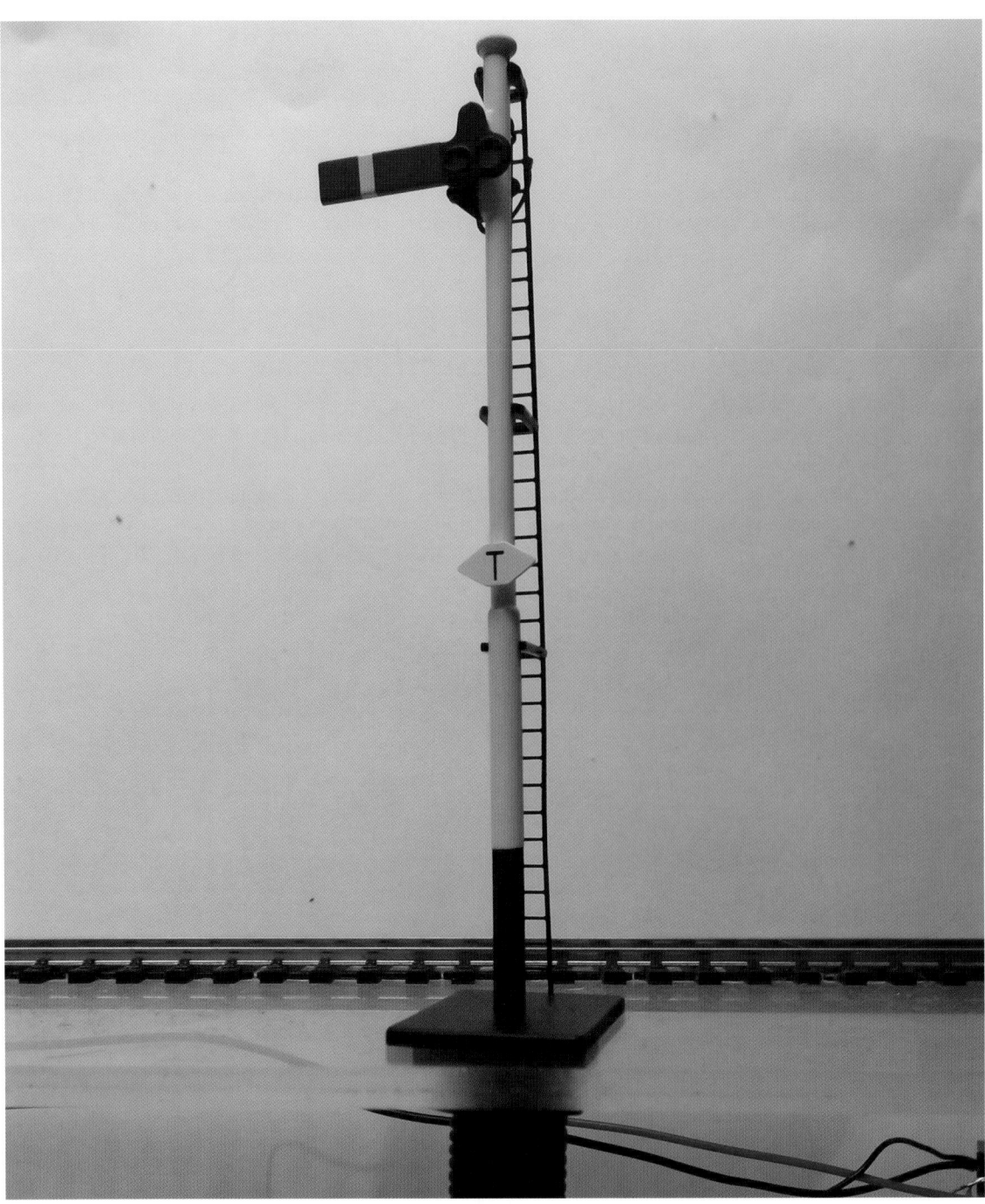

This Dapol upper quadrant semaphore signal is attached to the baseboard by a nut on the threaded tube, inside which is a very small electric motor that operates the signal arm. The T within the white diamond shape attached to the signal post is to indicate to the train driver that there is a telephone to call the signal box. When trains were stopped at signals the driver was required to phone the signalman to remind him he was blocking the line. Not all signals have this white diamond with a T: in this case the train driver sent his fireman to the signal box instead.

servo motor controllers make it possible to reproduce the signal bounce.

MEMORY WIRE

Memory wire is a proven method of getting a semaphore arm to move slowly and only requires an on/off switch to operate it. Nothing is commercially available, however, and the fine gauge of the wire, finer than a human hair, means that dexterity is required to assemble the mechanism. Memory wire cannot be soldered because too much heat destroys its crystalline structure and therefore its property of changing length. The ends of memory wire have to be crimped or wrapped around a nut and bolt. (For an explanation of how to make a mechanism using memory wire, see Chapter 2.)

ELECTRIC MOTORS

Dapol produces ready assembled model semaphore signals with miniature electric motors fitted in the base. The Dapol working semaphore signals must use only 16V AC electricity and they are damaged if DC is used. This is because they have electronic components to reverse the rotation of the electric motor and the circuit has been designed to only work with AC. An idiosyncrasy is the way they are operated using a single push-to-make push-button switch. If the signal is at danger pushing the switch changes it back to clear, but the same switch has to be pushed to change the signal arm from clear back to danger.

Electric motors have to be geared down to produce a slow movement. If electric motors are used in conjunction with a cam they can produce the characteristic bounce of a semaphore signal. A cam is a rotating irregular shape that pushes the lever to give linear motion. A correctly shaped cam will give the characteristic signal bounce.

SOURCES OF SEMAPHORE SIGNALS

Dapol: Ready-built working models of semaphore signals in N, OO and O gauge. Currently models of LMS home and distant signals and GWR home and distant signals are produced. As well as a moving arm, these signals have a light behind the spectacle plate. The mechanism is a tiny DC motor geared down to move the arm.

Ratio kit for an upper quadrant home semaphore signal. Ratio also makes kits that allow more complex signals to be built.

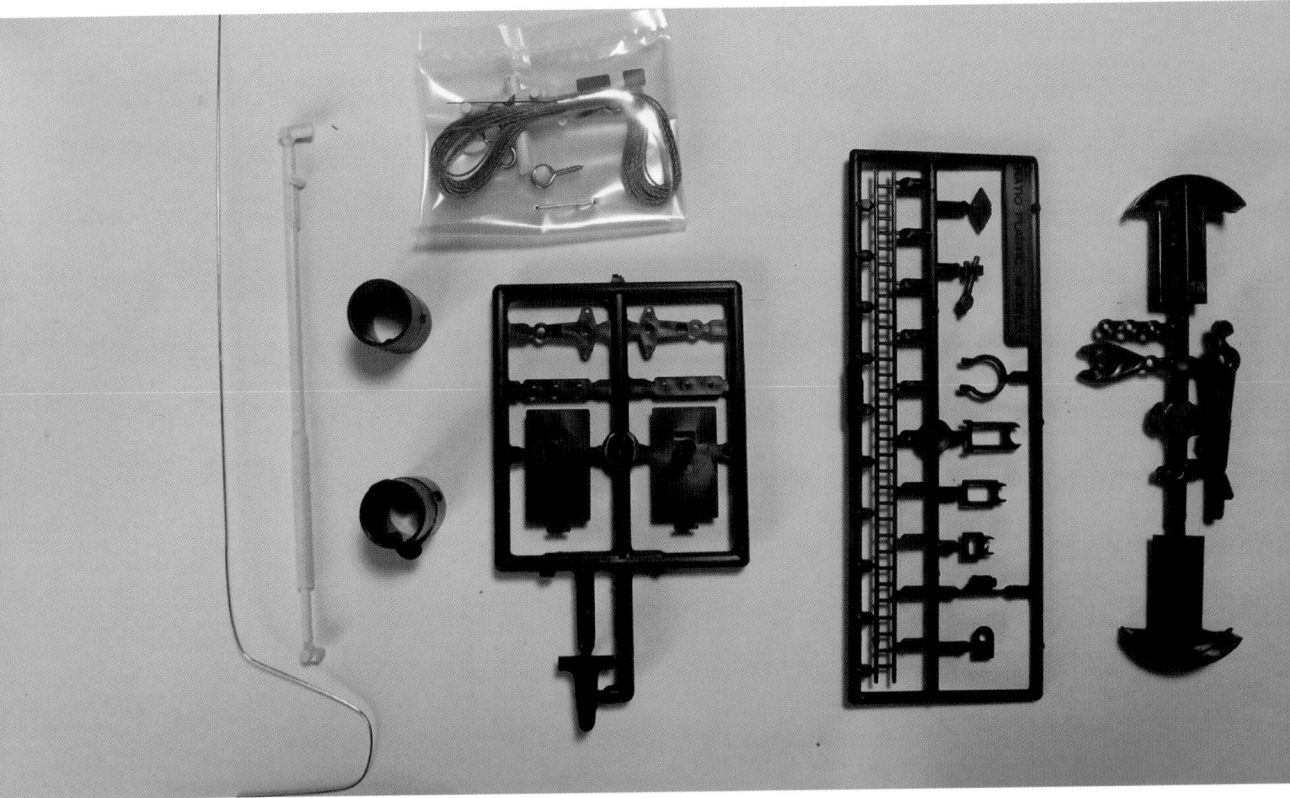

The contents of the Ratio kit, including eyelets and thread to allow the signal to be operated by a model lever, the components for which are on the right. Note that the semaphore signal arm is ready coloured.

Ratio: Plastic kits of LMS, GWR, LNER and LNWR OO gauge semaphore signals. Some of the kits can be built up into many different types of signal as parts are supplied for brackets to make junction signals and different length of posts. A small range of N gauge kits is also available.

Tomix: Working N gauge semaphore signals. Although they are based on Japanese signals, these signals have an appearance that is very close to British semaphore ones.

Hornby: Ready-made home, distant and junction semaphore signals without a motor are available. They are easily motorized with a servo motor and a servo motor controller.

Model Signal Engineering: An extensive range of kits is available, mostly made of etched brass and cast white metal. Some kits are presently sold ready assembled.

In addition, various German manufacturers make good-quality working semaphore signals, but German semaphore signals are very different in design from those in use in the UK.

COLOUR LIGHT SIGNALS

Nearly all colour light signals use light emitting diodes (LEDs) instead of miniature bulbs. The advantages of LEDs are that they have a very long lifespan and do not need replacing, they consume less current than bulbs, they do not get hot, so there is no danger of melting plastic fittings, and they produce pure colours. In fact LEDs are so good the full-size railways have now started using them.

WIRING A TYPICAL COLOUR LIGHT LED SIGNAL

A model colour light signal is going to have two, three or four LEDs, each of which has two connecting legs for wires. To reduce the number of wires inside the signal tube, one connection of the LED is shared or common. It can be on the positive or the negative side of the LED. Depending on which side is chosen, signals are called common negative or common positive. Whether the signal is common positive or common negative affects its wiring. Signals manufactured in the UK are normally wired common negative, while elsewhere they are normally common positive.

The accompanying diagram (see bottom of the page) shows two resistors, one in each of the red and green wires. If preferred, these could be replaced by

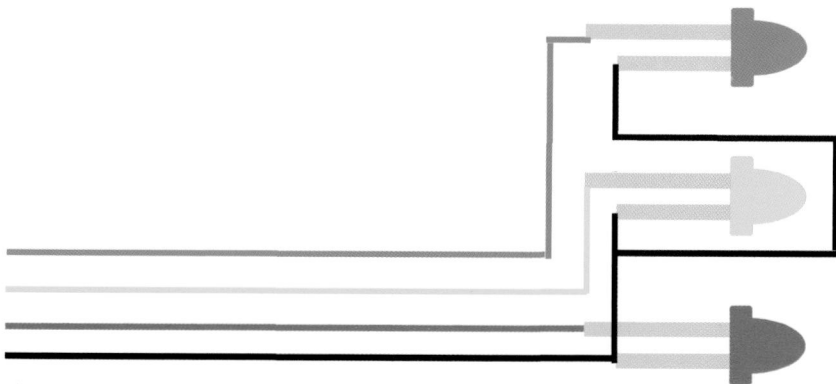

The usual wiring of the LEDs inside the signal head for a three-aspect common negative signal. For a three-aspect signal there will be four wires coming out of the signal. One is common (usually black) and there is one wire to activate each of the red, green and yellow LEDs.

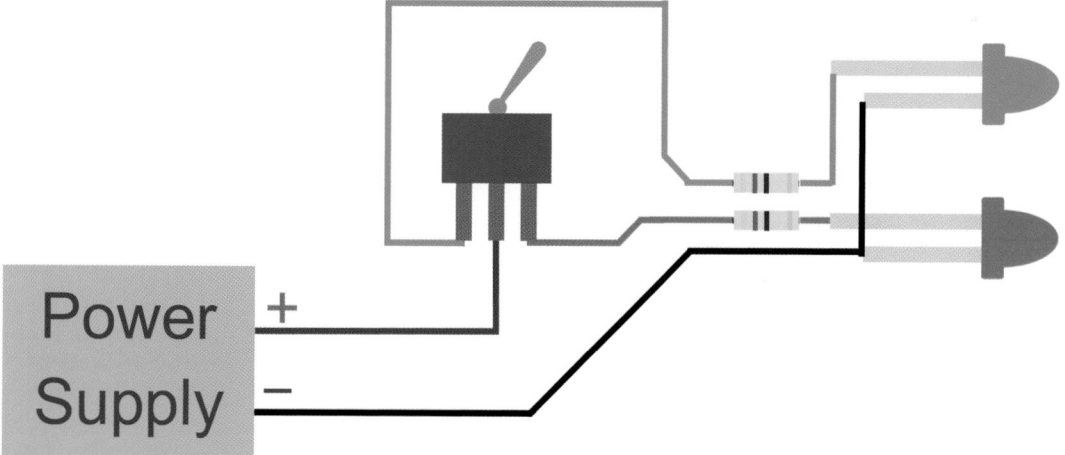

Diagram showing how the LEDs are wired together inside a two-aspect signal. The short legs of each LED are wired together and connected to the black wire. Wiring together the short legs of the LEDs will make this a common negative signal. (If the long legs were wired together it would be a common positive signal.) The long legs of each LED each have a separate wire. The common wire will be connected to the negative terminal of a power supply. The colour of the signal can be selected depending on whether red or green is connected to the positive terminal via a switch. To protect the LED a resistor should be used in each of the coloured wires. The black (negative) wire does not need a resistor if there are resistors in all the coloured wires.

a single resistor in the common wire. In either case the current always travels through a resistor as well as an LED. In the case of a four-aspect signal, two yellow LEDs can be lit at the same time. There must be a resistor in every coloured wire and not in the common to prevent two lighted LEDs sharing the same resistor.

EXTENDING WIRES FROM SIGNALS

Some signal manufacturers use enamelled copper wire for their signals. Instead of having plastic insulation on the outside, enamelled wire has a type of varnish or enamel that provides a thinner layer of insulation, so allowing smaller diameter wires. Because a lot of wires need to fit into the signal's post, the wires need to be of a very small diameter.

You may have seen this wire used for the windings on an electric motor or transformer. If you are lucky the varnish can be removed by the heat of a soldering iron so that you can make connections to the wire. For other types of varnish you may have to scrape the insulation off with a knife blade. With most makes of signals you will probably find the connecting wires to be too short and you will therefore need to extend them.

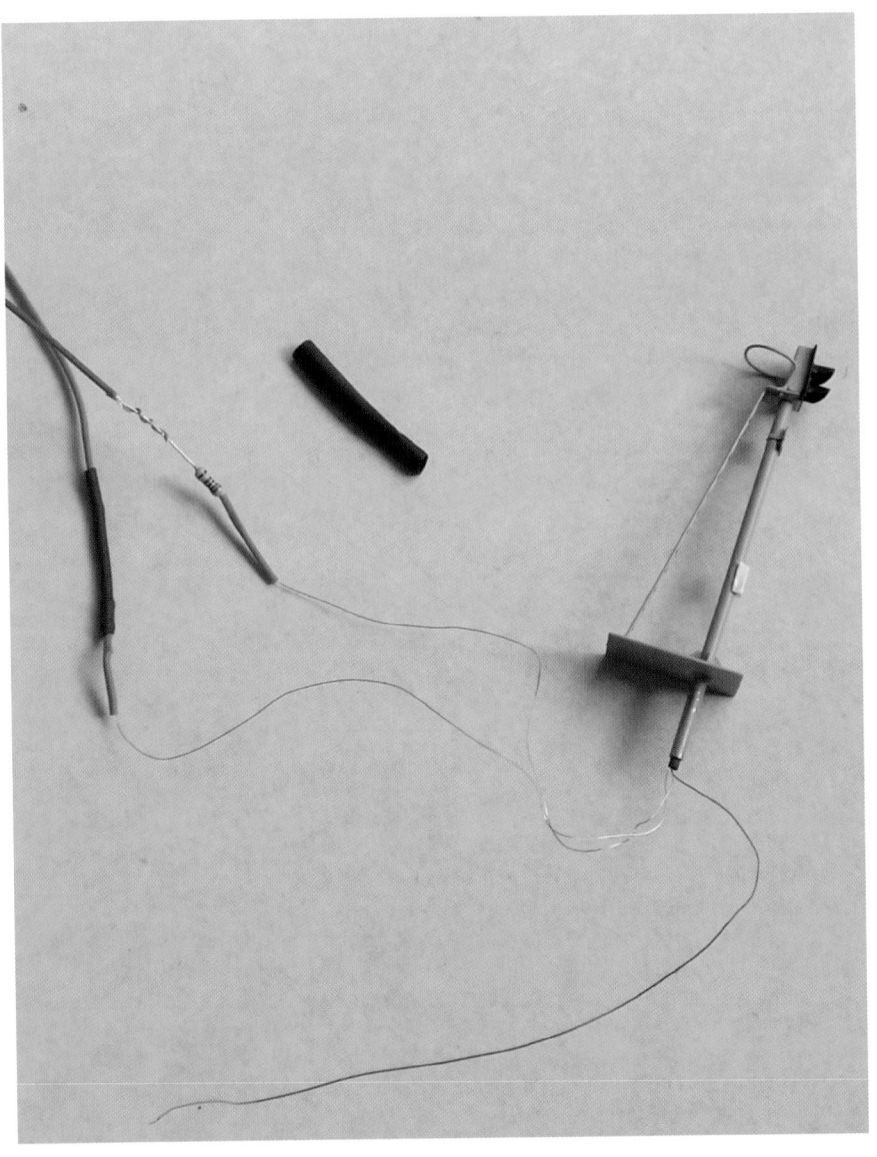

Extension wires being attached to a two-aspect signal. The green wire's joint has been covered in heat shrink. There is an unshrunk piece of heat shrink ready to be put over the joint of the red wire to cover the joint, resistor and original red heat shrink placed by the signal manufacturer. As well as preventing bare joints shorting together, the heat shrink gives the joint extra mechanical strength.

The photograph here shows how to connect the enamelled wire to 7/0.7mm wire (seven strands of 0.7mm diameter each), which is thick enough for currents up to 1.4A and commonly used by railway modellers. After stripping the insulation, the 7/0.7 wire can be wound around the leg of the resistor. Twist the strands together first, as individual strands have a tendency to splay out when soldered. Twisting the wire around the resistor leg keeps it firmly in place while soldering. This prevents the joint being weakened by the resistor leg and the wire moving before the joint has cooled.

It is best to insulate all the bare metal to prevent different wires touching. This can be done with heat shrink as shown in the photograph, where 2.4mm heat shrink was used. Slip a length of heat shrink over the joint and then heat it up with a hot air gun. The heat shrink will shrink to up to half its original diameter. The signal's common wire has no resistor and you may also wish to remove the resistors from the other wires if the signal is being used with a control board with built-in resistors, such as the MAS-Sequencer. In this case, wrap the thinner enamelled wire around the stripped twisted 7/0.7 wire. The heat of the solder will remove the enamel from the wire at the joint. Again insulate with heat shrink. If you do not possess a hot air gun, you can get away with heating the heat shrink tubing with a soldering iron or match. A hairdryer does not get hot enough to do this job. An acceptable but less satisfactory way to insulate the joint would be to wrap insulating or adhesive tape around it.

WIRING A SIMPLE SWITCH FOR A TWO-ASPECT LED SIGNAL

A two-aspect colour light signal can be controlled with a single pole, double throw switch sometimes called a changeover switch. These switches are moved by levers and are collectively known as toggle switches.

Signals using LEDs need DC type power and only light when the current flows in one direction, not the other. AC type power can damage LED signals. If an AC power supply is the only one available, it can

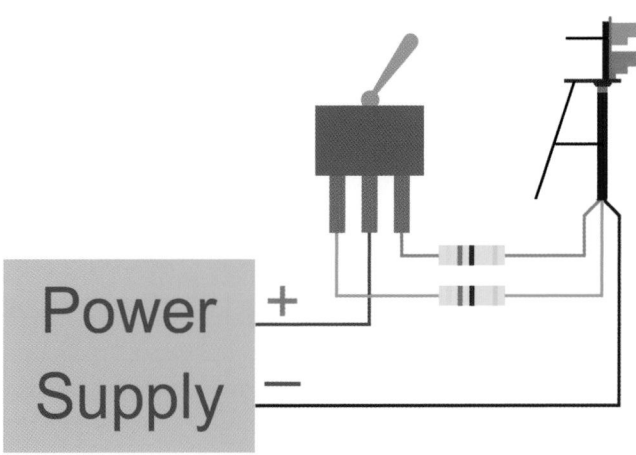

Wiring a two-aspect signal to a single pole, double throw switch is relatively simple. Make sure that the polarity of the power supply is the correct way round or the LEDs will not light.

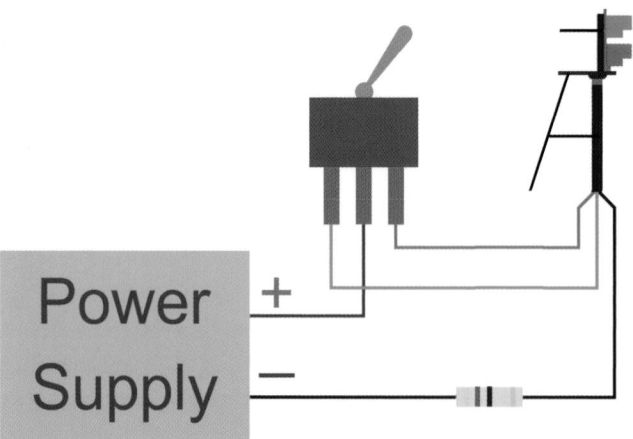

A single resistor can be used in the common wire instead of wiring two separate resistors in the red and green wires. In either case the current must pass through the resistor on its journey from the positive to the negative power supply. It does not matter if the resistor comes before or after the LED as it still does its job of limiting the current.

be converted to DC by using a diode. (For further explanation, see Chapter 8.)

Resistors need to be added to the wires of LED signals to limit the amount of current that flows through them. These may have already been fitted by the manufacturer. The higher the value of resistor used the lower is the amount of current that flows. As a higher current produces brighter LEDs, a lower current dims the LEDs. An extra resistor can be added in series to cause the signal LEDs to be dimmer if they are too bright.

With the switch in the position shown on the accompanying diagram, the positive power from the power supply will be connected between the centre and left-hand solder tags on the toggle switch and so the green LED will light. If the switch is thrown to the other position, the green LED will be disconnected from the power and the red LED connected and thereby lit.

This diagram also shows how a single resistor can be used in the common wire. As the current flows

round the circuit back to the power supply it has to pass through the resistor, regardless of which LED is lit.

If you want the track to be isolated in front of the signal when the signal is at red, you could use a double pole, double throw toggle switch. One pole of the switch could be used to operate the signal and the other to isolate the track in front of the signal. This would stop the trains when the signal is at danger, so ruling out any chance of a SPAD (Signal Passed At Danger) occurrence on your model railway.

WIRING A ROTARY SWITCH FOR A THREE-ASPECT LED SIGNAL

As with two-aspect signals, three aspect signals have a common wire (either positive or negative) to save space within the signal tubing. Resistors are usually already fitted by the signal manufacturer.

A toggle switch cannot do the job for a three- or four-aspect signal as three switch positions are required, one for each aspect. A suitable type of

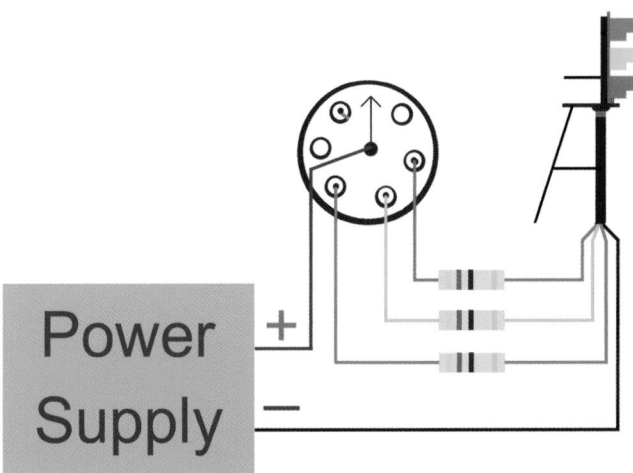

The rotor on the rotary switch is always connected to the positive of the power supply. As the switch is turned, it will connect the rotor to the red, green or yellow wire, thus lighting the red, green or yellow LEDs.

switch that has a number of outputs is called a rotary switch. This has a knob that is rotated from one position to the next. The accompanying diagram shows how a rotary switch is connected to a three-aspect LED signal.

WIRING A FOUR-ASPECT LED SIGNAL

There are now four LEDs to connect, meaning that a rotary switch is again the most suitable type. When the switch is at position three it needs to light yellow and double yellow together. So that the brightness of the LEDs is consistent, each LED has its own resistor. If the LEDs were to share a resistor, as in the previous two examples, the LEDs would be less bright when both yellows were lit together (see diagram overleaf, on page 81).

SOURCES OF COLOUR LIGHT SIGNALS

CR Signals: An extensive range of N and OO gauge signals, including both the older type of signal with a ring at the top of the ladder and the newer type with a safety cage on top of the ladder.

Traintronics: An extensive range of N and OO gauge signals. The firm also supplies kits for signal gantries.

Eckon: Easy-to-assemble kits for OO gauge.

Berko: Ready-assembled OO gauge signals.

Hornby: Signals made by Hornby have been available for a long time, but they are aimed at the train set market rather than for scale modelling.

Absolute Aspects: This company has taken over the well-respected range of signals made by Roger Murray.

New model signal manufacturers seem to appear all the time, so it is worth investigating what is available.

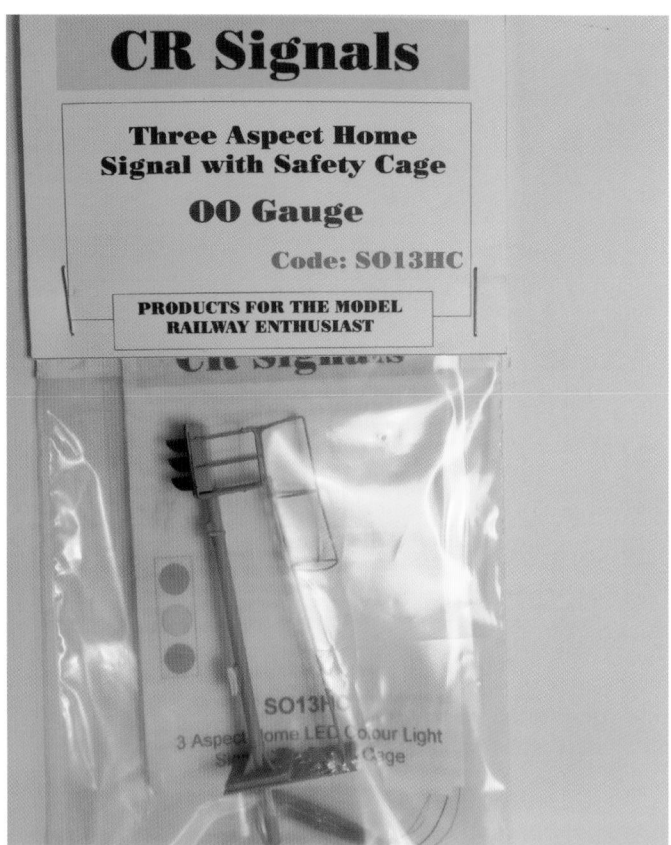

OO gauge cage three-aspect signal colour light signal made by CR Signals. Most of the model's construction is in brass.

A train travelling through glorious open countryside in this busy scene.

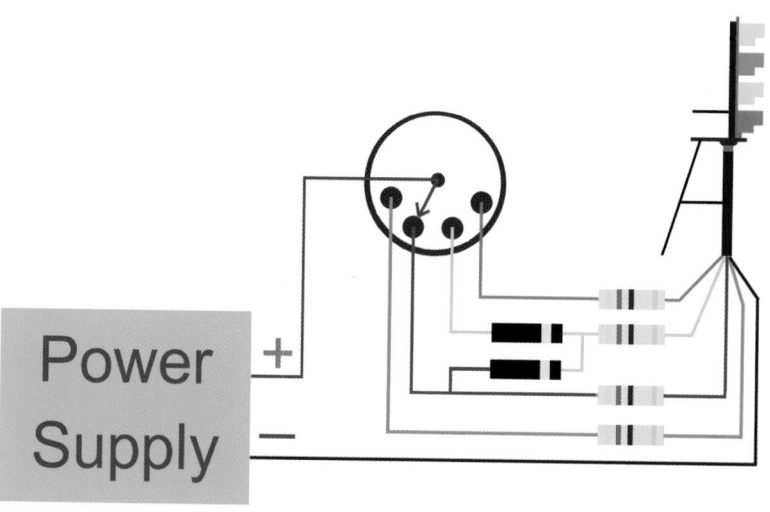

A four-aspect signal is more complicated because in one position we want to light just one yellow LED, but in the next position we want to light this LED plus an additional yellow LED. The problem is solved by using diodes, as shown in the diagram. When the rotor is turned to the yellow wire the current can flow through the first diodes, but the second diode prevents current flowing to the blue wire. So the single yellow LED is lit. When the rotor is turned to the blue wire the diodes will conduct electricity to both yellow and blue wires, so making the signal display double yellow.

SIGNALS MADE AT HOME

Colour light signals are fairly easy to make yourself as 3mm diameter LEDs are very close to the scale size of OO gauge signal heads. Brass tubing can be used to make the post. The only part that is difficult to make is the ladder, although it may be worth buying this one component.

CHAPTER SIX

MORE ADVANCED OPERATION OF SIGNALS

WIRING LED FEATHERS

Feathers are used to show where there is a diverging route. Models of feathers usually use white LEDs and can be operated by a contact connected to a point. When the point moves to the diverging route the feather lights.

This does not give a completely accurate operation, however, as feathers could light when the signal is red and this would not happen on a full-size railway. The accompanying diagram shows how to prevent the feather lighting when the point is set to the diverging route, but the signal is at red.

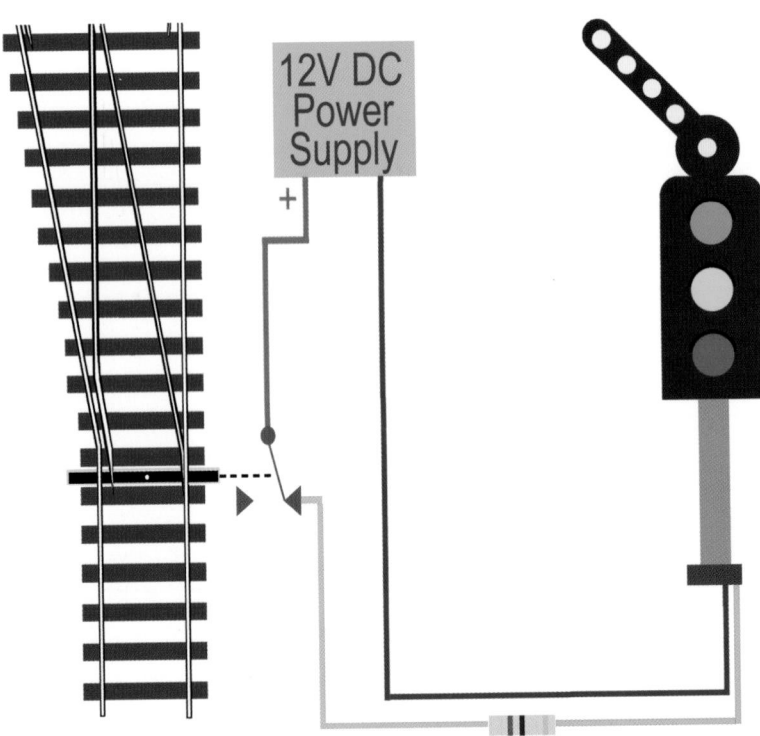

12V DC Power Supply

The light blue wire is connected to the feather LEDs inside the signal. This shows how a contact operated by the point supplies current to the light blue wire only when the point is set to the diverging route. If the point is set the other way the feather cannot light.

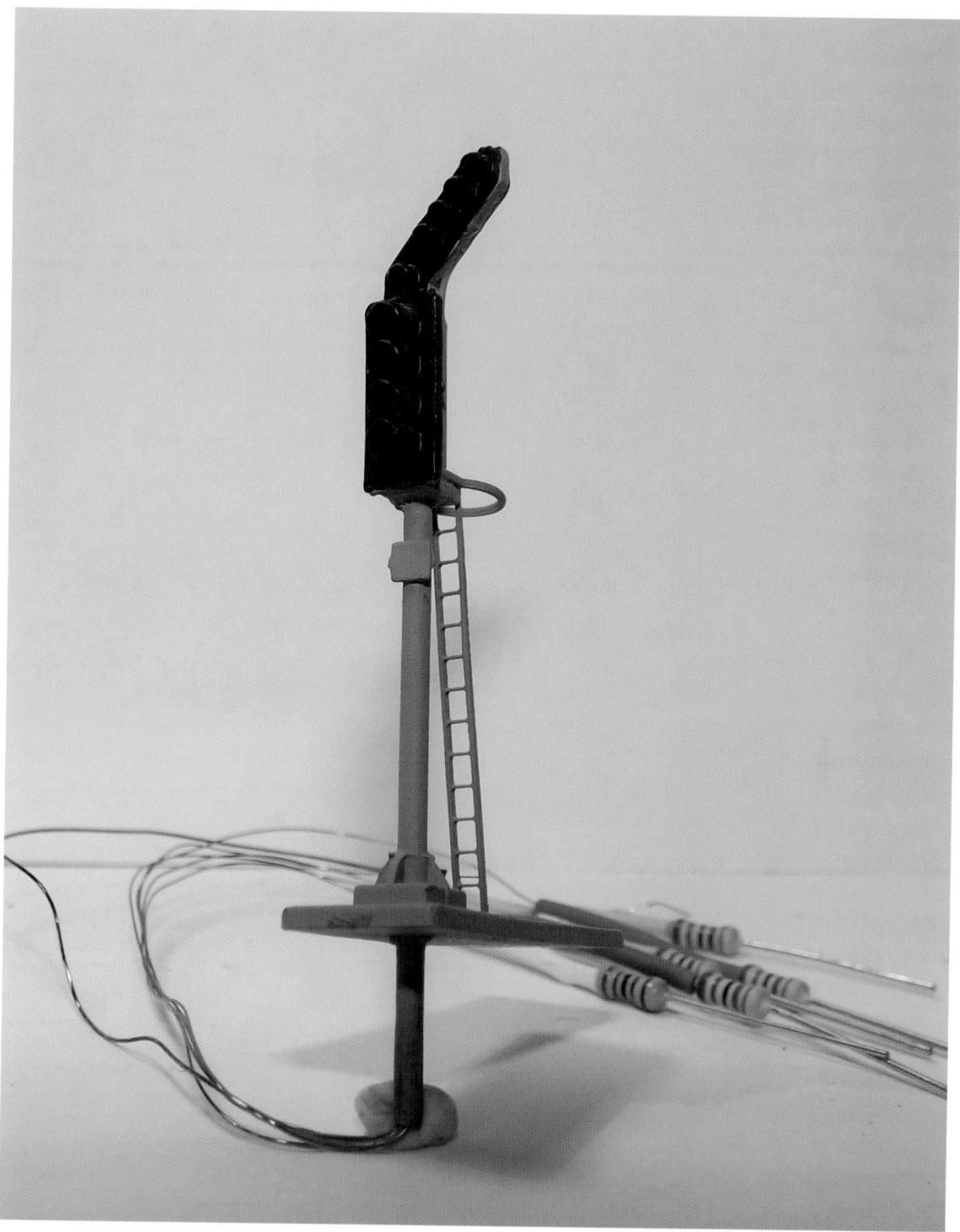

An N gauge four-aspect signal with a right-hand feather made by CR Signals. The extremely fine wires are necessary so that all five wires will fit in the signal post. At the end of the wires are the resistors to limit the current through the LEDs.

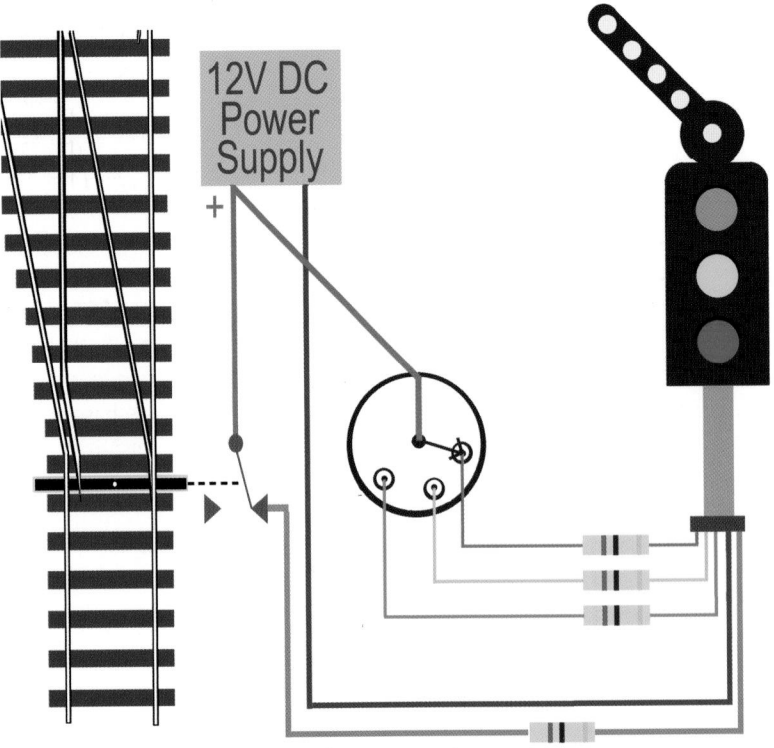

The wiring for both the feather and the rotary switch that selects the red green or yellow light on the signal.

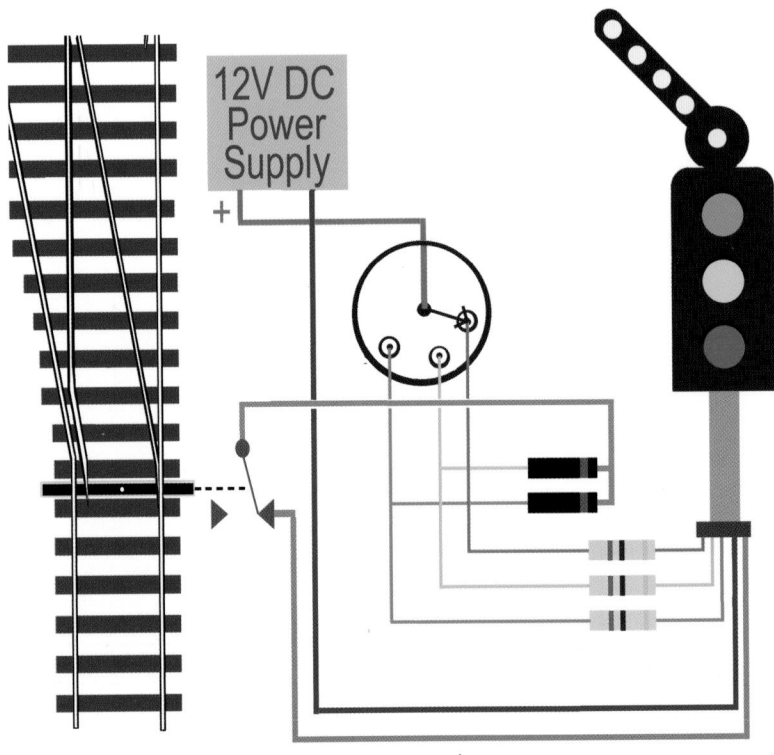

The wiring to get the feather to operate correctly. Instead of connecting the light blue wire directly to the positive terminal of the power supply, it is connected via the rotary switch. Connections are only made to light the feather if the rotary switch is in the yellow or green position. Diodes are used to prevent unintended connections between the green and yellow wires.

INTERLOCKING

SIMPLE TWO-ASPECT COLOUR LIGHT SIGNAL AND POINT INTERLOCKING

On full-size railways interlocking signals and points is essential for safety. The interlocking will not allow the signals to change to clear until the points are set for the correct route.

A simple representation of this interlocking is to have the signals operated by the directional setting of the points. When the points are set correctly for the train the signal will be at green and when the points would derail the train the signal will be at red.

This is a compromise between realism and simplicity for model railways because on a full-size railway the signalman is required to change the signal back to danger after the train has passed. This cannot happen on the model railway when the signals are only operated by the position of the points. Another snag is that the signal will incorrectly be at clear when there is an obstruction down the line or when there is no train approaching. Nevertheless a lot of modellers are happy with the effect of this simple interlocking circuit.

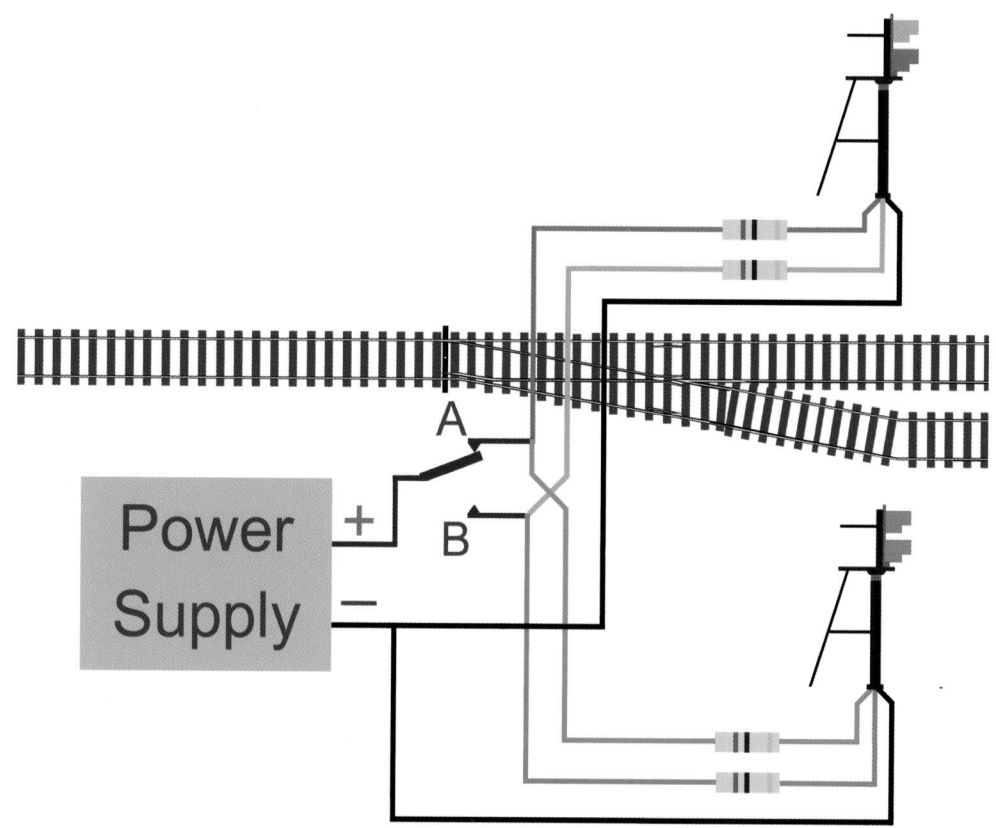

The diagram shows the point set to the lower line. The setting of the point causes the contact (switch) operated by the point's movement to connect the positive terminal of the power supply to contact A. Contact A connects the positive supply to the red light of the upper signal and the green light of the lower, so illuminating these two lights. When the point changes position to the upper line, the positive supply will be connected to contact B. This will light the green LED of the upper signal and the red LED of the lower signal.

You need a changeover contact, also known as a single pole, double throw contact (SPDT), operated by the points movement. Alternatively this contact may be built into the point motor (see Chapter 2). The diagram here shows how this contact is wired so that the signal changes to green when the point is set for the train to run down that line. A single pole, double throw contact could be used to interlock semaphore signals with the point in a similar way.

SEMAPHORE SIGNAL AND POINT INTERLOCKING

The accompanying diagram shows how to interlock a semaphore signal with a point. The semaphore signal is moved by a servo, which requires a servo motor controller. The servo has two positions. When terminals O and S on the servo motor controller are connected or disconnected, the servo moves between its two positions. The semaphore signal arm moves to the danger position when terminal O is not connected to terminal S. It moves to the clear position when terminal O and terminal S are connected.

There is also a contact operated by the movement of the point. This contact is open when the point is set to the other track.

For the semaphore signal to be changed to clear (pulled off) terminal O needs to be electrically connected to terminal S. For this to happen the point first needs to be set in the correct position to close its contact and in addition the operator's switch has

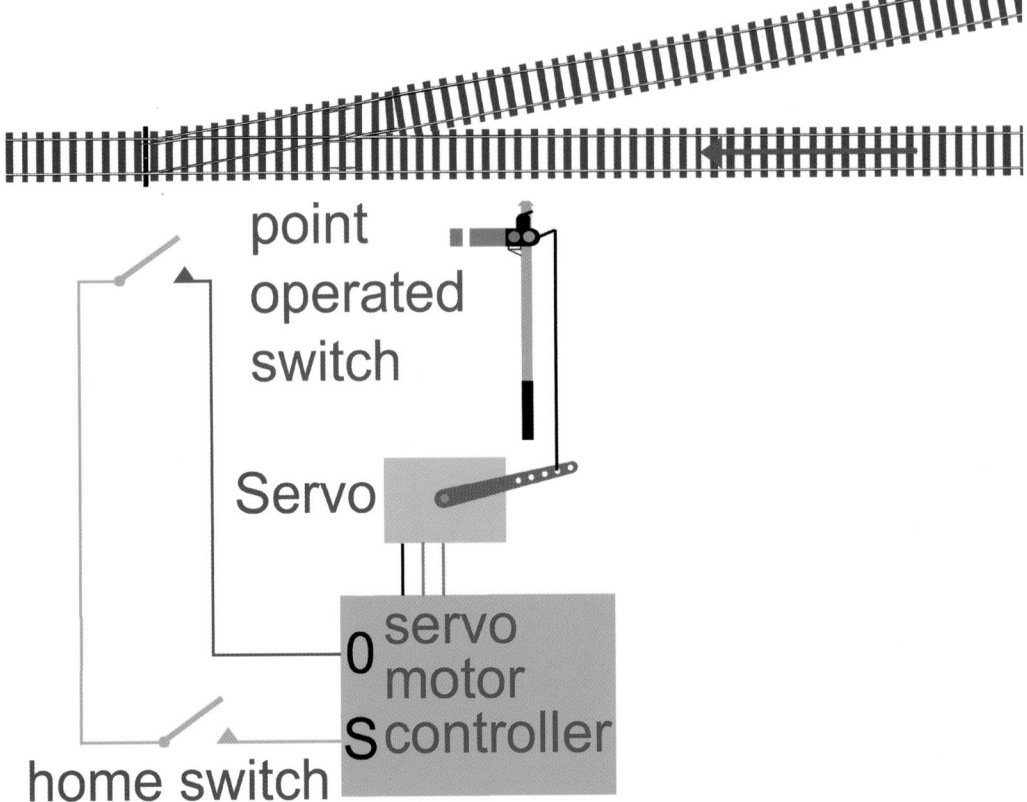

How to interlock a semaphore signal to the directional setting of the points. The connection between terminals O and S on the servo motor controller pass through two switches. The home switch is controlled by the operator and the point-operated switch only closes when the point is set to the lower track. Both switches need to be closed before the signal will move to clear. This type of circuit is an example of a series circuit.

to be moved to the closed position. When the point is not correctly set the signal will remain at danger, regardless of the position of the operator's switch. This is because the point's contact prevents the electrical connection between terminal O and terminal S being made. It is impossible to set the signal to clear until the point is in the correct position.

If there is more than one point along the route the electrical connection between terminals O and S can pass through all the contacts operated by these points. This means that every point has to be set to the right position before the signal will clear. Apart from realism, derailments will be avoided provided model train drivers obey the signals. This can be taken a stage further by using double pole switches. The second pole of the switches could be used to switch power on and off to a section of track in front of the signal. This would make it impossible to drive a train past the signal while it is at danger,

We have shown a signal on only one of the lines, but it would be easy to have a second semaphore signal on the other line with its own home switch but sharing the point-operated switch.

DISTANT SIGNALS

Distant signals should only show clear if the home signal is at clear. The diagram here shows how to add in the switch for a distant signal so that it is interlocked with the points and the home signal. For the distant signal to show clear, the point must be set to the correct track and the home signal must be set to clear.

These methods can also be applied for use with two-aspect colour light signals.

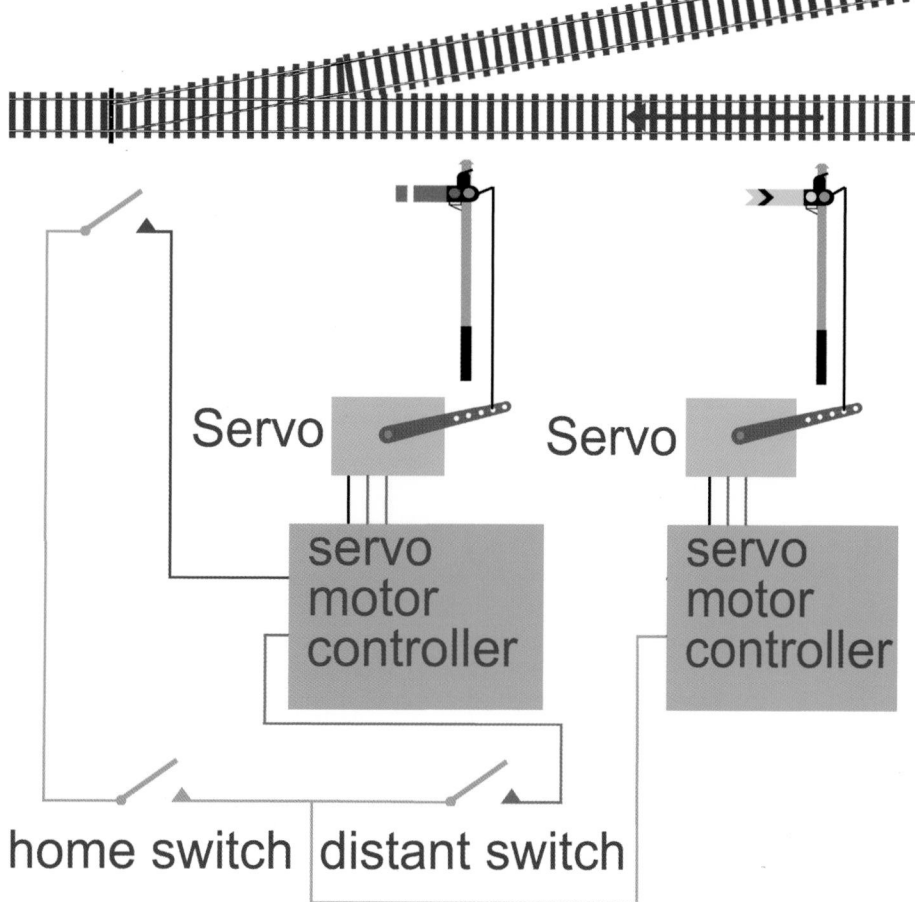

The home signal is controlled in exactly the same way as in the previous diagram. There is an extra operator switch, servo motor controller, servo and distant signal. For the distant signal to be at clear there needs to be an electrical connection passing through all three switches. This provides the interlocking with quite a simple circuit.

Servo

Servo

servo motor controller

servo motor controller

home switch | distant switch

AUTOMATING SEMAPHORE SIGNAL OPERATION

By automating semaphore signals we mean that the signals change in response to the train's movements without the operator needing to do anything. In order to be able to automate the signals the electronics need to know the positions of the trains on your layout. There are a number of ways to detect trains.

REEDS AND MAGNETS

These have probably been around for the longest time. A reed switch consists of a springy piece of ferrous metal encased in a glass tube with connection leads protruding from each end. When a magnet comes close to a reed switch, the ferrous metal bends towards the magnet and the two leads are electrically joined as long as the magnet is close. If you have, for example, a circuit to control a signal and the circuit is wired to a reed switch located beyond the signal, when the circuit senses the reed switch closing it knows the train has passed the signal and will be able to set it to danger. The typical range of magnet to reed switch is about an inch, but this will depend on how powerful the magnet is. The reeds are small enough to fit between the sleepers of the track and the magnets are fitted to the trains.

Reed switches and magnets are fairly inexpensive. The disadvantage is that every train needs to be fitted with a magnet and the detector cannot tell how long the train is or where the magnet is located on the train.

The reed could be replaced with a Hall effect device, an electronic component that detects magnetic fields. Hall effect devices have the advantage of being less conspicuous, but they are not commonly used.

(Left) a magnet and reed switch alongside a length of OO gauge track; (right) a smaller reed and magnet suitable for the N gauge track they are alongside. Note that the reed switch is encased in a glass tube.

LIGHT DEPENDENT RESISTORS (LDRS)

LDRs are an electronic component with the characteristic of a resistance that changes substantially when light falls upon it. By locating the LDRs in the centre of the railway track, a train crossing above them will cast a shadow over them. Associated electronics will distinguish between the resistance present when no train is above and that resulting when there is less light as the train is above.

An advantage of LDRs is that the whole of the train is detected and nothing has to be fitted to the train. The disadvantage is that this system will not work in the dark or at low light levels. A commercial LDR system is available from All Components.

CURRENT SENSORS

These use the fact that no current flows along the rails unless there is an engine on the line. When an engine is moving on the track there is a current present to power the engine's electric motor. This system requires some electronics to sense the current flowing into the rails and insulation breaks have to inserted along the rails to split the track into sections.

This method can only detect that an engine is somewhere along a particular section and not at an exact spot. If you wish to detect whether or not the wagons overlap into the previous section, you will need them to cause a current to flow from one rail to the other. Carriages fitted with working lights will activate the sensors, but otherwise you can fit resistors across an axle causing a current to flow. Very small surface mount resistors are generally used.

INFRARED DETECTION

Our eyes see only a limited range of colours. Some animals see a wider range than we do. Infrared is the colour before red in the spectrum. Although it is invisible to us, it behaves in the same way as visible light. Some phone cameras can be switched to see infrared.

A primitive method of infrared train detection is to shine an infrared beam across the track onto an infrared detector. When a train comes along the beam is blocked from reaching the detector and so the presence of the train is registered. A major disadvantage of this method is the conspicuousness of the infrared detector and emitter at the side of the track.

More sophisticated methods of infrared detection involve reflecting the beam off the underside of the rolling stock by locating the infrared emitter and detector between the sleepers of the track. Only a tiny amount of infrared is reflected back to the infrared detector. Since larger amounts of infrared may already be in the background from sources such as room lights, it is better to use a commercial system that uses sophisticated electronics for amplification and filtering rather than design and build your own. An advantage of infrared detection is that the whole of the train is detected and no modifications to the rolling stock are required. Heathcote Electronics supplies an extensive range of infrared detectors known as IRDOT (Infra Red Detection Of Train), which are available for lighting control panel LEDs for train detection. Some have relay contacts for train control and interfacing to computers on DCC systems. Other units use infrared detection for automatic signal and point control.

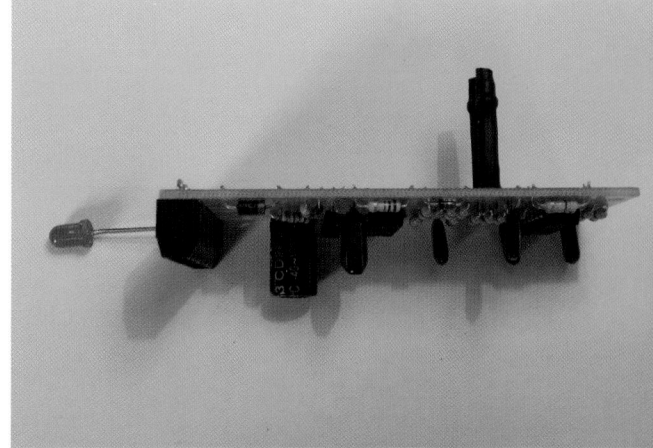

An IRDOT-1 unit, manufactured by Heathcote Electronics. IRDOT is an acronym of Infra Red Detection Of Trains. The two black tubes on the top of the board contain the infrared emitter and detector. These are located in a hole in the baseboard and the infrared beam is reflected off any rolling stock above it.

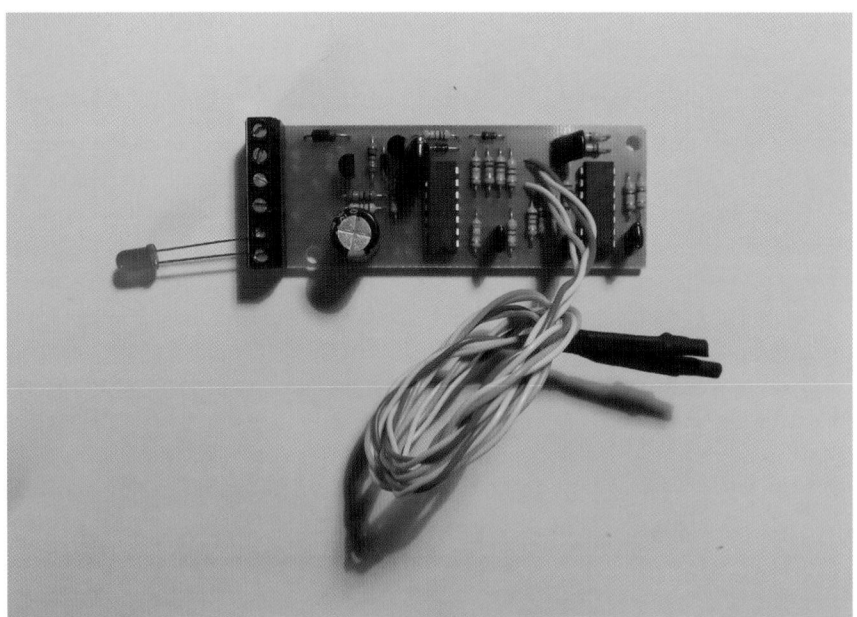

The IRDOT-1 can be supplied with the emitter and detector on the ends of extended wires. This allows the infrared system to be located in positions where there are obstructions under the baseboard.

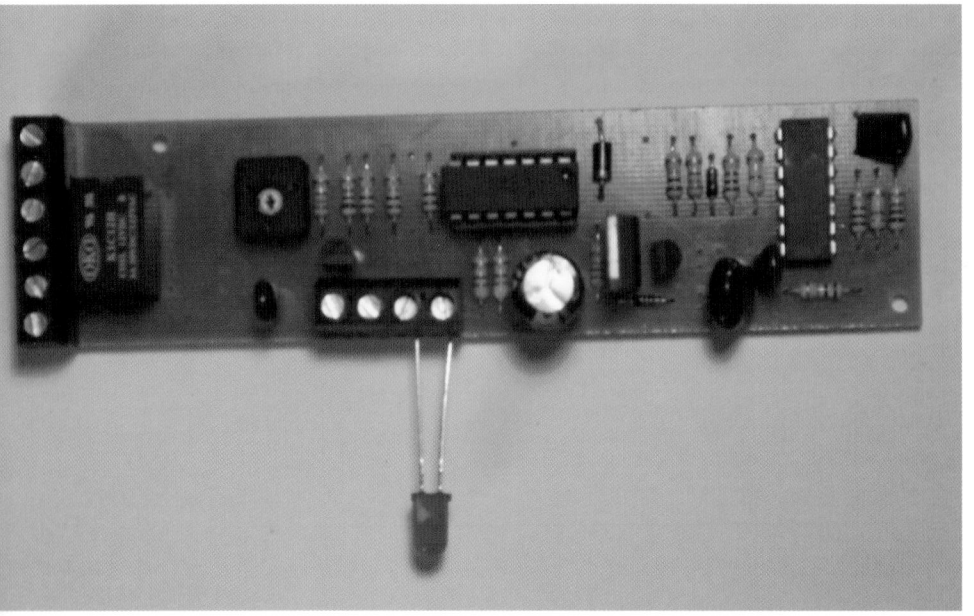

The Semaphore Sequencer incorporates infrared detection with semaphore signal control. Note the potentiometer (pot), which is rotated with a small screwdriver to adjust the time taken for the signal to return to danger. The red LED on the side is to indicate train detection when setting up the board.

MERG (Model Electronic Railway Group) sells the Hector kit to its members for building an infrared detector.

A simple way of automating semaphore signals is to use the Dapol semaphore signal models in conjunction with Heathcote Electronics's Semaphore Sequencer, which is located under the baseboard before the signal and has built-in infrared detection. Its infrared emitter and detector are located in a hole in the baseboard between the sleepers. When a train is detected by the Semaphore Sequencer the signal changes to clear and an adjustable timer is started. When the selected time has elapsed the signal returns to danger. Provision is made for interlocking to points, if required.

AUTOMATING COLOUR LIGHT SIGNALS

Imagine you are a signalman on a double-track line (the majority of railways are double- not single-track) sitting in your signal box. All your signals are at danger for safety. The telegraph asks you, using a bell, if you can accept a train. You check up the line that the next signalman can accept the train. If he can you pull your signals to clear and communicate back down the line by tapping the telegraph that you can accept the train. You watch out of the window until the train has passed and then you return your signals to danger. A trainspotter sitting on the fence by the side of the line will see a signal change from danger to clear. After a while a train passes and the signal returns to danger. This is the effect you can create by making your signals change automatically with the movement of trains.

MAKING A TWO-ASPECT COLOUR LIGHT SIGNAL WORK AUTOMATICALLY

This circuit can be made at home and is a simple method using reed switches to detect the train approaching and leaving the signal.

How the Circuit Works

The signal is initially at red. As a train approaches the signal and is detected by reed 1, the signal changes to green and remains green until the train passes the signal. The train is then detected by reed 2 and the signal changes from green back to red.

The circuit uses a 74HC132 chip, which consists of four logic gates. A logic gate is a digital component that works in binary. It recognizes a voltage close to 5V as a Logic 1 and a voltage close to 0V as a Logic 0.

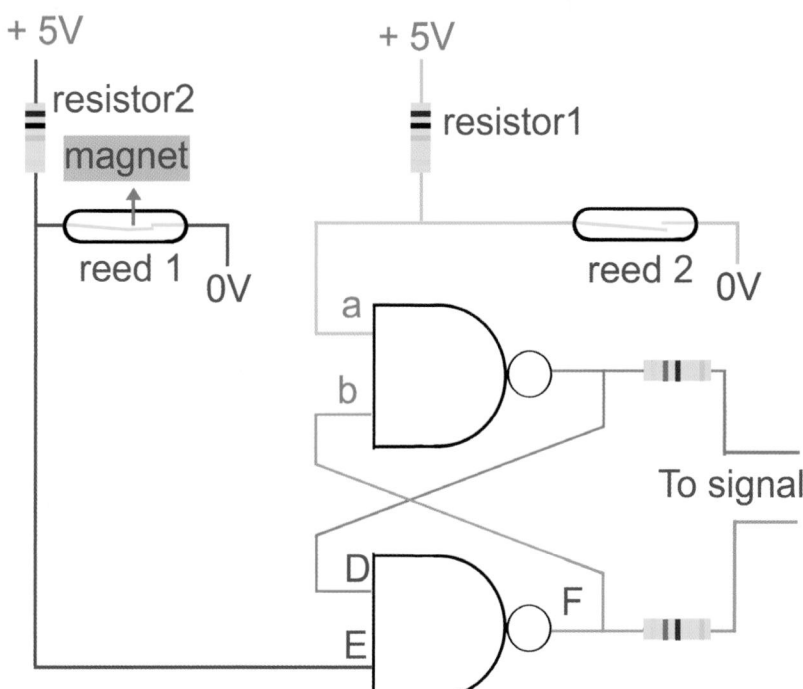

Schematic diagram for automatic signal control, showing how the electronic latch works to remember the train is between the two reed switches.

The four logic gates in the 74HC132 chip are called NAND gates. Each gate has two inputs and one output. The output is Logic 0 if both inputs are Logic 1. For all other combination of inputs the output is Logic 1.

For example, if a was Logic 0 (0V) and b was Logic 1 (5V) the output c would be Logic 1. If a was Logic 1 and b was Logic 0, the output c would be Logic 1. If both the inputs a and b were Logic 0, the output would be Logic 1.

Two of the gates are connected together to form a latch. This is a very simple memory that remembers the train being between the two reed switches. You will see that when the reed switches are not activated inputs A and E are held at 5V by resistor 1 and resistor 2. When one of the reed switches is activated it will connect the input to 0V. A small current will flow through the resistor. The resistor prevents a short circuit that would result from the reed connecting across the power supply when it is operated by a magnet. A value of 10 kilo ohms would be a good selection for the resistors as this would result in a flow of just 0.5 milliamp.

What Happens When the Train Reaches Reed 1

When the train reaches reed 1, the reed closes connecting 0V to input E. Regardless of whether input D is 0V or 5V, output F will be 5V (as explained above).

Output F is connected to input b making it 5V, and input a is 5V as reed 2 is open (because reed 2 is not detecting the train).

With input a and b both at 5V, output c will be 0V.

Output c connects to input D making input D 0V.

Since reed 1 opens as the train moves past the reed, output F will remain at 5V, even though Input E has returned to 5V because input D is now at 0V.

The two logic gates are in a stable state where the signal will remain at green. When the train reaches reed 2 this will close, making input a 0V and therefore output c 5V.

As output c connects to input D, input D will be at 5V. As both inputs D and E are at 5V, output F will be at 0V. With input b at 0V the latch will again be in a stable state, but this time with the red lit in the signal. This condition will last until reed 1 is activated again.

Power for the Circuit

The 74HC132 chip requires a stable DC voltage of 5V. If the voltage is higher than this the chip will be destroyed, lower and it will not function.

The best way to obtain the 5V is to use a voltage regulator chip. A popular example of these is the 7805 Voltage regulator, which needs at least 8V on the input side. (For more information on power supplies, see Chapter 9.)

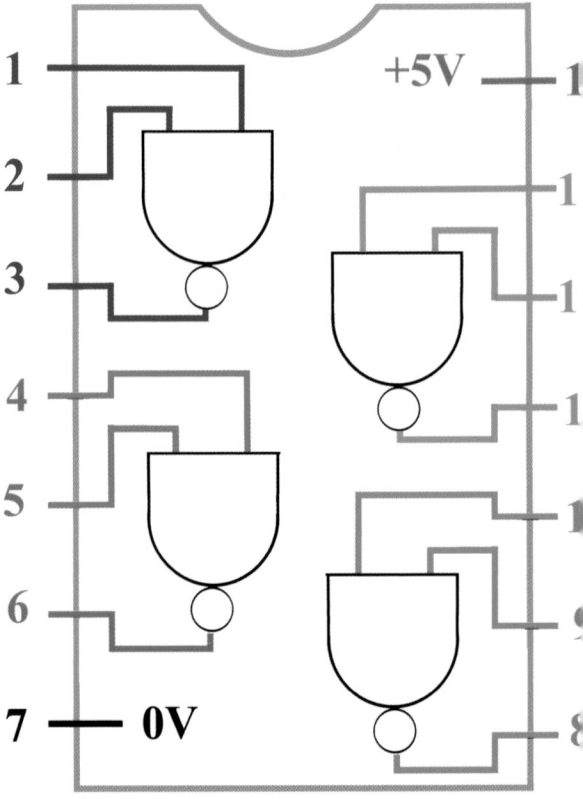

The internal arrangement of the 74HC132 integrated circuit. There are four NAND gates, each with two inputs. Pins 7 and 14 supply power to the integrated circuit. Each NAND gate is shown in a different colour.

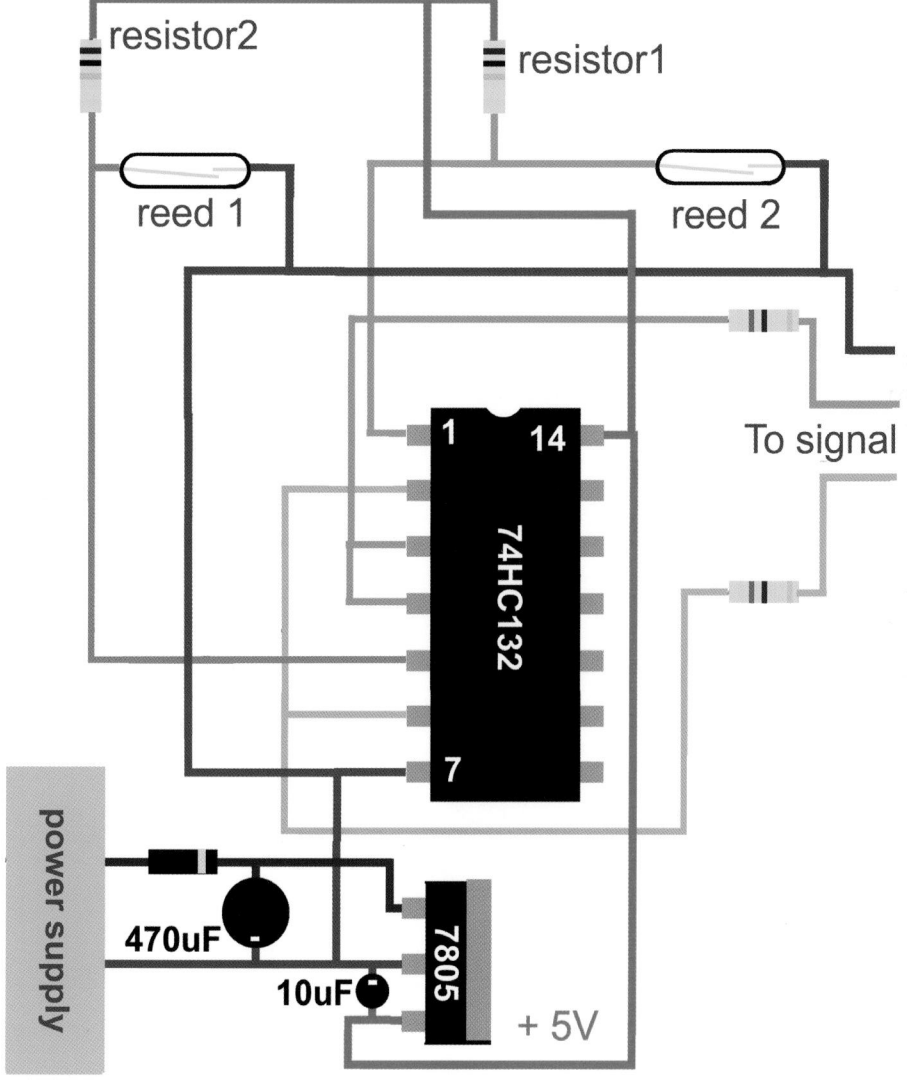

This diagram shows how all the components are connected to build the circuit. It can be powered from either AC or DC. The 7805 is a voltage regulator to ensure the 74HC132 gets a regulated 5V to power it.

How to Build the Circuit

The circuit is built on stripboard (trade name Veroboard).

The stripboard is a piece of Paxolin with holes on a 0.1in grid. On one side are copper strips running the length of the board. Soldering connections are made to these strips.

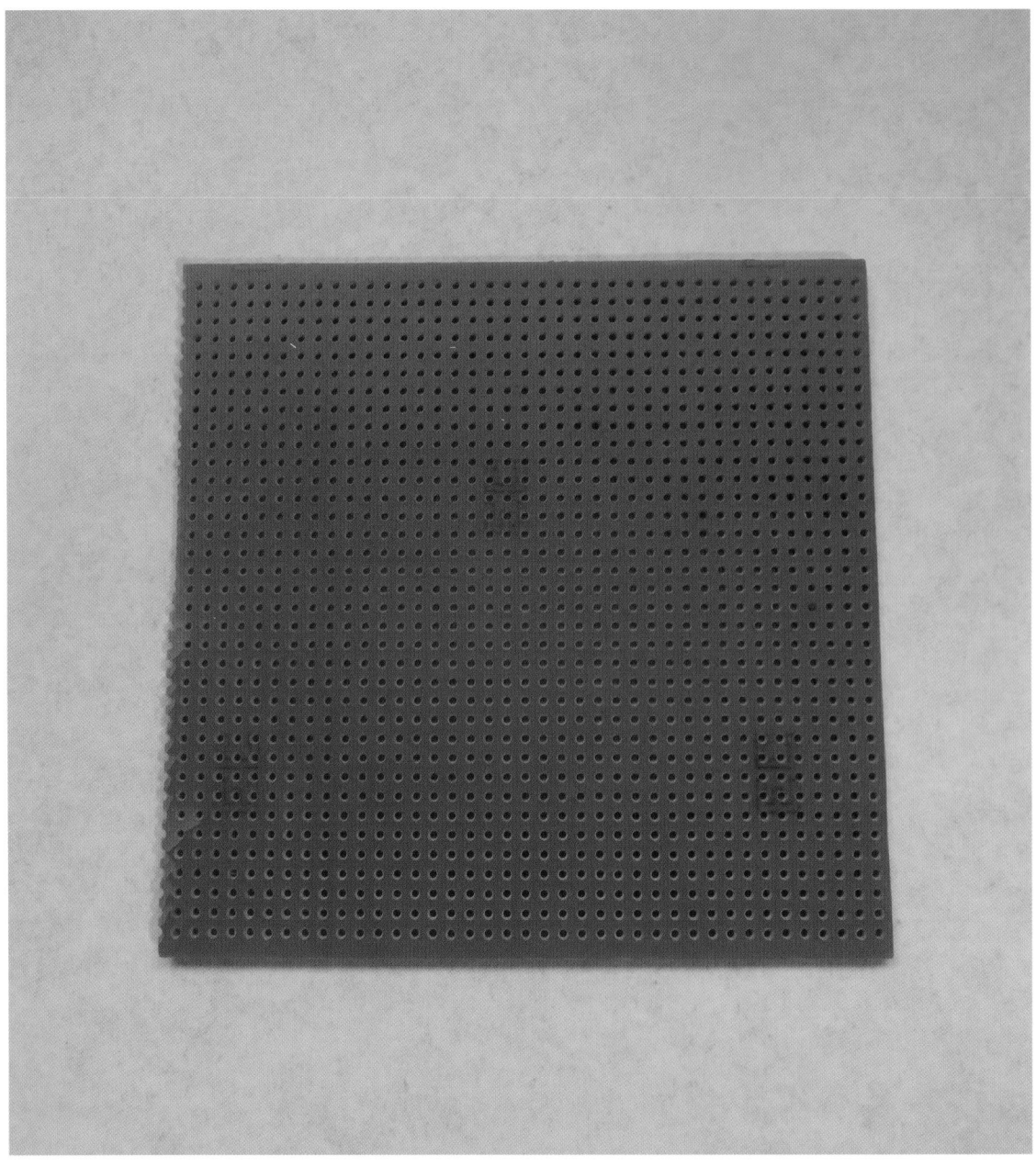

The top of the stripboard. The components are placed on this side.

There is plenty of detail in this model railway bridge and signals.

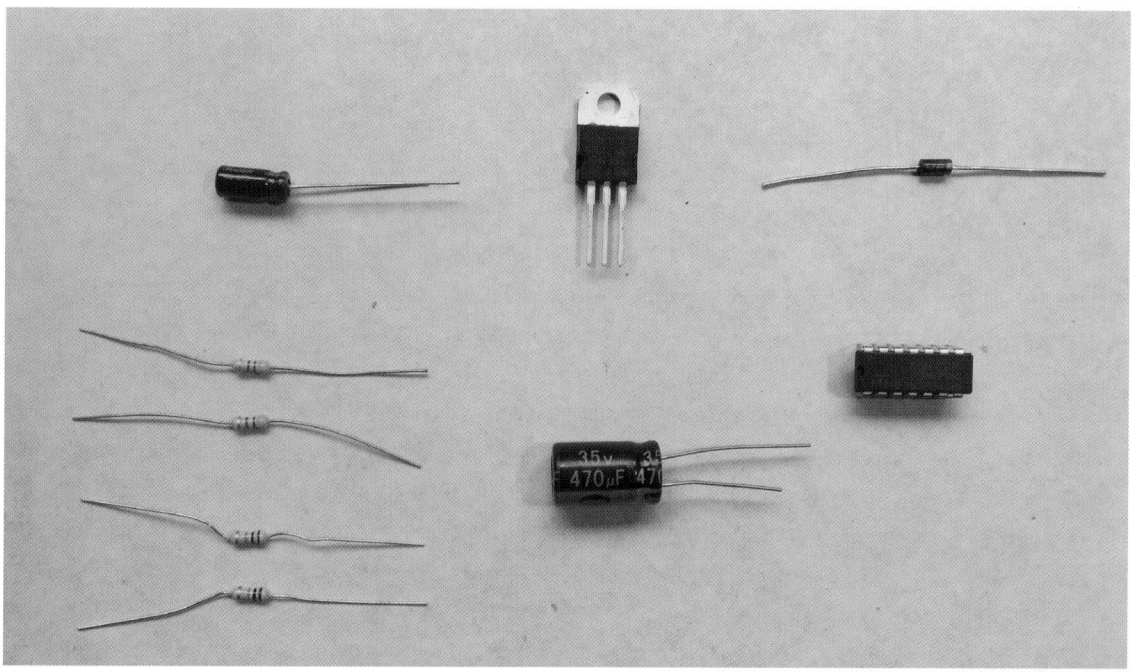

The components to build the circuit board. At top left is the capacitor. Below it are four resistors. The top middle is a voltage regulator and below it is a 470 microfarad capacitor. Note the white stripe that indicates the negative side of the capacitor. At top right is the diode and below this the 74HC132 chip. Note the notch in the end of the chip, which shows which way round to fit it.

Another busy model railway scene.

The bottom of the stripboard. The components' legs poke through and are soldered to the copper strips. Note how the copper strips run across in horizontal lines with an insulation gap between each strip.

The 74HC132 chip soldered into position. The copper tracks on the stripboard have been cut by rotating the tool to prevent pins on opposite sides of the chip being electrically connected. The special tool is seen placed on top of the board.

A special tool is used to cut the strips in order to prevent pins on opposite sides of the integrated circuit being unintentionally connected together. A drill bit with some tape wrapped around it could be made into a suitable tool.

The grey and orange wires are twisted together to connect to the reed switches, so reducing the chance of electrical interference being picked up.

A manufactured model signal would work in the same way as the two LEDs used in the circuit. Two resistors have been used on the left of the stripboard

to limit the current to the LEDs in the signal. but these could be omitted if the model signal has built in resistors. The two LEDs have been used instead of a signal just to test the board.

This has used only two of the four NAND gates, so a second signal could be controlled with the addition of a couple of resistors. In fact we have broken a rule by leaving the inputs to these two gates unconnected. This is bad practice because the gates will consume much more power if their inputs are left unconnected.

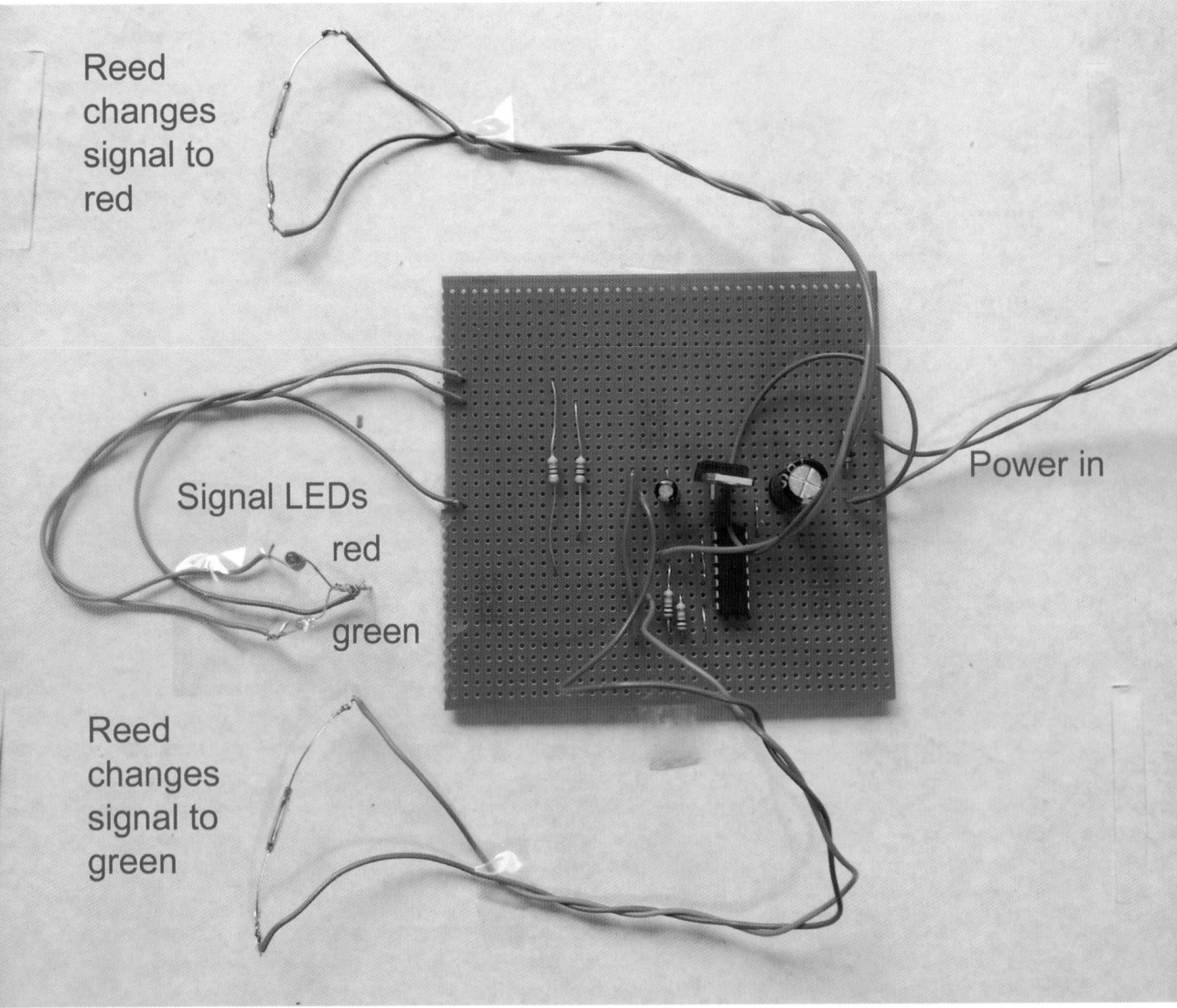

Reed changes signal to red

Signal LEDs red green

Reed changes signal to green

Power in

All the components have been soldered into position and can be seen labelled. You could drill two or more fixing holes to the circuit board so it can be held in position on the underside of the baseboard with wood screws.

COMMERCIALLY AVAILABLE SYSTEMS FOR AUTOMATIC SIGNAL CONTROL

Heathcote Electronics produces products to automatically control two-, three- and four-aspect signals together with route indicators, also known as feathers. These range from the MAS Sequencer, which controls a signal on its own, to IRDASC boards that control several signals along the line, keeping them in the correct lighting sequence. Infrared detection is used and interlocking to the points is simple.

There is a lot to be said for controlling signals automatically as continually throwing switches for manually controlled signals can become tiring, not to say taxing on the memory.

The MAS Sequencer controls multi-aspect colour light signals using infrared detection built into the board. The MAS Sequencer is positioned a realistic distance past the signal. When a train passes a signal at green and reaches the MAS Sequencer, it is detected by the infrared and the signal is changed to red. Once the train has cleared the infrared detection the MAS Sequencer starts its adjustable timer, causing the signal to change through its aspects and then back to green again.

An IRDASC-4 is a circuit board to control multi-aspect signalling. Unlike the MAS Sequencer, it sets its signal depending on the signal ahead. If, for example, the signal ahead is yellow it sets itself to double yellow (assuming it is controlling a four-aspect signal). The signal ahead may be controlled by either another IRDASC-4 or a MAS Sequencer. The information about the signal's aspect is carried between the boards by a single wire. In fact the MAS Sequencer and IRDASC-4 are very simple to wire.

CHAPTER SEVEN

LEVEL CROSSINGS

GATED CROSSINGS

A level crossing is, as the name suggests, a place where the railway track crosses a road, bridleway or footpath at the same level.

As a result of various Acts of Parliament, different regulations apply to level crossings on roads as compared to footpaths and bridleways (pathways where horses are also allowed). On level crossings at footpaths and bridleways, individuals are responsible for making sure it is safe to cross by themselves. There

A crossing for a footpath, showing the wicket gate at the far side and the warning notice. There are also slatted wooden pieces on the sides of the crossing to prevent cattle from straying on the track.

A private road crossing the Churnet Valley Railway. It is the responsibility of the public to open the gates and make sure it is safe to cross. Warning signs are provided.

has to be at least a warning sign and a stile or gate leading on to the track.

Where a railway meets a public road at a level crossing there originally had to be gates and a 'fit and proper person' to operate them. This means that it would be the signalman's responsibility to open and close the gates if the crossing was near to a station with a signal box.. Inside some signal boxes there is a windlass for opening and closing the level crossing gates, so the signalman would not have to leave the

box. Where there was no signal box alongside the crossing a crossing keeper would be employed. The railway company would usually build him a crossing keeper's cottage alongside the crossing.

On little-used lines the train stops before the crossing and the guard jumps out, opens the gates to let the train through and closes them afterwards. In fact some crossings didn't even have gates and the train would stop so the guard could jump out and hold up the road traffic with a red flag.

This crossing keeper's house, built by the North Staffordshire Railway, is now in use as a private house. You can see where the track used to be, heading towards the tunnel mouth. When in use the crossing keeper would have been responsible for the safety of the public on the road crossing the railway line.

An old concrete warning sign. Signs were also made in cast iron, a very popular material on railways.

PRIVATE AND PUBLIC CROSSINGS

There is an important difference between private and public crossings. A private crossing is where a private road, such as a farmer's track or road to a hamlet, crosses the railway track. A public crossing is where a public road crosses the railway track. Private crossings have field gates that normally block off the road and are opened only when the railway needs to be crossed. It is the responsibility of the person crossing to look out for trains. Unlike public crossings, private crossing gates do not block off the railway track as they open away from the track to prevent members of the public from blocking it.

Public crossings have a distinctive style of crossing gate that features a large red circular target shape where the gates meet in the middle. Both roads approaching the track need to be blocked by the gates. Single or double gates can be used, depending on the width of the road. There also had to be a wicket gate for pedestrians.

Public crossing gates are interlocked to the signals. This means that there are stop signals just before the crossing and the crossing gates cannot be opened to traffic until the signals are at danger. Associated with stop signals are distant signals to warn the driver to be ready to stop.

The crossing gates at Cheddleton Station, Staffordshire. Unlike a private road, the gates on this public road remain closed to trains when not in use. Note the characteristic red target shape on the gates, which overlap here as the road is wider than the railway tracks.

The gates on the station side of the crossing at Cheddleton Station. The pedestrian gates give access to the platforms.

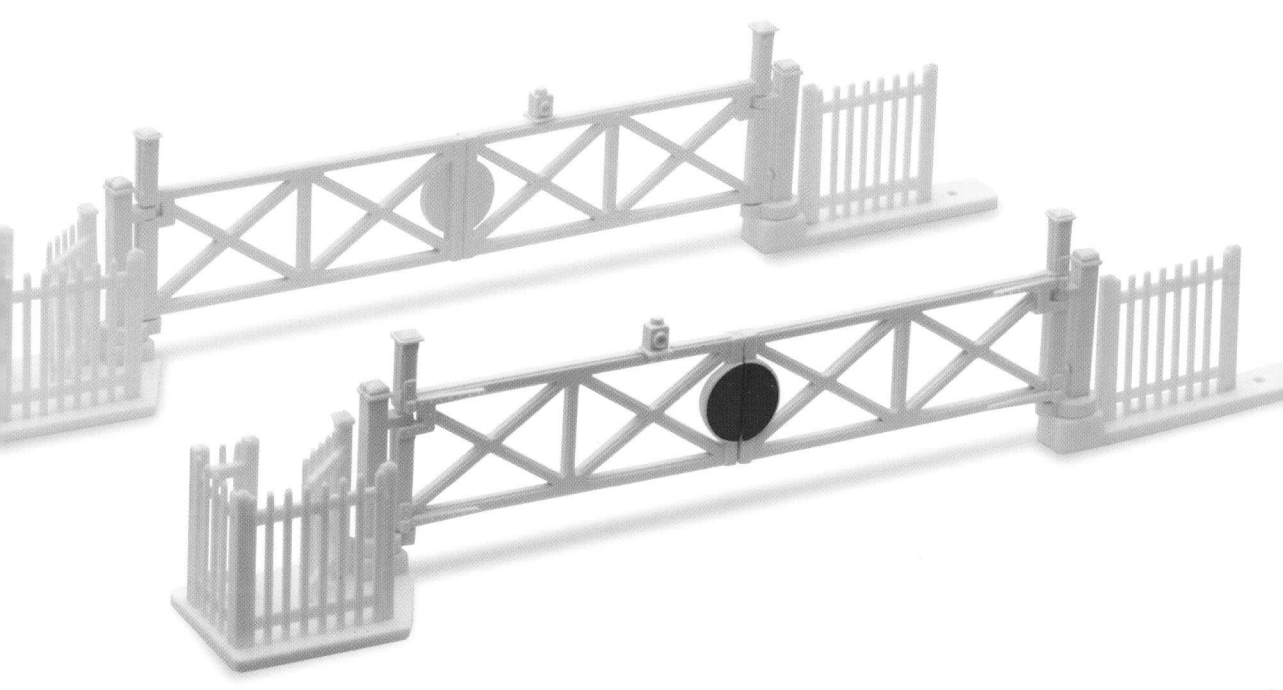

Peco's model of a public gated crossing with four gates. The wicket gate for pedestrians can be seen on the left. There is also an oil lamp on top of the gate. PECO PUBLICATIONS

BARRIER CROSSINGS

From the previous section it can be seen that a great many people were required to operate all the public level crossings. Automatic level crossings with barriers were introduced from 1961, partly as a measure to reduce the wage bill. Rather than being operated by a person, these were generally automatically activated by the front wheel of an approaching train striking a treadle alongside the rail. The early barrier crossings had full lifting barriers that went all the way across the road. Initially these had only red flashing lights but later, as a response to accidents, an amber light was added that displayed for five seconds before the red lights on the barrier began to flash and the barrier lowered.

The full barrier crossing at Oakham, seen here, is still managed by the signalman. A road junction on the crossing requires two sets of lights, one facing each

road. There is a footbridge for pedestrians in addition to wicket gates on the pavement to ensure safe crossing. As the barriers descend, the nearside barriers come down first to prevent traffic being trapped between the gates. Both barriers lift together. Full barrier crossings can also be remotely controlled, for example at Blythe Bridge, Staffordshire.

From 1972 a new category of unmanned crossings appeared with full barriers interlocked to signals and with CCTV.

Half-barrier crossings were then introduced on roads used by more than a thousand cars per day to prevent cars being trapped on the line. These have a barrier that blocks the approaching lane of the road but not the exit. They also have warning lights: the sequence is that the amber lights for five seconds and then the red lights flash as the barrier falls. The time between the start of the barriers' operation and the arrival of the fastest train is about twenty seconds.

Oakham barrier crossing shows four barriers, making it a full barrier crossing. In 2013, when this photograph was taken, the signal box was still manned and controlled by the signalman. Because it is manned, all the barriers can be lowered together as the signalman can see he is not trapping a car between the barriers on the road. There are two sets of traffic warning lights on the roads to cater for the road junction just before the crossing. PECO PUBLICATIONS

A CCTV camera can be seen above the direction sign to Blyth Bridge Station on the right hand side. This allows the signalman in his power box to check that the crossing is not blocked and the signals can be cleared for the trains to go through.

On an automatic half-barrier crossing, such as this example at Cresswell, Staffordshire, only the approach side of the road is blocked when the barriers are lowered. As this is an unmanned crossing, there are yellow cases on short posts to contain telephones that can be used to contact the signalman controlling this section of line directly if there is a slow-moving road vehicle or an emergency.

A model half-barrier crossing made by Peco. Although the majority of crossings have the warning lights on a post separated from the barrier mechanism, there were some, like the Peco model, with both combined. It would be possible to drill out the plastic warning lights and insert LEDs.

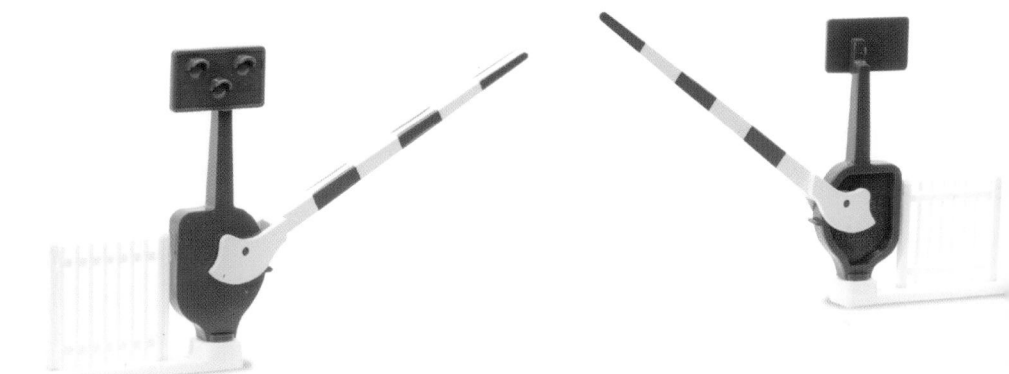

Automatic half-barriers do not have railway signals interlocked to them.

At around this time AOCL (automatic open crossings locally monitored) were also introduced. These have no barriers but do have the characteristic amber lights and flashing red lights associated with other barrier crossings.

MOTORIZING LEVEL CROSSINGS

GATED CROSSINGS – TWO GATES

If your gated crossing has two gates they will need to open and close one after another. If you try to open them at the same time they will bump into each other. Slow motion point motors can be used to motorize the gates. By using a DPDT centre off switch wired to reverse the polarity, it is possible to wire the switch so that the motor turns to open the gate, turns to close the gate or, in the mid-position, shuts off electricity so that the gate is stationary. A separate switch is needed for each gate. If a coil spring is inserted in the linkage between the motor and gate, it should prevent damage to the gate if a train accidently runs into it when the gate is closed across the line.

A dual servo motor controller made by Heathcote Electronics could be used to motorize the gates with servo motors. This has the advantage of an output that allows the gates to move one at a time under the control of a single switch.

Using a dual servo motor controller (made by Heathcote Electronics) to move a two-gated crossing. The green and brown wires go to an on/off switch. The red and black wires go to a power supply. The yellow link wire causes the second servo motor to move after the first servo motor has come to rest.

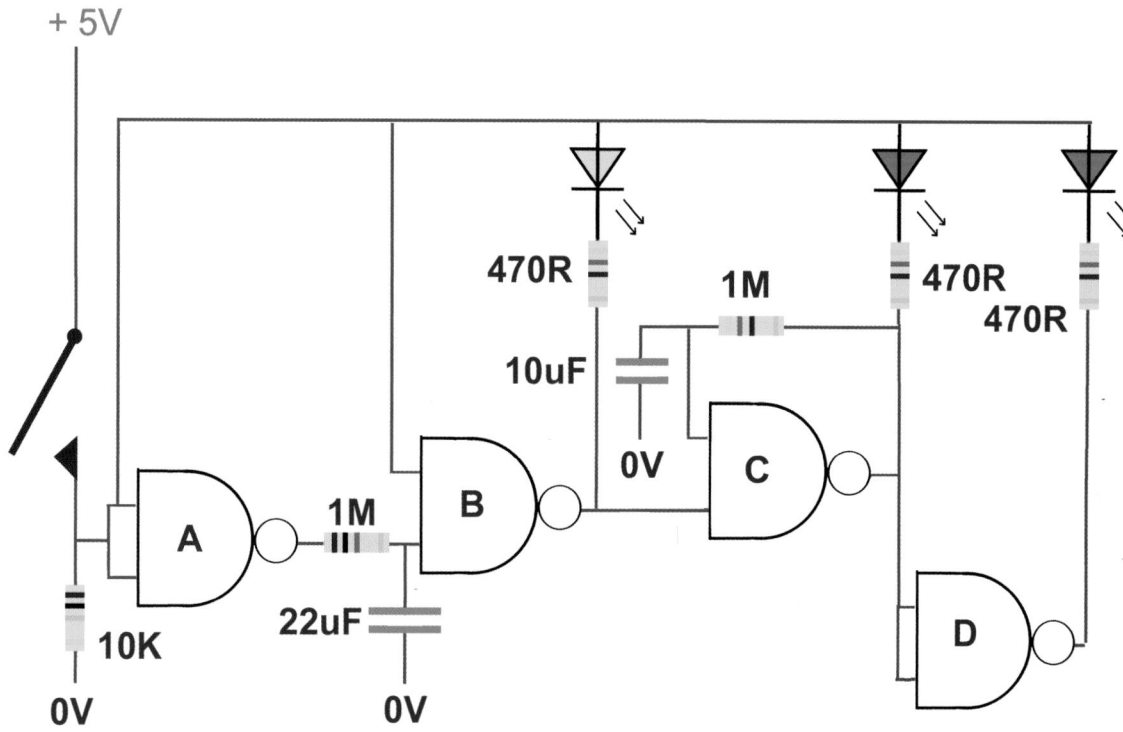

As the on/off switch is connected to the anodes of all the LEDs, they cannot light until the switch is thrown. When the switch is open NAND gate A has 0 at its inputs, its output is high and the 22 microfarad capacitor will be charged up. When the switch is thrown the amber LED will light for 5 seconds while the capacitor discharges. When the capacitor is discharged NAND gate C will start to oscillate, causing the red light to flash. NAND gate D causes the other red LED to flash out of synchronization.

GATED CROSSINGS – FOUR GATES

All four gates can be made to open at once with a single switch as there is not the collision problem inherent in level crossings with two gates. Either servo motors or slow motion point motors can be used to operate the gates.

BARRIER CROSSINGS

As with gated crossings, slow motion point motors or servo motors are suited to making the barriers move. The motorized kits made by Faller are based on European crossings, but they can be adapted to look more British. The barrier works automatically as the trains approach by using reed switches in the track to cause the motor to start moving. The motor works off AC, not DC.

HOW TO MAKE WARNING LIGHTS FLASH

It is fairly simple to build an electronic circuit to make a pair of red LEDs flash alternately to represent flashing lights on the traffic light warning board of a

Suppliers of Model Railway Crossings

N gauge

Ratio make a gated level crossing kit. Their product code is Ratio 234. This is a plastic kit with four gates and it is not motorized.

Kato make a working barrier crossing. This is a Japanese style crossing. It uses their design of track which has the ballast moulded in. This may make it difficult to use if you are using another manufacturer's track.

OO gauge

Wills make a plastic kit of a two gated crossing which is not motorized. It includes parts for the roadway and wicket gates. This kit also includes one pair of gates, a sheet of plastic cobbled stone and a sheet of planked track crossing. It is possible to shorten the gates for use with a single track line by cutting out a section of the gate. The product code is SS56.

Wills also make a crossing keeper's cabin kit which is useful if there is no signal box nearby. Their code for this kit is SS29. Alternatively, you could use the Wills kit for a crossing keeper's cottage. The product code is SS39 for the crossing keeper's cottage.

Dapol supply a gated crossing which has two gates. It is a plastic kit that has a roadway moulded in and is for a single track line.

Hornby make non-working ready assembled models for both single and double track crossings. They have models of both gated and barrier crossings. The model parts are designed to clip onto their track.

Peco kit LK46 supplies two field gates, two stiles and one wicket gate. This might be useful for making a model of a private crossing. Peco model LK50 uses a four gated crossing with wicket gates. This would be suitable for a double track line.

A half barrier crossing model is also made by Peco. The model code is LK51.

The above models do not have the roadway moulded in. However, Peco make other models which do.

barrier level crossing. In the example shown here, the circuit has been built so that the amber lights before the red lights start flashing. The circuit is worked by an on/off switch, but it could be modified to be operated by the automatic signal circuit to give automatic operation.

At British crossings there is an amber light before the red flashing lights which lights for five seconds. The 1M resistor and the 22uF capacitor determine this time.

AUTOMATING LEVEL CROSSINGS

By automating level crossings we means making them work automatically as the train approaches. Two sources of electronic boards for automating level crossings are Express Models and Heathcote Electronics.

AUTOMATING ROAD VEHICLES

Faller make model road vehicles with an internal rechargeable battery. Steering is done by laying a strip of iron wire under the road surface which guides the magnet on an arm on the front axle of the vehicle thereby steering the wheels. There is a reed switch built into the vehicle. When it passes over a magnet in the road the reed switch opens so stopping the vehicle. It is relatively easy to arrange for an electromagnet just before the crossings to turn on when the barriers lower thus stopping the vehicles in front of the barrier or gates.

CHAPTER EIGHT

HELPFUL ELECTRICAL AND ELECTRONIC CONCEPTS

Model railways use concepts from both electrical and electronic engineering. Relay switches and transformers, for example, are considered to be electrical devices, while LEDs, diodes and transistors are considered to be electronic devices. Both electrical and electronics derive from the name of the sub-atomic particle that carries electrical charge, the electron. This in turn is derived from the Greek word for amber, which has electrostatic properties.

ELECTRONS, CONDUCTORS AND INSULATORS

All materials are made up of atoms. An atom has a nucleus around which orbits a number of electrons. The nucleus has a positive electrical charge and the electrons carry a negative electrical charge. A lump of metal, for example, will normally have an equal number of positive and negative charges overall and therefore you will not get a shock off it. You may notice, however, that you sometimes get a shock when you get out of your car or step off an escalator because a surplus of electrons has built up and charged up the car or escalator, and that you have discharged it by stepping out or off. The electrons have flowed through your body. This movement of electrons is an electrical current. Materials that allow electrons to flow easily, such as metals, are called conductors. Those that are very difficult for electrons to flow through, such as plastics, are called insulators.

VOLTAGE AND CURRENT

Current and voltage can be compared to water flowing along a pipe. The voltage is similar to water pressure and the current is similar to the amount of water flowing along the pipe per second. In other words, the number of electrons flowing down the wire every second is current and the energy contained in each electron is voltage. High voltages kill you because there is a lot of energy in each electron, but low voltages can't even be felt.

Electrical current is measured in amps, with small amounts in milliamps. There are a thousand milliamps in one amp. Voltage is measured in volts. To give some idea of the units, a typical OO gauge engine would use 0.25A at 3V to move very slowly and 0.25A at 12V to move very fast, so getting more energy to move faster. If you attach more carriages behind your model engine you will find it requires even more current to make it move because, although the voltage sets the speed, the current sets the torque (pull) of the electric motor.

The electricity that comes into the home is 240V AC and would just vaporize your models if it became connected to them. There are several good reasons why electricity companies prefer to supply AC and not DC, and 240V not 12V. To get the same amount of power down the line at 12V they would need to send twenty times more electrons, so all the wires would have to be twenty times as thick. Copper is not cheap so this would be very expensive. In fact the electricity companies have a trick to save copper by sending electricity long distances in small wires at extremely high voltages. Substations convert this down to 240V for households.

Transformers in the substations convert one voltage to another. They can convert high voltages to low voltages and vice versa. Transformers only work with AC electricity, not DC. The reason for this is that transformers require a changing magnetic field. A DC current would produce only a constant magnetic field and so the transformer would not produce a secondary voltage. The accompanying diagram

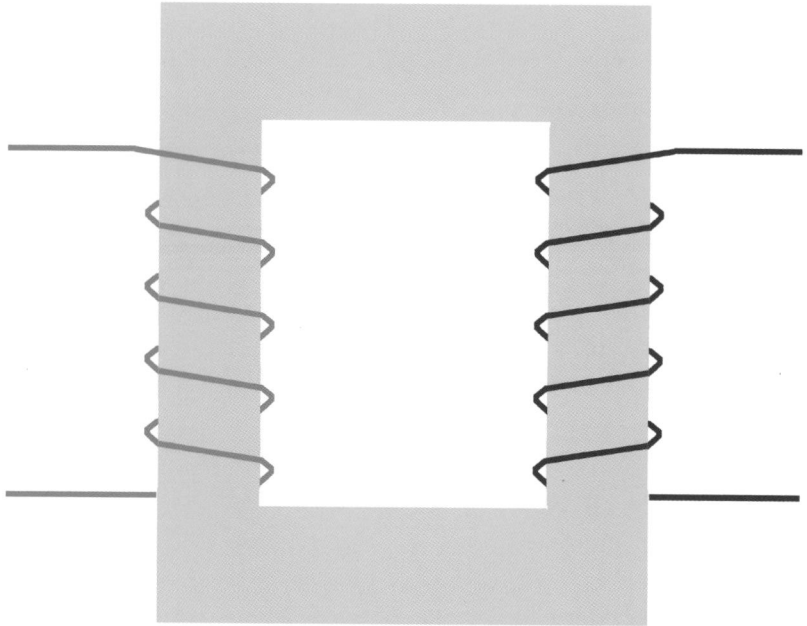

The green wire here represents the primary side of the transformer and the blue wire represents the secondary side. In an actual transformer there would be many more turns of wire than shown here. The pale blue rectangle represents the iron core of the transformer. Iron concentrates the magnetic field, which flows around it. If the core were wood, for example, the transformer would be very weak as wood is not a ferromagnetic material and would not concentrate the magnetism.

shows how the two coils of wire in a transformer are electrically isolated and the energy is transferred by the changing magnetic field.

ALTERNATING CURRENT (AC) AND DIRECT CURRENT (DC)

An alternating current (AC) does just that. It alternates in the direction it flows along the wire. For mains voltages it reverses direction fifty times a second. In other word the frequency is 50 Hertz. The unit Hertz replaced the old unit of cycles per second. If alternating current were to be connected to your model locomotive, even at the correct voltage the DC motor inside would reverse direction fifty times a second, emitting a low-pitched hum until black smoke and a burning smell indicated the demise of the electric motor. Smoke generators are a better method of obtaining smoke effects.

Before the invention of diodes it was very difficult to convert AC electricity to DC. Early model railway manufacturers therefore had to use AC electric motors inside their locomotives. The disadvantage to using AC electric motors is that it is very difficult to reverse the direction in which the engine is travelling. With DC this is easy: you simply reverse the polarity of the electrical supply to the rails. From a desire not to upset existing customers who have invested in AC model railways, a few manufacturers, such as Märklin, have continued to manufacture AC model railways. Another German manufacturer, Faller, produces a large range of motorized kits using synchronous AC electric motors. These have the advantage that the speed of rotation depends upon the frequency of the power supply rather than the voltage (the speed of rotation of DC motors depends upon the voltage).

An example of direct current (DC) is the current supplied from a battery. This always flows in the same direction. It is possible to convert AC to DC with a power supply.

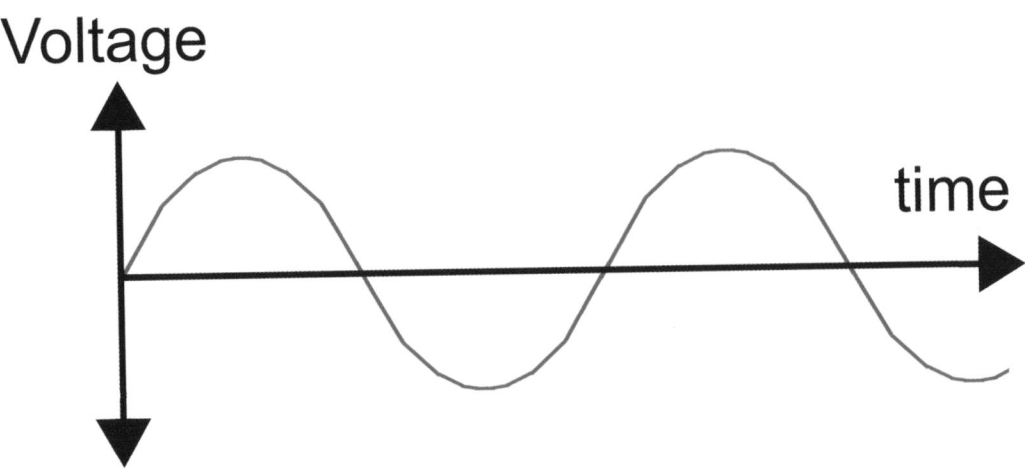

The red line in this graph plots the increase and decrease of voltage with time. This is AC electricity. The wavy line produced is a sine wave and this is a common natural occurrence. The waveform of the electricity from the sockets in your home will be a sine wave. The important thing is that the voltage changes between a positive and negative value and this will reverse the flow of the electricity. This is why AC is not suitable for powering DC electric motors and microchips, for example.

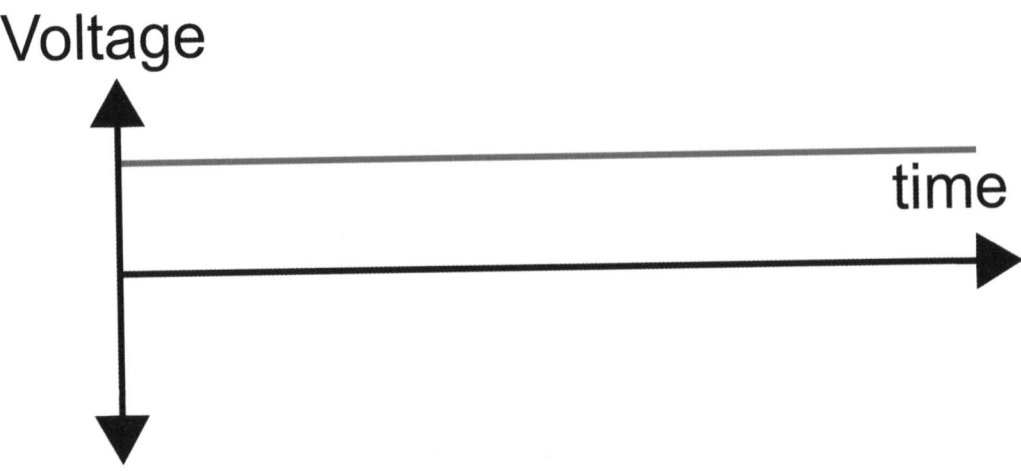

The red line here stays at the same voltage through time. This is DC electricity, which is obtained from batteries and regulated power supplies.

TRANSFORMERS

Transformers are used to change the electrical supply from one voltage to another. They only work with AC and not with DC electricity.

Transformers use the fact that a current flowing along a wire produces a magnetic field. A wire passing through an alternating magnetic field produces a current A large magnetic field is produced by winding many turns of wire around an iron core. This is called the primary coil. The secondary coil consists of another wire wrapped in many turns around the same iron core. The secondary core changes the magnetic field into an electrical current flowing along its wire. Enamelled wire, consisting of solid copper wire coated in varnish or enamel as an insulation, is generally used because insulation with plastic-coated wire takes up much more volume. Many more turns of enamelled wire will fit on an iron core. The iron core inside a transformer is used to concentrate the magnetic flux so that as much

as possible is concentrated through the secondary winding. The larger the number of turns in the wire wound around the core the greater the magnetic field. By having a different number of turns of wire in the primary and secondary coils on the iron core, the voltage is transformed between the wires going in and out. A practical example is if you had 240 turns on the primary coil and 16 on the secondary coil, this transformer would convert the mains voltage (240V) into 16V and make it suitable for your model railway. As there is the same magnetic field through each set of windings, the power through each winding will then be the same. (This example assumes a perfect transformer. Fortunately transformers are close enough to perfect for this assumption to be reasonable.) Remembering watts is the unit of power, then the current multiplied by voltage will be the same for each winding. Therefore, if 1 Amp at 16 Volts is drawn out of the secondary only 16/240ths of an Amp is supplied by the mains into the primary. Just as well, or you would get enormous electricity bills.

The steel laminations are visible on this mains transformer.

The iron core of the transformer is usually made out of laminations of steel. This is to reduce the eddy currents that can be induced in the iron laminations (one of the reasons transformers are not quite perfect). There is a limit to how concentrated the magnetic field can be in the core of the magnet: if there is too much magnetic field the core is saturated. To get around this you need a larger cross-sectional area of laminations, resulting in a heavier, bulkier and more expensive transformer. Sometimes these laminations become loose, resulting in the characteristic buzzing noise caused by the laminations vibrating as they are magnetized in opposite directions fifty times a second.

The main use of AC electricity on model railways is for operating solenoid point motors and lighting. Transformers, however, are a building block of DC power supplies and both DC and DCC controllers. (For more information on DC power supplies, see Chapter 9.)

SOLENOIDS AND ELECTROMAGNETS

The principle that an electric current produces a magnetic field is also employed by solenoids and electro-magnets. If you put a number of turns around a steel rod, a DC current flowing along it will produce a north and south pole at each end of the rod, just like a bar magnet but with the advantage that you can switch the magnet on and off by switching the electricity on and off. This would be useful on a model railway for uncoupling certain types of couplings designed to be uncoupled by magnets. If you make a metal rod move then you have a solenoid; this is the principle used by some point motors.

Wrapping enamelled wire around a 6in nail will make a home-made electromagnet, but it will probably need at least one hundred turns of wire. The factors governing the strength of the magnetic field created are:

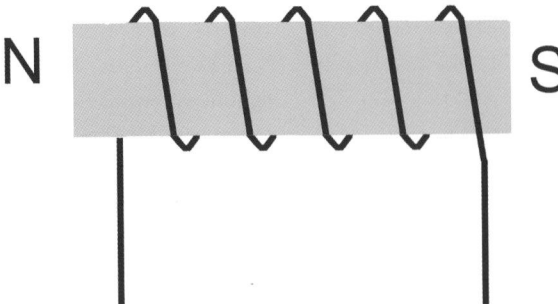

This diagram shows an electromagnet. A real electromagnet would have many more turns of wire around an iron core, since more turns produce a stronger magnetic field and therefore the magnetic force it exerts will be stronger. DC current passing through the turns produces a north and south pole, just like a bar magnet. This is shown by the N and S at the ends of the core. AC electricity put through these poles will reverse at 50 times per second. The electromagnets used in solenoid point motors, however, work equally well with AC or DC electricity. This is because iron is equally attracted to a north or south pole.

Permeability of the core. This is to concentrate the magnetic field. A ferromagnetic material is required: 6in iron or steel nails are satisfactory ferromagnetic materials for home construction. Brass nails would be useless as they have no ferromagnetic properties.

Cross-sectional area of the core. The greater this is the stronger the electromagnet will be. Therefore the thicker the nail, the stronger the force of the finished electromagnet.

Number of turns of wire. The more turns of wire, the more powerful the electromagnet. In fact the strength is proportional to the number of turns squared. This has the helpful result that 141 turns would produce an electromagnet with twice the strength of one with 100 turns. Fine wire is needed in order to pack lots of turns together. This is the reason that enamelled copper wire is used as its insulation takes up a tiny amount of space.

Current flowing through the windings. The larger the current, the stronger the magnet. There are, however, practical limits on supplying a large current and there is the disadvantage that the wire from which the turns are made has a resistance.

A simple electromagnet can be easily made by winding thin enamelled wire around a thick iron nail, using adhesive tape to hold the coiled wire in place. Enamelled copper wire comes in different thicknesses measured in SWG (standard wire gauge). We have made electromagnets using very fine 36 SWG enamelled copper wire, which is approximately one third of a millimetre in diameter and allows a lot of turns to be fitted. You will find that when you solder the ends of enamelled copper wire the enamel sometimes melts and a good solder joint is made. With other types the enamel withstands a higher temperature and it is necessary to scrape it off the ends with a sharp knife before it will solder well. A satisfactory power supply will be 12V AC or DC, although if you use AC, instead of getting one north and one south pole, the poles will alternate with the frequency of the supply. For some purposes this isn't a problem but it would not be useful for attracting a permanent magnet, for example, as it would repel and attract the permanent magnet fifty times a second.

WATTS

A watt is the unit used to measure all types of power. Watts are the modern equivalent of horse power. As well as measuring the power of a car engine, watts are used to measure electrical power: a 100W light bulb, for example, gives out more light than a 60W bulb but will also use more electricity.

The correct current and voltage are needed for electrical devices to work. Too high a voltage can result in damage, too low a voltage and the electrical item will not work. The current rating is slightly different in that we need enough current for the job. Suppose, for example, that we wish to power fifty LEDs for model building lighting. We are using a regulated 12V DC power supply and have calculated resistor values so that each LED is supplied with 20 milliamps of current. We will need a total current of 50 × 0.02 (20 milliamps is 20/1000 of an amp, 20/1000 = 0.02). So the total current required will be 1 amp.

If the power supply's maximum current output is 0.5A, then it cannot supply enough current and will cut out after a short time or will supply a much reduced voltage, causing the LEDs to shine dimly.

If the power supply is rated for a current of more than 1A then everything will work as expected as the LEDs will only take the current they require. The lighting system would work with a 10A power supply but not with a 0.5A supply.

Often power supplies are specified by their voltage and wattage. For electrical items watts are calculated by multiplying the current and voltage. It is important to keep all the units consistent: the current must be in amps and the voltage in volts. Hence if we have a power supply or transformer specified as a 10W 5V unit, we can do the calculation in reverse to find the maximum current the unit can supply: 10/5 = 2. This means that the unit can supply any current up to 2A, but no more. As a matter of cost, it is best to select the minimum wattage that will do the job.

CHAPTER NINE

ELECTRICAL AND ELECTRONIC COMPONENTS AND ASSEMBLY EXPLAINED

CAPACITORS

Capacitors are a device for storing electrical charge. Capacitance is measured in farads. There is a huge range of values from pecofarads to farads themselves. A pecofarad is 10 to the [minus]12 farads: in other words, 1 pecofarad is 0.000000000001 of a farad. Capacitors have many uses on model railways. They are used for smoothing DC when AC is being converted to DC. They are also used for the suppression of electrical interference from electric motors. Large value capacitors are used for storing electrical charge for carriage lights and for capacitor discharge units.

To obtain large values of capacitance electrolytic capacitors need to be used. These are generally polarized and have to be connected with the polarity the correct way round. Connecting them the wrong way round results in a hissing sound, followed by a large bang as the end flies off. They are usually marked with minus symbols on one side of the case to indicate which way round they should be fitted.

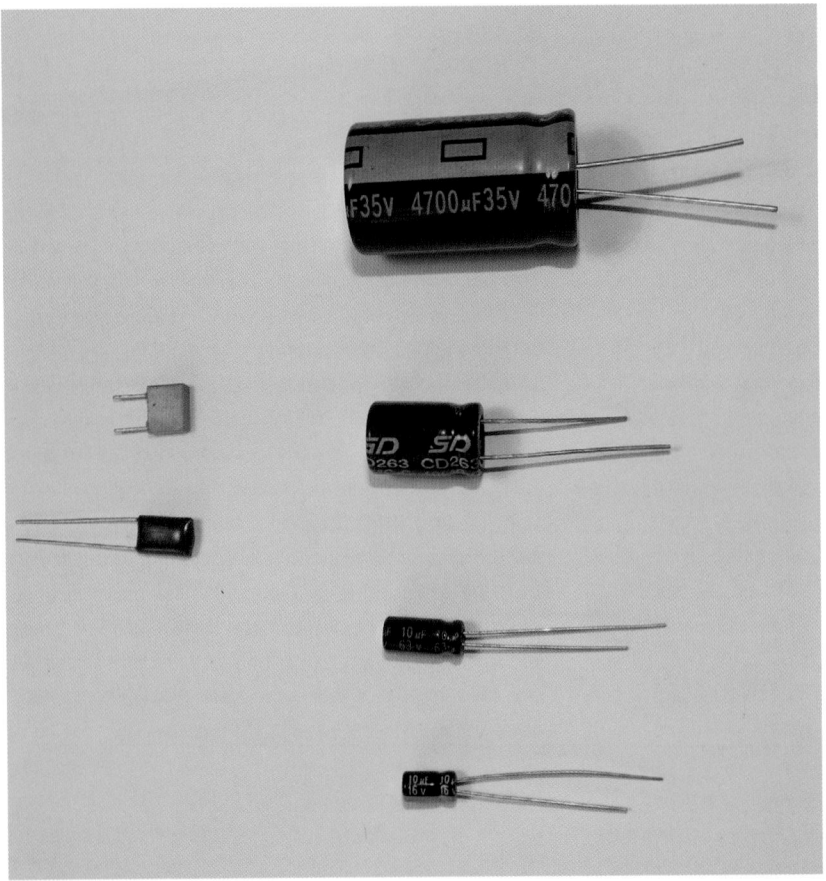

The four capacitors on the right are all electrolytic capacitors of different values. Electrolytic capacitors need to be connected the correct way round. Each is marked on one side with a negative symbol. They range in value from 4700 microfarads to 1 microfarad. As well as the capacitance, a value for voltage is marked. This is the maximum voltage the capacitor can be used at. The other two capacitors are not polarized and you do not need to worry about their orientation. The green capacitor is 10 nanofarads (a nanofarad is one billionth of a farad, i.e. 10 to the power of −9).

RESISTORS

Resistors are components made of a material that limits the current passing through them. This current can be calculated using Ohm's Law. Apart from the resistance, you sometimes also have to take into account the wattage that the resistors can handle: if you had 1A flowing through a 2 ohm resistor rated at 0.25W (a common size), the resistor would rapidly vaporize. This is because there would be a difference of 2V between the ends of the resistor. Ohm's Law states that multiplying current times resistance (measured in ohms) gives volts: 1A × 2 ohms therefore gives 2V. Watts are obtained by multiplying voltage and current: 2V × 1A gives 2W dissipated by the resistor as heat. When the current

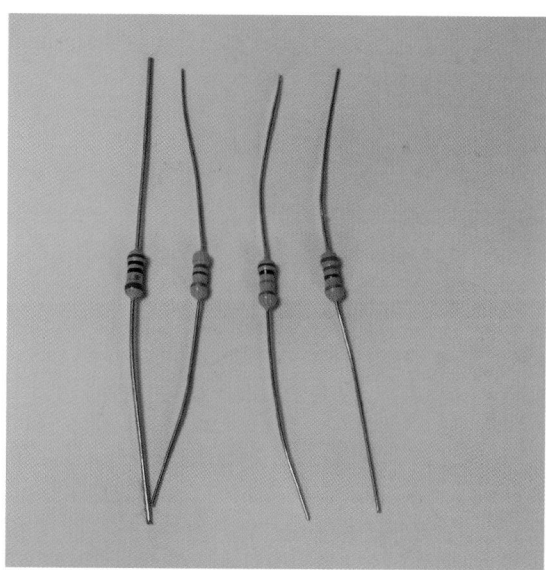

The three resistors with the beige background colour are quarter watt carbon resistors. This means that the most power they can dissipate is 0.25W and you may need to calculate power dissipation to make a choice of the correct resistor. Far greater wattages are available. The resistor with the light blue background is a half watt metal film resistor. These can be made with greater precision than carbon resistors.

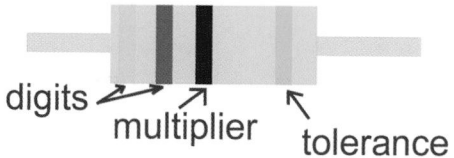

digits ↗ ↗
multiplier ↖
tolerance

black = 0
brown = 1
red = 2
orange = 3
yellow = 4
green = 5
blue = 6
violet = 7
grey = 8
white = 9

In this diagram of a resistor the brown and green bands indicate the digits one followed by five, and the red band indicates that there are two noughts after these digits. Hence the value is 1500 ohms.

flows through a resistor there is a voltage difference between the two ends. (Think of water flowing down a narrow pipe: the pressure will be higher at one end than the other.) As voltage is energy per unit charge, this lost energy is converted into heat, making the resistor hot.

As well as being available with different wattages, resistors come in values ranging from fractions of an ohm to tens of megaohms. The values are generally identified by coloured bands encircling the body of the resistor.

Manufacturers cannot produce resistors with an exact value: 10 kilo ohm resistors, for example, are sold with a 10 per cent tolerance. When measured these resistors can be found to have any value between 9 kilo ohms and 11 kilo ohms. Five and ten per cent resistors have a metallic band at one end signifying the tolerance of the resistor. More expensive resistors can be bought with a tolerance of 1 per cent or less, but 10 per cent resistors are fine for most purposes such as limiting the current to an LED. The human eye cannot detect a 10 per cent difference in light.

There are usually four bands on a resistor, one of which indicates the tolerance to which the resistor is made. The other three bands are used to indicate its value. The first two of these indicate the digits in the value and the final band indicates how many noughts follow these digits. On a resistor with yellow, violet, orange and gold bands, for example, the yellow and violet would indicate the first two digits four and seven. The orange would indicate three zeros following these digits. The value would therefore be 47,000 ohms. This value might alternatively be referred to as 47K, shorthand for 47 kilo ohms.

DIODES

Diodes are components that allow electricity to flow in one direction but not the other. One use of this property of diodes is to convert AC electricity into DC electricity. In other words, diodes are a one-way valve for electricity. This can be done with just one diode, producing half wave rectification. A more efficient method is to use four diodes arranged as a bridge rectifier to produce full wave rectification. Another use for diodes within model railways is the diode matrix for switching solenoid point motors.

Electric motors and LEDs generally work satisfactorily with unsmoothed DC. If you were to power a relay from unsmoothed DC, however, you would hear a chattering noise. This is because the relay is switching on and off very rapidly each time the unsmoothed DC is approaching zero. This is why a smooth supply is required to operate relays.

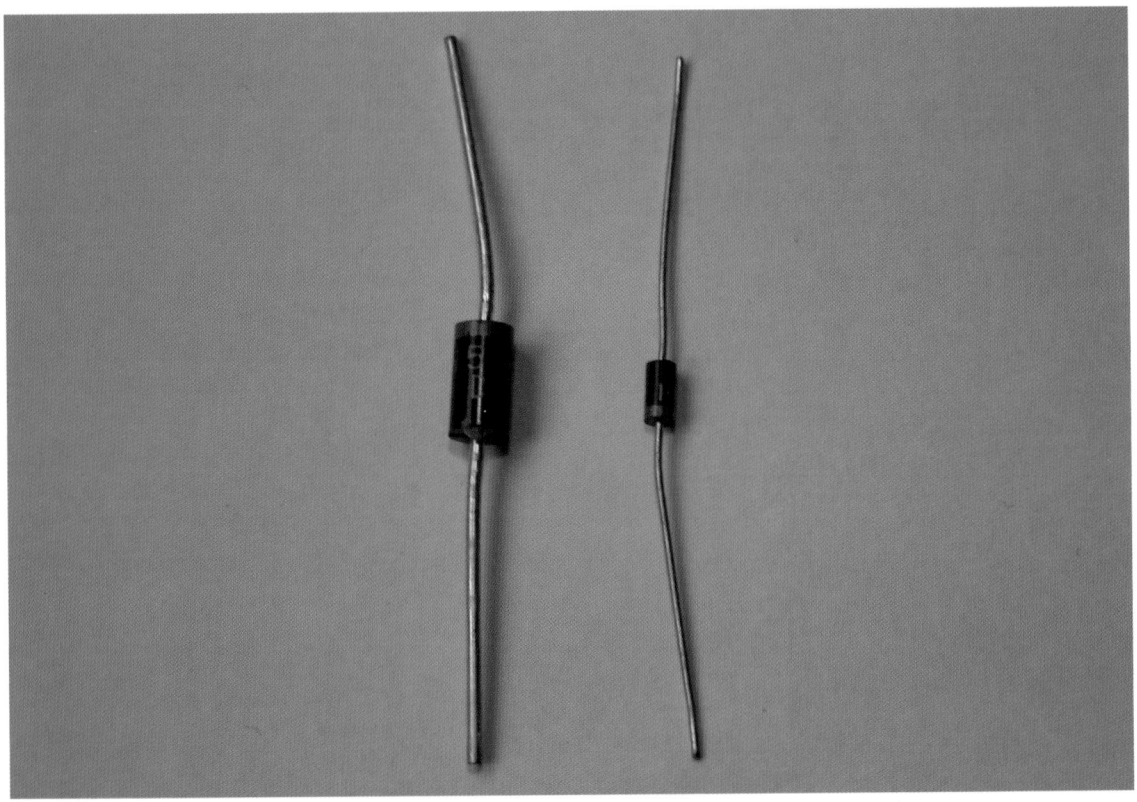

The larger diode is rated for a maximum current of 3A and the smaller diode is rated for a maximum current of 1A. The silver bands indicate which way the electricity flows through the diode.

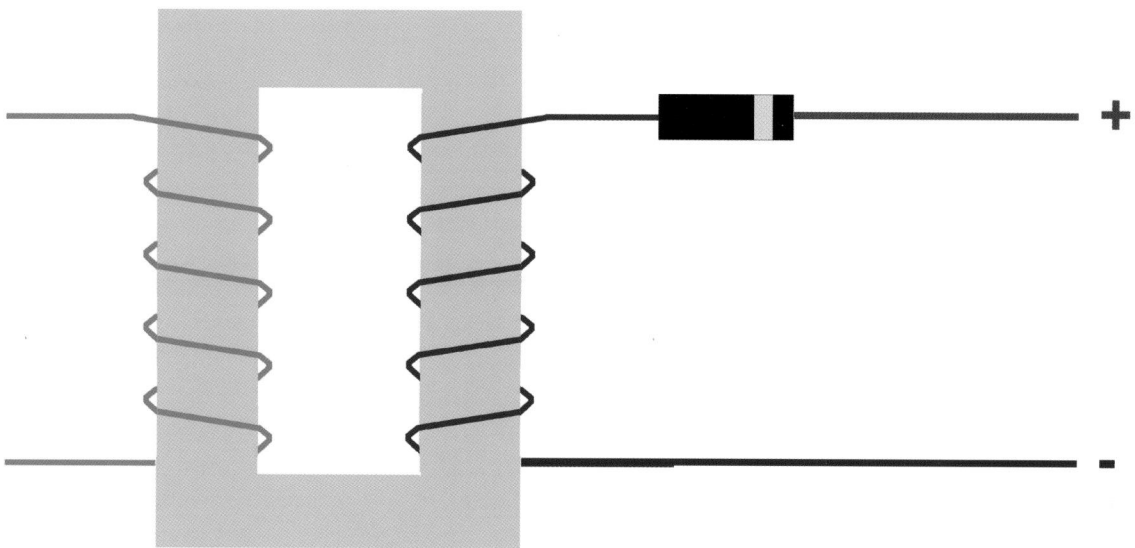

A single diode changes AC to DC. Here the AC is obtained from the mains with a transformer.

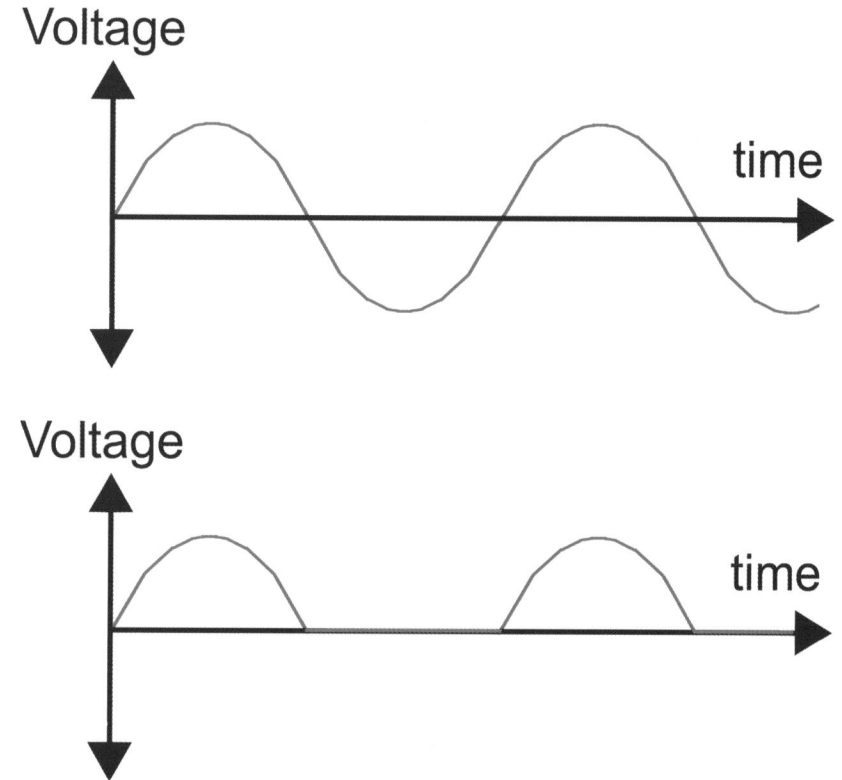

The waveforms of the AC voltage and the DC output obtained by using the diode. The diode can only conduct when the AC voltage is positive, so a very lumpy waveform is obtained. Using a single diode is called half wave rectification. Half the power is lost.

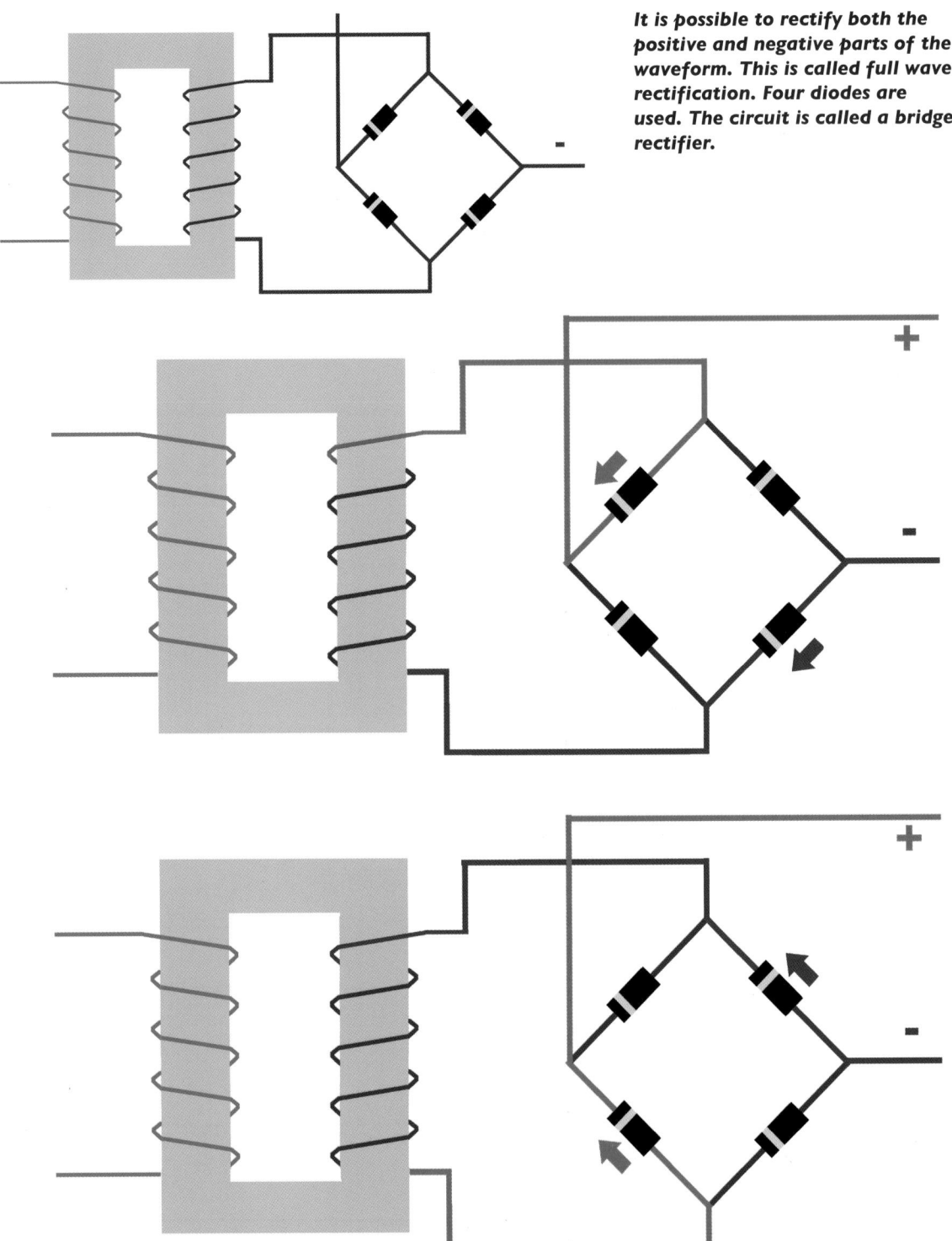

It is possible to rectify both the positive and negative parts of the waveform. This is called full wave rectification. Four diodes are used. The circuit is called a bridge rectifier.

How the bridge rectifier works. For both positive and negative portions of the AC waveform there is a path through the diodes to the positive output.

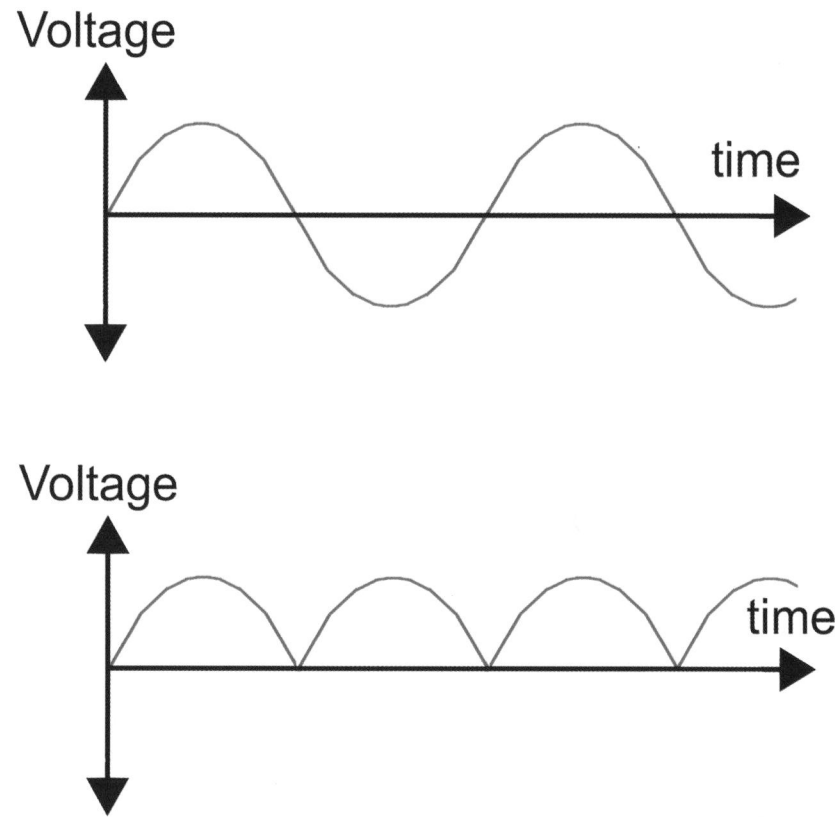

The waveform demonstrates that with a diode bridge both parts of the AC waveform are rectified, but the voltage still drops away to zero 100 times a second.

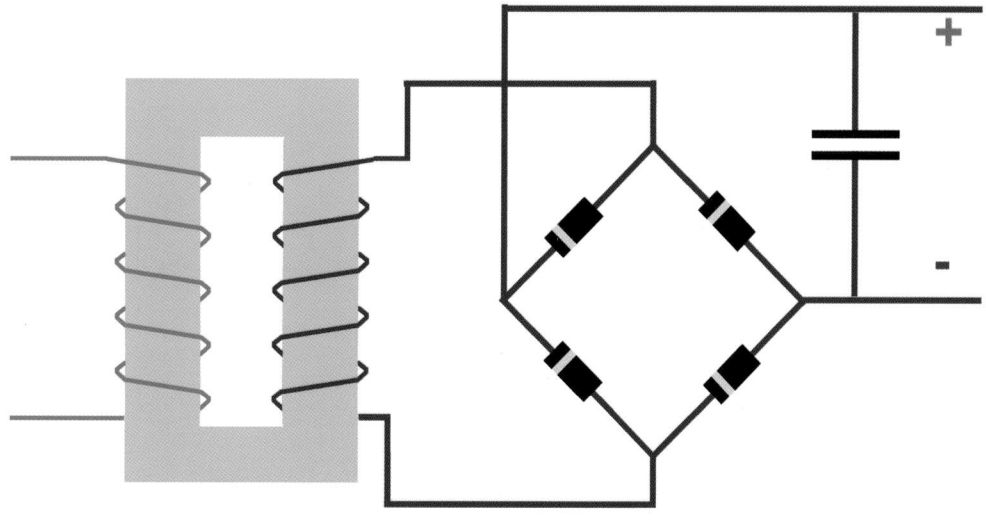

Putting a smoothing capacitor in the circuit smoothes out the DC voltage. As a fairly large value of capacitor is required an electrolytic capacitor is normally used.

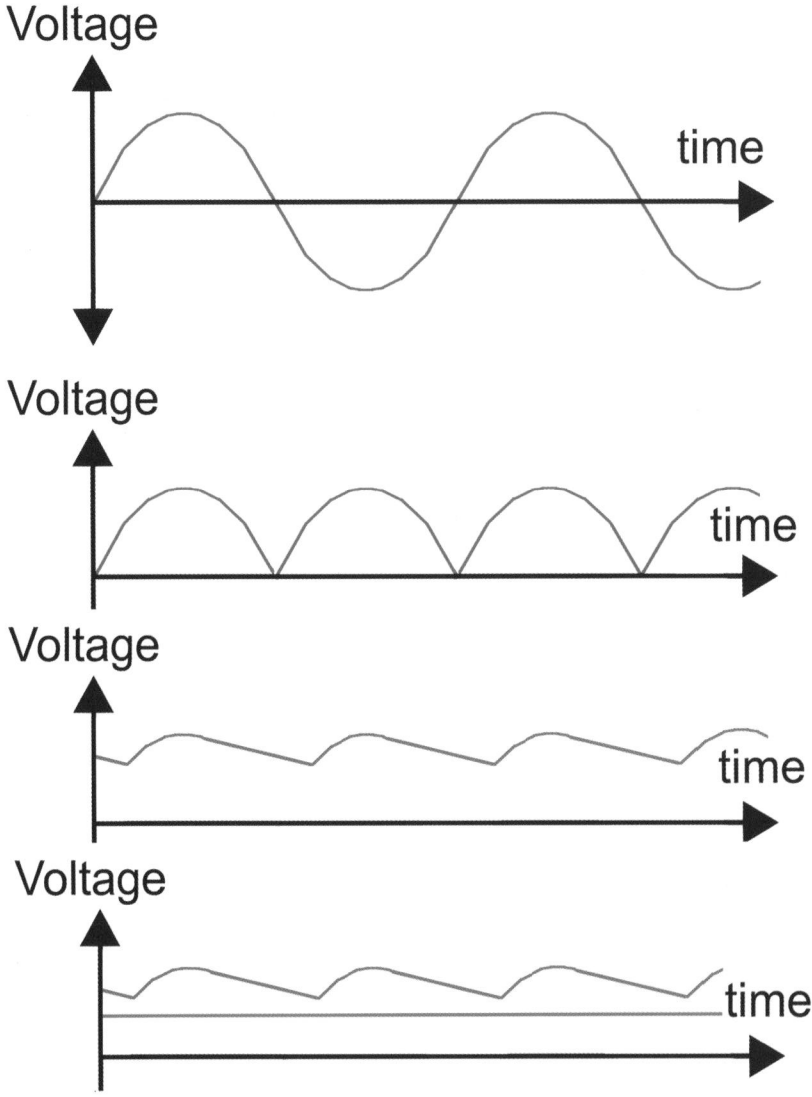

The waveform obtained when a smoothing capacitor is used. The smoothing capacitor charges up when the rectified waveform is at its maximum voltage and releases this stored charge as the rectified waveform diminishes. The result is to smooth out the waveform. The larger the capacitor, the smoother the waveform will be. The greater the current consumption of the circuit, the lumpier the waveform will be. The green waveform shows smoothed regulated DC obtained by using a voltage regulator chip.

LIGHT EMITTING DIODES (LEDS)

LEDs are used on model railways for colour light signals, head and tail lights on trains, lighting for coaches and buildings and for indications on control panels. They have also been used by the hundred for landing lights on model airfields.

Light bulbs produce light by having a piece of metal wire that becomes white hot when electricity flows through it, making it glow. LEDs work on a more efficient principle. The material (semiconductor) that forms the LED converts some of the energy of the electron (voltage) into a particle of light called a photon. Depending on the material used, a different colour of light is emitted by the LED. Nowadays you can get white LEDs and white is a mixture of all the colours of the rainbow. In actual fact there are several LEDs within a white LED, each emitting a different colour and combining them together to give white light. White LEDs originally had a harsh blue tinge, but LEDs can now be obtained that are described as warm white. Cool white and neutral white are also available. Some LEDs have bodies tinted in the same colour as the one they emit; some are clear and may emit a white or a coloured light. Common colours are red, yellow, green, amber and blue.

LEDs are manufactured in several sizes ranging upwards from tiny surface-mount ones that are typically 1.2 × 1.6mm. They are harder to work with because the connection has to be soldered to the side of the LED. Surface-mount components have no legs and are intended for soldering directly to the track of circuit boards. Typically they are much smaller than the older 'through hole' components. Surface mounts are more suited to assembly by machine, although it is possible to assemble them by hand. Common sizes for through hole LEDs are 3mm and 5mm diameter.

In LED specifications brightness is measured in mcd (millicandellas): the higher the number, the brighter they are. The light from an LED is emitted in a cone shape. Different LEDs have wider or

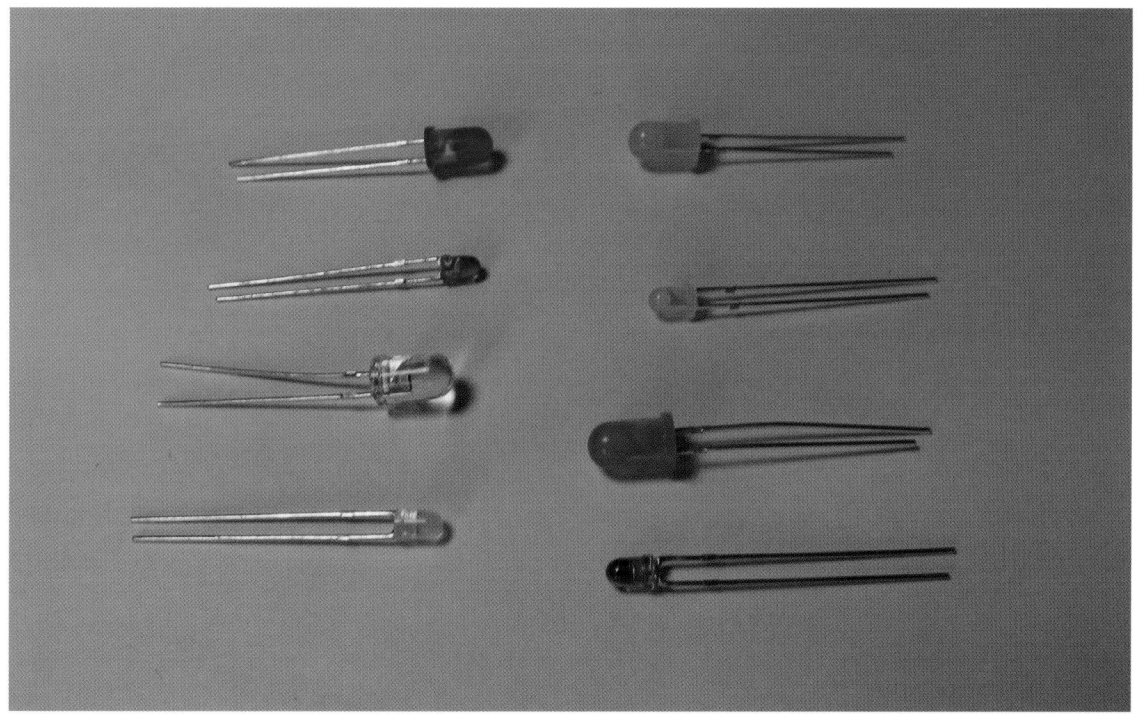

5mm and 3mm diameter LEDs. LEDs are available either with the body tinted or made using a clear material. Many more sizes and colours are available. Some very closely resemble model brake lamps.

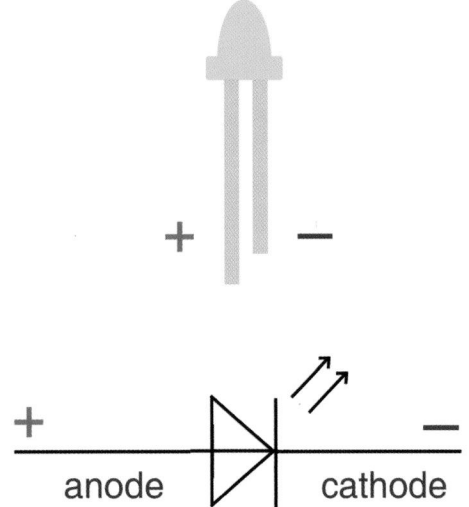

At the top of the diagram a LED is represented realistically. An actual LED has the anode (the leg connected to positive) identified as the longer leg. The symbol used for a LED is in the lower part of the diagram.

narrower cones, typically varying between 30 and 140 degrees. The width of the cone affects where the LED can be seen from and also its apparent brightness. LEDs have a long lifespan and do not get hot when lit. They also use less electrical current than bulbs and this becomes significant if a large number of lights are required.

LEDs are a special kind of diode designed to emit visible light. They only light when the electricity flows in one direction because they are diodes. LEDs have two legs of different lengths to identify how the LED is connected. An LED only lights if its long leg has a positive voltage and the short leg has a negative voltage. LEDs should be powered from a DC voltage. Excessive current will destroy an LED. The current is limited by using a resistor. The lower the value of the resistor the greater the current that will flow, so resulting in the LED being brighter. A typical value for a resistor used with an LED would be 1 kilo ohm, sometimes shortened to 1K. LEDs can be bought with built-in resistors.

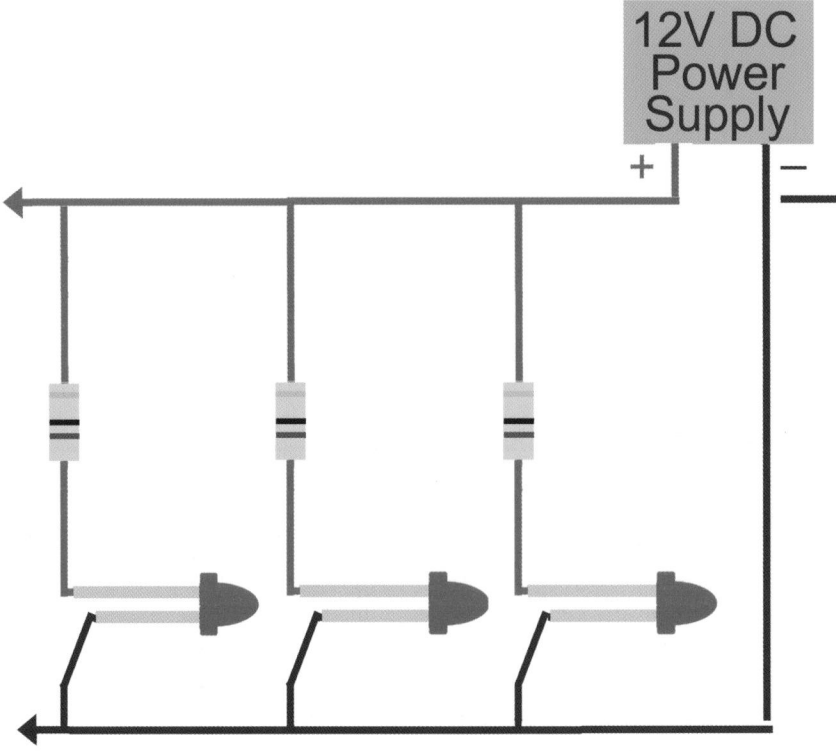

How to wire three LEDs to the same power supply. Some LEDs already have built-in resistors and these are sold as either 5V or 12V LEDs.

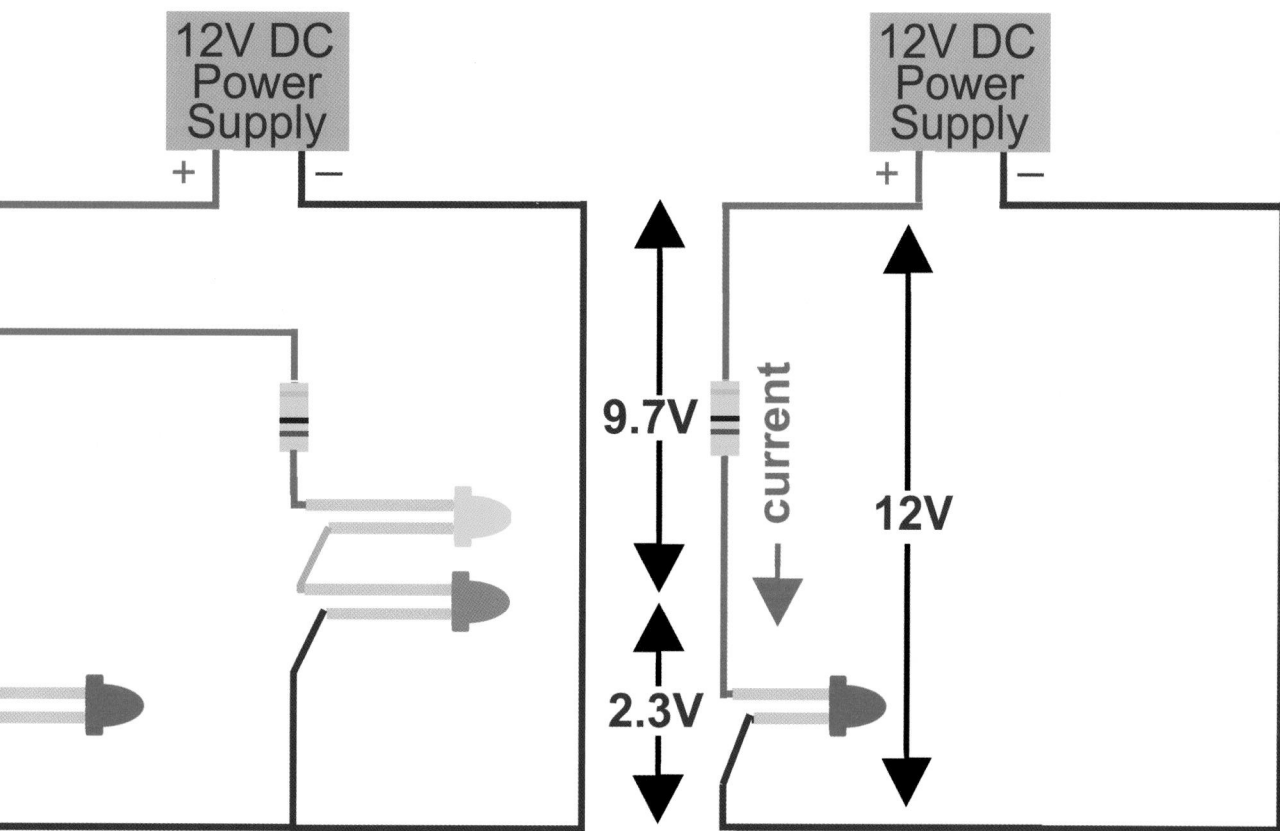

(Left) the short leg of the red LED is connected to negative and the long leg is connected to positive via a resistor to limit the current. (Right) a yellow LED and a green LED wired in series, sharing the same resistor. The power supply and the voltage of each LED limits how many can be wired in series.

These are called 5V or 12V LEDs. As these need a power supply of 5V or 12V, they are not very flexible and external resistors are normally used in signals.

Depending on the colour, each LED needs a certain voltage. Examples of typical values are 1.9V for red, 2.1V for yellow, 3.2V for blue and 2.2V for green. You do not need to produce these voltages, however, because the resistor will automatically adjust the voltage so that the correct voltage is across the LED.

CALCULATING THE CORRECT VALUE OF THE RESISTOR TO USE WITH AN LED

- You need to know the voltage of the power supply.
- Subtract the voltage of the LED from this.
- Using the diagram this would be 12V [minus] 2.3V = 9.7V.
- Divide this voltage by the current you want to flow through the LED.

- Refer to the data sheet to find the maximum current the LED is designed for.
- From the diagram 9.7V/25mA = 9.7V/0.025A = 388 ohms.
- Convert to amps to get the result of the calculation in ohms.
- Find the nearest resistor value to the calculated one, in this case 390 ohms.

This calculation uses Ohm's Law, which states that V=IR or R=V/I, where V = voltage measured in volts, I = current measured in amps and R = resistance measured in ohms.

LEDs can be bought with built-in resistors. These 5V or 12V LEDs need a power supply of 5V or 12V, respectively. They are not very flexible, so external resistors are normally used in signals.

BI-COLOUR AND TRI-COLOUR LEDS

These are LEDs that can be made to change to different colours. Bi-colour LEDs actually have two LEDs encapsulated in the LED package. Often, but not always, these are red and green. There are two ways they can be connected.

Bi-colour LEDs with two legs have both ends of the internal LEDs connected together. However, they are connected so that the red LED lights when the current flows from A to B and the green LED lights when the current flows from B to A. To make the current flow from A to B, A has to be a positive voltage and B negative voltage. To make the current flow from B to A, B has to be a positive voltage and A has to be a negative voltage. A situation where this occurs is with a slow motion point motor. If you

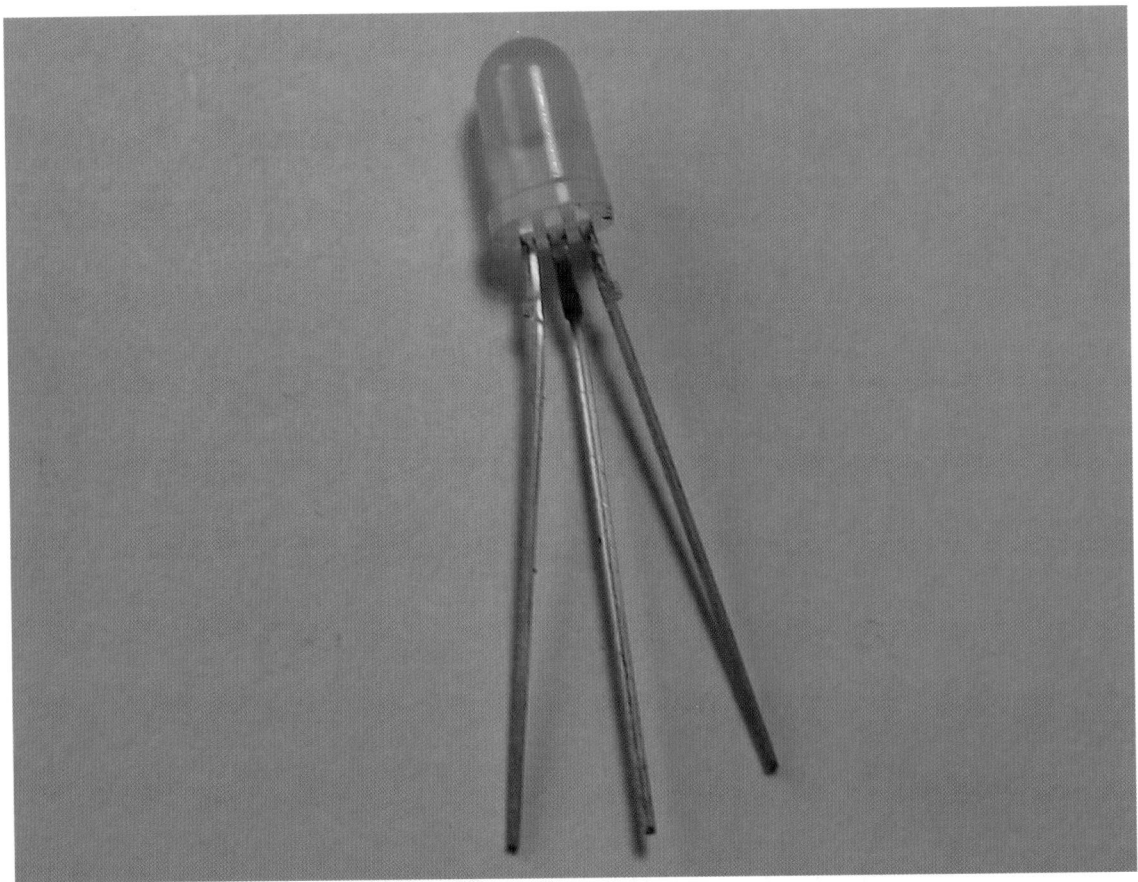

This tricolour LED has three legs identified by their different lengths. The LED can display red, green or yellow.

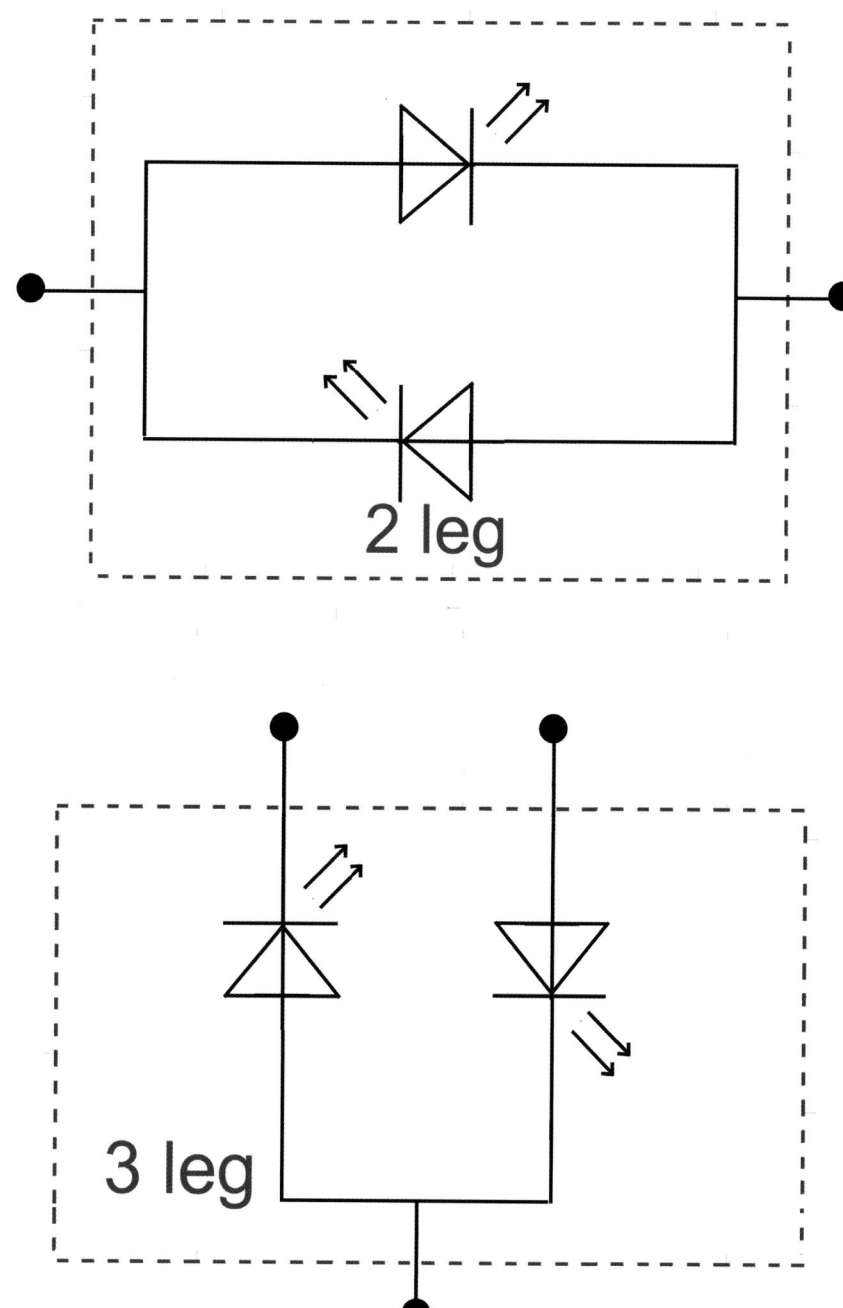

The internal wiring of bicolour LEDs. The two-legged version requires the polarity of its supply to be reversed for it to change colour. The colour of the three-legged version is changed by connecting different legs to the power.

connected a resistor and a two-leg LED between the wires going from the switch to the point motor, the LED would change colour depending on which way the point was set.

Three-leg LEDs have only one end of the internal LED connected. Tri-colour LEDs are usually red, green and yellow. In the diagram here the cathodes are connected together. To make the LEDs light, C is connected to a negative voltage. If A is then connected to a positive voltage the LED will light as green. If B is connected to a positive voltage the LED will light red. If you connect both A and B to a positive voltage, both the red and green LEDs will light and the LED will appear to be yellow. The resistors have been omitted from the diagrams and would have to be included in a practical circuit.

The model railway applications for bi-colour and tri-colour LEDs are models of searchlight signals and for control panel indications.

AC POWER SUPPLIES

AC power supplies consist simply of safely boxed transformers.

In principle, a low voltage can be produced from the mains using a transformer, but we would recommend that a manufactured sealed unit is purchased for safety reasons. This, however, is going to give you AC and you often require DC for your model railway.

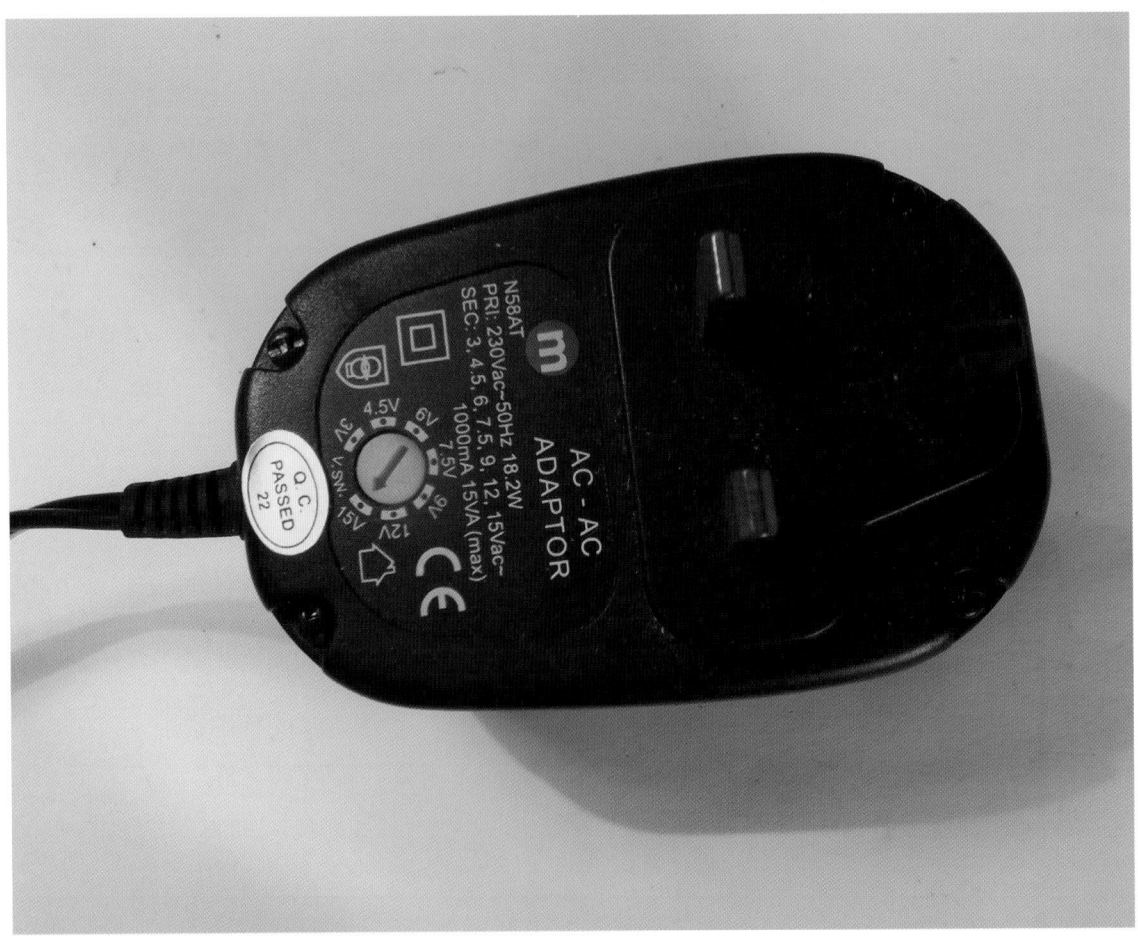

An AC power supply is really a transformer safely encased in a plastic casing. Rotating the slotted rotary switch with a small screwdriver allows different voltages to be selected.

DC POWER SUPPLIES

If you have a low voltage AC power source it is easy to convert it to DC using a diode. Only the positive cycles will flow through the diode, so we are left with lumpy or, to use the technical term, unsmoothed DC.

This unsmoothed DC is fine for some uses. It will, for example, power LEDs safely that would otherwise have risked damage from AC. It is not the same, however, as the smooth, stable DC electricity obtained from a battery. Every half cycle the electricity disappears and while it is present it is changing all the time. This happens so quickly that your eyes just see the average light output from an LED and cannot discern the changes in brightness as the electricity flowing through the LED changes. This is a similar effect to how your eyes watch a film and perceive a series of still frames passing very quickly as a moving image. This unsmoothed DC is not suitable for purposes such as powering coreless electric motors, which would overheat, or most electronic circuits, which want a constant electrical supply rather than one that switches on and off rapidly.

To turn the unsmoothed supply into a smoothed one, some of the electricity has to be stored when it is at its maximum. The stored electricity will then release itself when the AC has become negative and the diode is blocking off the negative. A device that stores a charge is called a capacitor.

We are now a lot closer to having a DC supply but it is still not as stable as that obtained from a battery. To provide a stable voltage a voltage regulator chip is used. These are available with different output voltages. A LM7805 voltage regulator, for example, will maintain the output of your power supply at a stable 5V even when the current taken varies. This type of power supply is called a linear power supply. Its disadvantages are its large size and its inefficient energy conversion.

SWITCH MODE POWER SUPPLIES

Remembering that it is the changing magnetic field that causes the electric current to be induced in the secondary of the transformer, in fact the more rapidly the magnetic field changes the greater the current

A 12V 1A switch mode power supply. A conventional linear power supply would be much larger in size. On the right are the different adapters for the mains sockets of various countries.

that will be induced. If the mains frequency were a lot higher than 50Hz, much smaller transformers could be used to convert the mains into large currents. This is what switch mode power supplies do, initially converting the AC to DC, then switching it at a high frequency so a small transformer can be used. There is an even cleverer advantage. An electronic circuit to monitor the output of the switch mode power supply varies the switching frequency to keep the output voltage stable. This means that the efficiency of the energy conversion is very high. Saving energy means that the power supply does not get hot and can be made in a smaller size.

SWITCHES

Imagine you have a battery connected to a light bulb by two wires. The bulb will be lit at all times until the battery eventually becomes flat. If you cut one of the wires in half the light bulb will no longer be lit. If you rejoin the cut wires the bulb will light again. An electrical switch does the job of connecting and disconnecting the wires. This is the simplest type of switch and is known as an on/off switch.

Apart from being operated by humans, switches on model railways may also be operated by mechanical movement or magnetism.

MICROSWITCH

An example of a switch operated by mechanical movement is a microswitch. This consists of a switch operated by a steel lever. The steel lever has a spring pushing the switch into position one. The mechanical movement presses against the lever to put the switch into position two. This type of switch can be used to allow the movement of the points tie bar to operate signals. Microswitches can also be used for preventing accidents with hinged

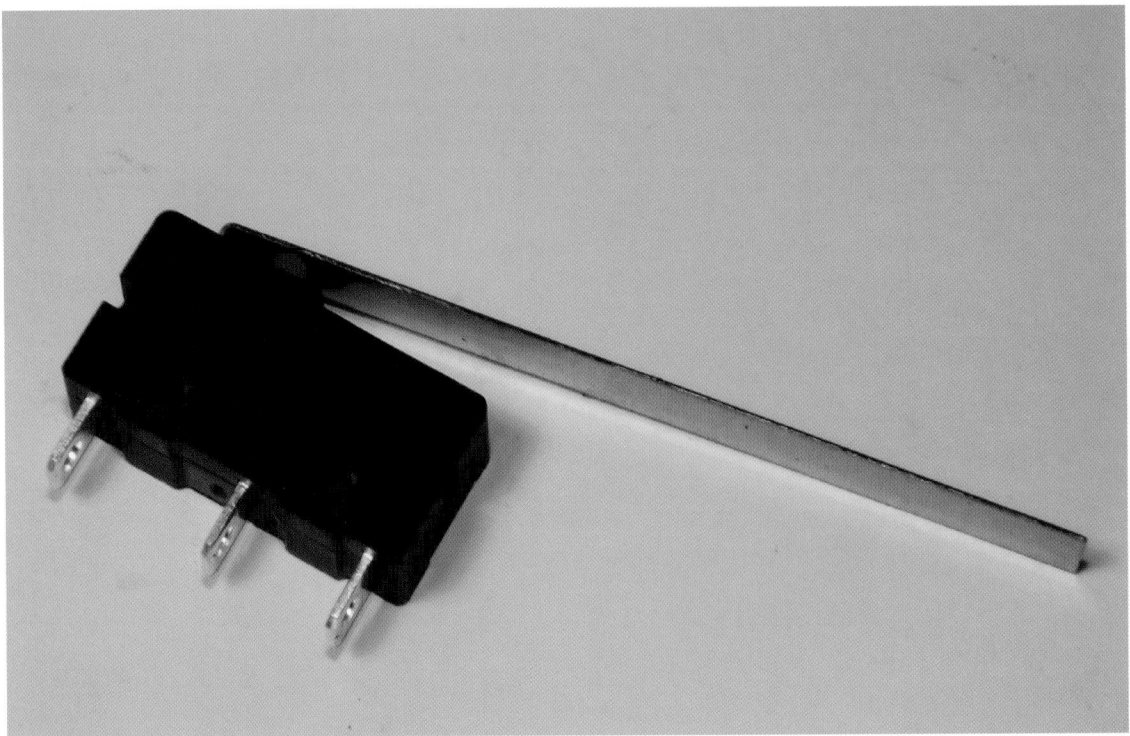

The microswitch is operated by a lever. The switch changes over when the lever is pressed by the movement of an object. A spring returns the microswitch to its original position when the pressure is taken off the lever. The microswitch acts as a single pole, double throw switch. It is commonly used to sense the position of point tie bars.

baseboards. The switch can be arranged so that it disconnects electricity to the tracks when the flap is raised, saving trains from accidently being driven over the edge. A third use of microswitches is the aligning of tracks on a turntable. For this microswitches can be obtained with a roller on the lever that can be arranged to drop into slots as the turntable rotates. When the microswitch drops into the slot, power will be cut off from the electric motor used to rotate the turntable. Microswitches are generally single pole, double throw.

REED SWITCH

Reed switches are switches moved by magnetism. They consist of a springy piece of iron inside a glass tube. Wire extends out of the ends of the glass tube in order to make electrical connections to the reed switch. When a magnet is near the reed switch the springy iron is attracted by the magnet.

There are two types of reed switch. In one type the springy piece of iron is closed but springs open when a magnet is nearby: this is called normally closed. The other type of reed switch is the one

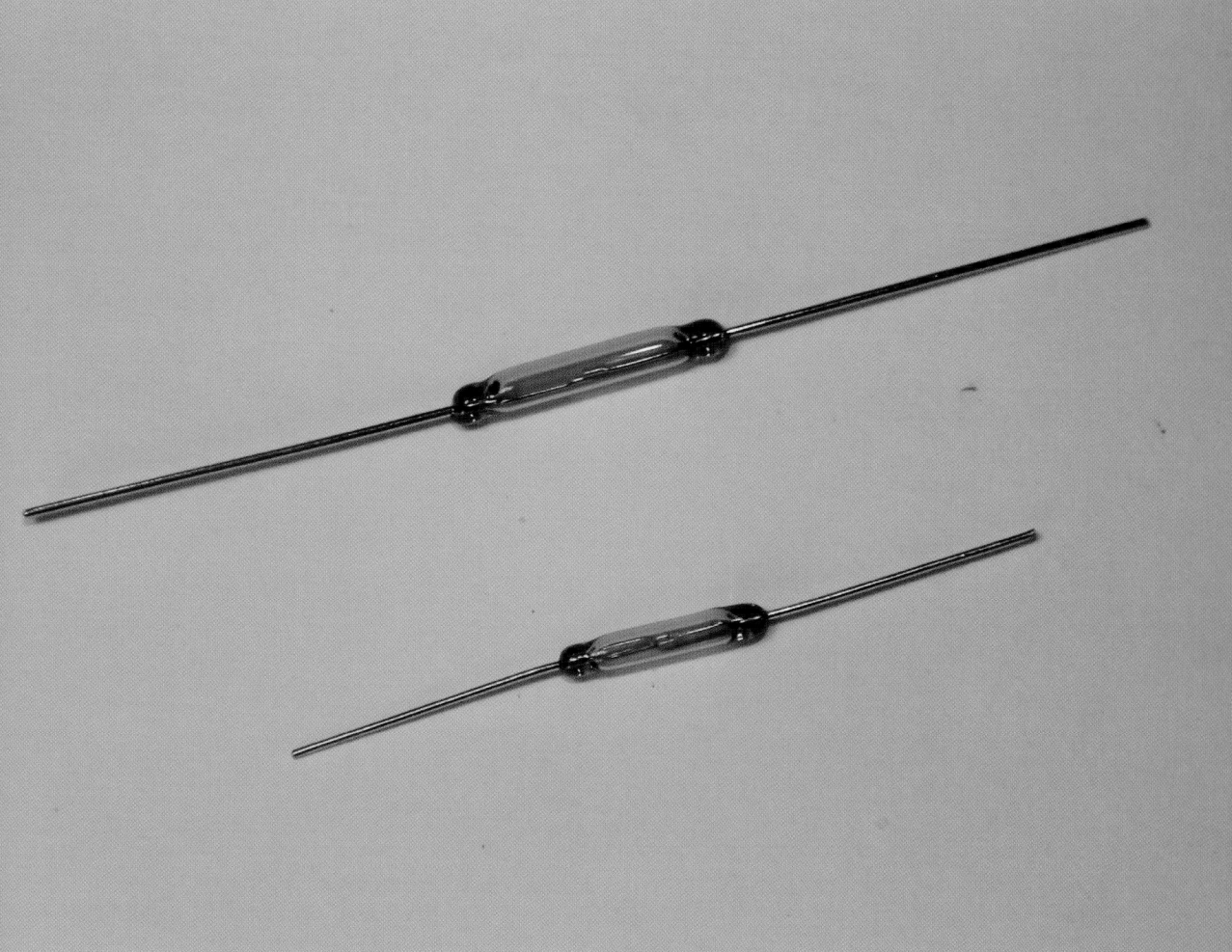

The glass tubes that contain the working part of a reed switch. These are normally open reed switches. The two wires coming out of the ends of the reed switch are electrically disconnected until a magnet is brought near to the reed switch.

more commonly used in model railways. It is known as normally open because the springy piece of iron stands apart and makes no connection until a magnet is nearby. The magnets are usually on the undersides of the trains and the reeds are located between the sleepers. A disadvantage to reed switches is that they can handle only a low current. You will probably find that either the contacts (pieces of springy iron) will fuse together or melt if you try to switch solenoid point motors with reed switches due to the high current solenoid point motors require. It takes approximately 3A to switch a solenoid point motor. A way around this problem is to use the reed switch to switch a relay with contacts rated for a high enough current to suit the solenoid point motors. Inexpensive relays can be obtained with contacts rated at 10A, which is more than sufficient.

The electronic versions of reed switches are Hall effect devices. These are electronic chips that sense a magnetic field. Surprisingly these are not in popular use on model railways.

TOGGLE AND MOMENTARY SWITCHES

There are several types of hand-operated switches that are useful for model railways. Toggle switches are available in several sizes, of which the miniature size is the most suitable. They consist of a small lever that moves from side to side and rests in two or three positions. They generally have a threaded section beneath the toggle lever. The base consists of a rectangular block containing the contacts and on the bottom of which are a number of lugs to which the connecting wires are soldered. These

Four toggle switches. The switch on the left has just two solder lugs and is an on/off switch. With the lever in the position shown the switch is off. This means the two solder lugs are not connected together. The centre left switch is a single pole, double throw switch. The centre solder lug is the common and, with the lever as shown, the centre solder lug is connected to the left solder lug but not to the right solder lug. The two switches on the right both have six solder lugs and so are both double pole switches. The centre right switch is a centre off switch. Its lever is upright and in this position none of the solder lugs are connected together. The right switch is a double pole, double throw: the two rows of solder lugs are electrically independent of each other.

switches are very easy to mount onto a control panel as you simply drill a hole of a slightly larger diameter and fasten them with the nuts and washers provided. There are two different washers. One is serrated to provide a good grip. This is called a lock washer and goes onto the reverse of the control panel. The second washer is called a locking ring and has an inner protrusion that locates in a vertical slot running along the switch's thread. The outer part of the locking ring has a bent-over protrusion that locates in a small hole drilled alongside the main mounting hole. The purpose of the locking ring is to stop the switch from rotating.

Connections are made by soldering wires to the tags on the back of the switch. Toggle switches can be obtained with many different contact arrangements to suit numerous model railway applications.

Contact Arrangements

Single pole, single throw (SPST) switches are probably better known as on/off switches. These have two solder tags on the reverse for attaching wires. When the toggle lever is in one position the two tags are electrically joined inside the switch. In the other position they are disconnected. These types of contacts are known as single pole, single throw. One use for this type of switch would be switching lights on and off in buildings.

Single pole, double throw (SPDT) switches are sometimes called changeover switches. The contacts have a similar operation to the SPST switch, but this switch has two contacts instead of one. When the lever is on the left the centre solder tag is connected to the right-hand solder tag. The left solder tag is disconnected. When the lever is on the right the centre solder tag is connected to the left-hand solder tag. The right solder tag is disconnected.

This type of switch is ideal for operating a two-aspect colour light signal. When the switch is in one position the green LED will be lit and in the other position the red LED will be lit.

Momentary single pole, double throw switches are available with an internal spring that returns the toggle lever to a central position where no contact is made. These are very suitable for switching solenoid point motors. By using just two of the three lugs, a single pole, double throw switch can be used as an on/off switch.

Single pole, double throw, centre off (SPDTCO) switches have three positions. With the lever in the middle upright position the switch makes no contact. The other two positions connect the solder lugs exactly as described for the SPDT switch.

Double pole, double throw (DPDT) switches consist of two single pole, double throw switches side by side. The two switches are electrically separate but are both operated by the same lever. One use for the DPDT switch is to reverse electrical polarity. This is useful for operating slow motion point motors. Slow motion point motors are usually powered by a DC electric motor. Reversing the polarity of a DC electric motor reverses the direction in which it rotates, therefore changing the point setting.

As the two sets of contacts are electrically separate, you can switch two different electrical circuits at the same time without any electrical conflict. For example, one set of contacts could switch power on and off to a section of railway line, while the other contacts could switch LEDs to indicate power on and off to the track.

Double pole, double throw, centre off (DPDTCO) switches are a three-position version of the double pole, double throw switches. When the lever is in the centre position no electrical connections are made between the lugs. When the lever is in the two outer positions it works exactly the same as the double pole, double throw switch. An example of its use is if it is wired to reverse the polarity to an electric motor. In one position the motor will rotate clockwise. In the second position it will rotate anti-clockwise. But in the centre position the electricity will be cut off from the motor, so stopping the motor moving.

Other arrangements

Toggle switches can be obtained with more than two poles. A four pole toggle switch, for example, is the equivalent of four single pole switches side by side operated by one lever. There are also momentary switches with more than one pole. Sometimes double pole momentary switches are useful on model railways.

PUSH-BUTTON SWITCHES

There are many types and styles of push-button switches. The simplest are in effect momentary on/off switches. Push-button switches can be obtained with two types of operation: push-to-make or push-to-break. With the push-to-make switches the two lugs are only connected when the button on the switch is pressed. A spring inside the switch returns the button to the off position as soon as you remove your finger. With push-to-break switches the lugs are connected until the button on the switch is pressed, disconnecting the lugs.

There are also more complicated push-button switches that use a mechanical latching principle. On the first push connections are made and stay made until you press the switch for a second time, which then disconnects the connections. These switches are available with more than one pole.

The threaded barrel and nut to attach the push-button switch into holes drilled into a control panel are here visible. This is a push-to-make switch, so the two solder lugs are connected together by the switch when it is pushed.

ROTARY SWITCHES

A rotary switch is used where you need more than two or three positions on a switch. For example, to operate four-aspect signals you would need four switch positions. A rotary switch is operated by turning a spindle that clicks into a number of positions as you rotate it. At each position the common of the switch connects to a different contact. Rotary switches can be obtained with a number of poles as each pole is on a different layer of contacts on the spindle. They are mounted on a control panel in a similar way to toggle switches. Once bolted into position, a knob is attached to the spindle. This usually has a pointer so that it is clear which position the switch is set to.

RELAYS

A relay is a switch operated by electricity rather than by hand. It generally consists of a coil of wire that forms an electromagnet and a number of contacts moved by the electromagnet. Everybody is familiar with an ordinary (permanent) magnet. An electromagnet behaves like an ordinary magnet when electricity flows through its coil. When the electromagnet is powered the magnetic field attracts the contacts to one position. When it is not powered there is no magnetic field, so the contacts return to their original position.

The more commonly available relays require smoothed direct current to operate the coil. Make

ABOVE: *A rotary switch is useful for operating multi-aspect signals and for selecting from several controllers to give different operators connection to a piece of track. There is a central common connection: as the switch is rotated the arm is joined to each of the outer connections in turn.*

ABOVE: *The smaller of the two relays shown here is designed for soldering directly into a circuit board. The larger is intended for plugging into a special socket, which may have screw connections for the wires or be intended for soldering into a circuit board. Relays have moving parts and they will only last for a certain number of operations, perhaps 100,000 or more. A push-fit base makes them easy to replace when they wear out.*

sure your power supply provides this. If the supply is not smoothed you will hear a buzzing noise as the contacts switch on and off very rapidly at 50 or 100Hz. Relays are made with coils designed for different voltages, commonly 5V, 12V and 24V. The manufacturers build in some tolerance so that a 12V relay, for example, will operate with a supply from 10V to 15V, but it would not switch with 5V and would probably burn out with 24V.

Relays have a number of pins connecting to the coil and the contacts. There are two types of pins: those designed for soldering a relay into a circuit board and those designed for clipping the relay into a relay base. The relay base may have screw connections to it. It is more convenient to use a relay base because then the relay can be replaced if it gets damaged and the base is designed so that wires can be easily connected. It is, however, a more expensive option. It is quite possible to connect relays designed for circuit boards directly to wires by gluing them upside down and soldering wires to the pins. Another factor to

bear in mind when choosing relays is the maximum current that the contacts are designed to handle. A relay with contacts rated at a maximum current of 100 milliamps will not last very long if you try to switch point motors with it. Also it helps with longevity to overrate the contacts. A relay with 10A contacts would be much more suitable for switching point motors. There are lots of 12V relays in your car, so if you build your layout in the garage your car is close by to strip for necessary spare parts. Just like switches, relays can be obtained with different arrangements of contacts.

SOLDERING

SOLDERING ELECTRONIC COMPONENTS

Soldering electronic components together is a lot simpler than soldering together brass model kits. A 25W soldering iron is required. The lead-free solder

The label on the reel of solder identifies the diameter as 22swg. This is lead-free solder and is 99.3 per cent tin and 0.7 per cent copper. Although this makes adequate joints, the best-quality solder also contains silver, but this makes it very expensive.

used nowadays has a higher melting point than the old lead/tin solder, so you should choose a soldering iron that gets hot enough and states on the packaging that it is suitable for lead-free solder. Suitable solder is supplied as a thin wire: we use size 22swg. Inside the solder is a flux intended to clean the surface of the metals being joined. This is the reason it is important to get solder intended for use in electronic assembly. Some solders, such as that used by plumbers, do not contain a flux. Others contain a corrosive flux that will damage the components over time.

SOLDERING A WIRE ONTO A SWITCH

The end of the wire that you wish to attach to the switch needs about 5mm of its insulation stripped off. Special wire strippers can be bought for this, although once the knack is obtained you can strip the wire with wire cutters. If you are using wire consisting of a number of strands, it is best to twist these together to prevent individual strands splaying out as you solder the wire. Once the wire is stripped, melt some solder onto the bare wire end.

This 25W soldering iron by Antex is designed for lead-free solder and is very suitable for assembling electronic circuits and soldering wires on to switches and tracks. It is a good idea to use a stand when the soldering iron is hot as otherwise it is very easy to have an accident.

This is called tinning. Also tin the lug of the switch to which the wire is to be attached by melting some solder onto it. Make sure there is a little solder on your soldering iron tip as this helps heat transfer from the tip to the joint. Heat up the lug by touching the tip of the soldering iron to it. Once it is hot hold the wire alongside. You will see all the solder melt and fuse together around the joint between the lug and the bare wire. Be careful not to let the wire move until the solder joint has cooled down, otherwise you will get a weak joint. Other reasons for getting a weak joint are if the wire or the lug is dirty or if the joint did not get hot enough. Do not wrap lots of wire around the lug before soldering as it will be harder to heat it up and the wire will possibly short onto other lugs. It will also be difficult to remove the wire if needed in the future.

It is a good idea to have a soldering iron stand to keep the hot soldering iron out of harm's way.

A desoldering pump (solder sucker) used for removing unwanted solder to allow components to be removed. The plunger is depressed and the nozzle held near the solder joint which has been melted with a soldering iron. The button on the side is then pressed, the plunger springs back and creates a vacuum behind the nozzle, causing the molten solder to be sucked up.

HEAT SHRINK

Heat shrink is used to insulate electrical joints. It is a rubber-like tube available in several diameters. Typically when heated it shrinks to half its original diameter. The best way of heating heat shrink is with a hot air gun. It is very useful for insulating extension wires that have been soldered to signals. Signal manufacturers generally seem to supply signals with wires that are too short. Without the heat shrink there would be a tendency for the bare joints of adjacent wires to touch and cause intermittent faults. Heat shrink is also useful for insulating the joint where a wire is attached to a LED leg.

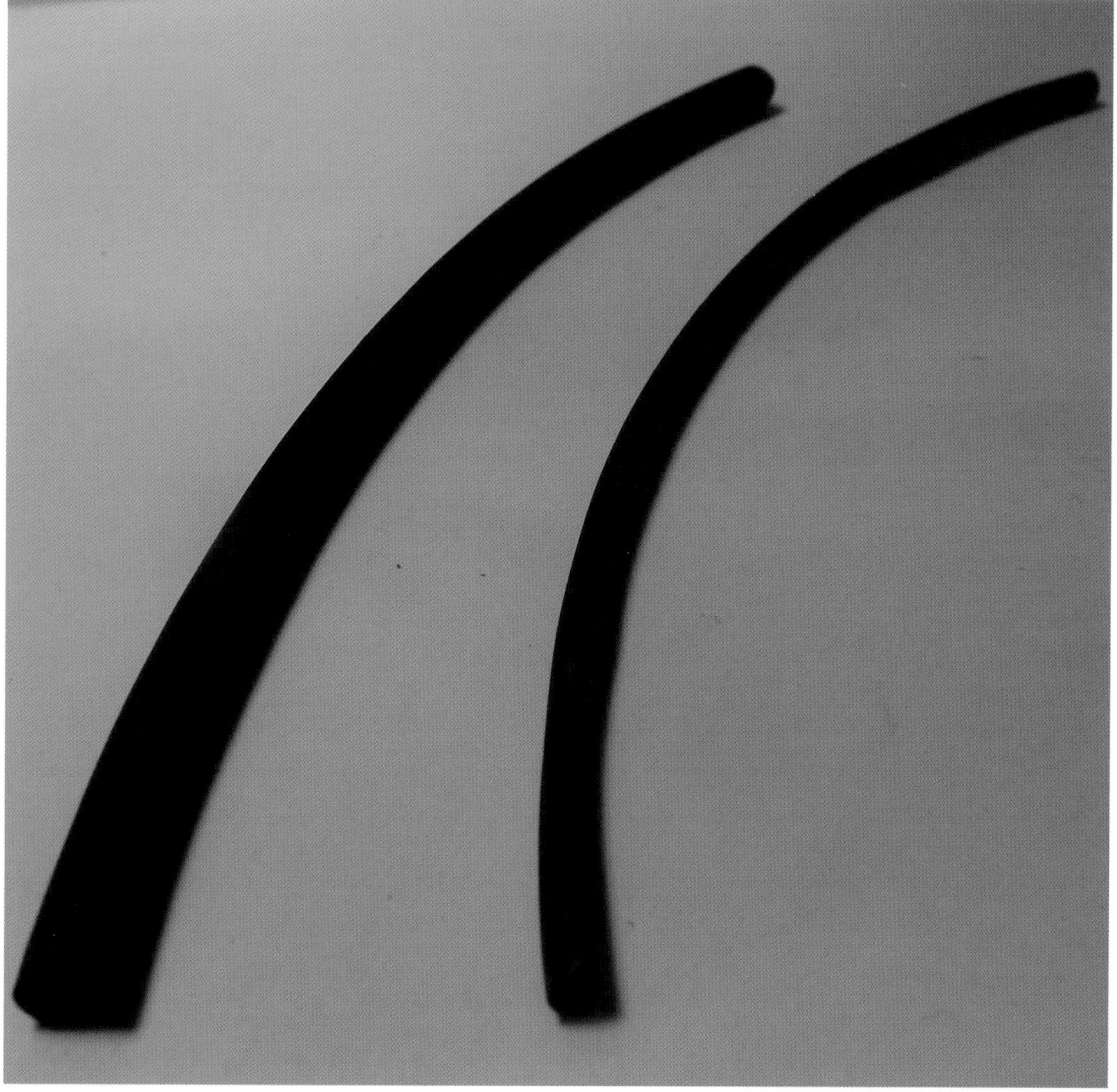

Two different diameters of heat shrink: 4.8mm and 2.4mm. Both will shrink to half their diameter when heated with a hot air gun. Other diameters and colours are readily available.

TERMINAL BLOCKS

These are a convenient way of connecting two or more wires together. They are sometimes called chocolate blocks. As the wire is screwed down rather than soldered, connections can be changed quickly and easily. Some modellers insert chocolate blocks in the wires leading to point motors. If a point motor fails at an exhibition, this allows it to be readily changed using a pre-prepared replacement. Terminal blocks consist of a plastic strip containing two rows of screws. Each pair of screws is electrically connected together by a brass connector. Each pair of screws is electrically isolated from the others.

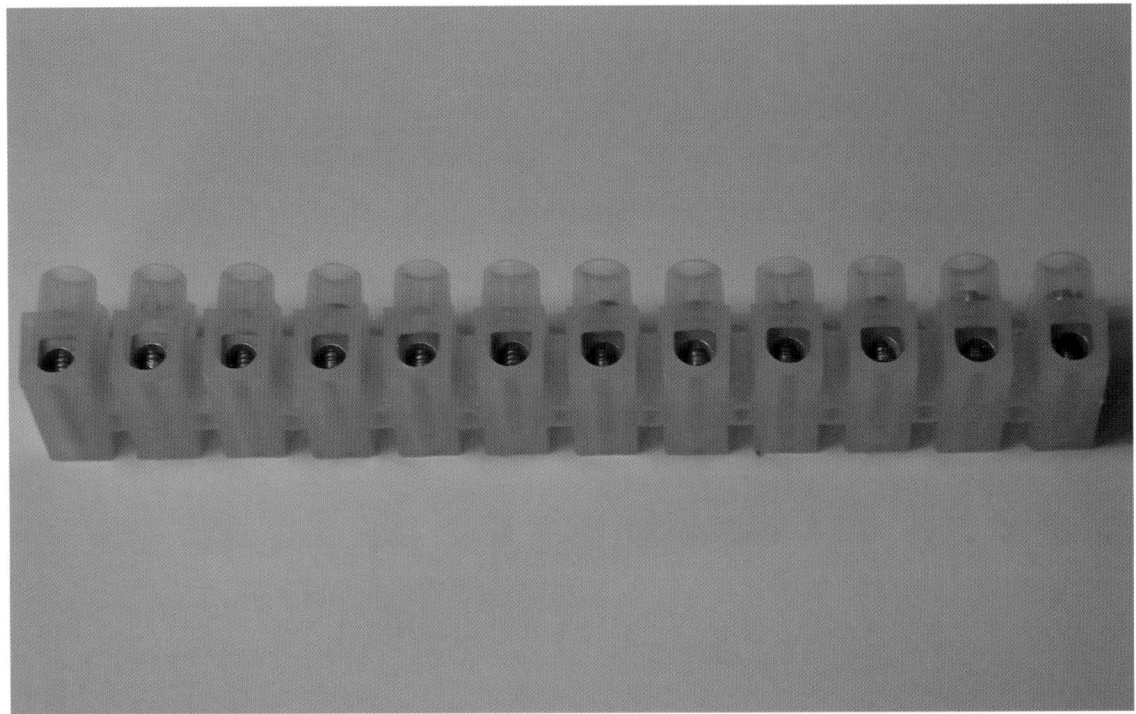

The clamping screws are tightened to hold the wire in place. Terminal blocks are also known as chocolate blocks.

INDEX